NOT IN SISTERHOOD

Not in Sisterhood

Edith Wharton, Willa Cather, Zona Gale, and the Politics of Female Authorship

Deborah Lindsay Williams

palgrave

NOT IN SISTERHOOD
Copyright © Deborah Lindsay Williams, 2001.
All rights reserved. No part of this book may be used or reproduced in
any manner whatsoever without written permission except in the case of
brief quotations embodied in critical articles or reviews.

First published 2001 by
PALGRAVE™
175 Fifth Avenue, New York, NY 10010 and
Houndmills, Basingstoke, Hampshire, England RG21 6XS.
Companies and representatives throughout the world.

Palgrave is the new global publishing imprint of St Martin's Press LLC
Scholarly and Reference Division and Palgrave Publishers Ltd (formerly
Macmillan Press Ltd).

ISBN 0–312–22921-6 hardback

Library of Congress Cataloging-in-Publication Data can be found at the
Library of Congress.

A catalogue record for this book is available from the British Library.

Design by Letra Libre, Inc.

First Edition: May, 2001
10 9 8 7 6 5 4 3 2 1

Printed in the United States of America.

*FOR MY GRANDMOTHERS,
DORA AND JUDITH,
AND FOR GREAT-AUNT ZARA,
THE SUFFRAGIST*

CONTENTS

ACKNOWLEDGMENTS

My first acknowledgment is to the feminist scholars who have come before me, whose groundbreaking work has not only enabled me to write this book but also helped me to appreciate the complexity and satisfaction of doing feminist literary scholarship.

My early work on Gale, during graduate school, benefited enormously from the incisive and witty commentary of Lauren Fitzgerald and Brian Culver. Also at New York University, I am grateful to Professor Josephine Hendin, who encouraged me to pursue my interest in Gale, and to Professor Perry Meisel, who first brought to my attention the similarities between Virginia Woolf and Willa Cather. Marilyn Gaull supported this project from the beginning and with her judicious editing attempted to wrestle my sometimes rebellious prose into submission. Any stylistic or syntactical infelicities in these pages are no fault of hers.

Within the community of Cather scholars whose work has so enriched my own, I owe particular debts to Bob Thacker and Merrill Skaggs for giving my ideas a forum. Ann Romines and Janis Stout have provided intellectual support and encouragement in myriad ways, through both their scholarship and their friendship. I am grateful to both of them. My knowledge of Wharton has deepened through conversations with Donna Campbell, Mark Eaton, and Katherine Joslin. I thank them for their collegiality.

At Iona College, my first debt of gratitude is to Laura Shea, for her companionship and conversation on our commute to and from New Rochelle and for taking the time, at the end of a busy semester, to read and comment on the entire manuscript. I am grateful to Warren Rosenberg, the Dean of Arts and Science at Iona, for asking me to present a portion of my work on Gale as part of the Spring 2000 Dean's Symposia. I could not have finished this project without research funding and a course remission, and for both of those I again owe thanks to Dean Rosenberg as well as to Iona's English Department. Robert Monteleone and Melaine Forsberg, at Iona's Ryan Library, provided invaluable assistance in tracking down hard-to-find materials through interlibrary loan.

My thanks to Abby Markwyn, who spent hours copying and organizing materials from the Gale Archives in Madison, Wisconsin when I could not get there myself. At at the State Historical Society of Wisconsin, I am grateful to Harry Miller, Lisa Hinzman, and the other staff members who have helped me with questions about Gale materials. My thanks to the various libraries where I read through manuscript archives: the State Historical Society in Madison, the Schlesinger Library at Radcliffe, the Butler Library at Columbia University, the Fales Library at New York University, the Morgan Library, and the Library of Congress. At the Schlesinger Library, I am particularly grateful to Jacalyn Blume, who patiently answered numerous email questions about suffrage photos.

Many friends and colleagues helped me with this manuscript. Celia Bland, Bridget Brown, Ann Brunjes, and Christopher Packard carefully read many early drafts of this material; their friendship, conversation, and energy have supported me during the entire process of writing this book. For information about women in the Klondike, I am grateful to Nancy Pope, and to the many other generous scholars who sent me references and details via the H-Amstdy listserv. I want to thank Rachel Adams and Jean Lutes, who provided much-needed commentary on the concluding chapter, and Barbara Bloom for her consistently sage advice. This book is much improved because of Shireen Patell's rigorous and insightful reading of it in manuscript; I am lucky to have such a keen scholar for a sister-in-law.

My life is immeasurably strengthened by bonds of sisterhood that I have with my real-life sister, Hannah Williams, and with my college sisters, the "Wheaties": Nina Brouwer, Sarah Bradshaw, Susan Byrd, Julianne Frawley, and Sarah Shannon. My Aunt Susan and Uncle Jim gave me a copy of *The Book of the Homeless,* a wonderful gift that let me see firsthand the scope of Wharton's war relief efforts. My family has constantly encouraged my work on this book and never once asked me, "are you done yet?" I am always thankful for their love and laughter. Lastly, I must thank my husband, Cyrus R. K. Patell, without whom I could not have written this book. His scholarship inspires me, his friendship sustains me, and his love brings me more joy than I have ever known.

I am grateful to the Watkins/Loomis Agency and the Edith Wharton estate for permission to quote from unpublished Wharton letters and to reprint photographs of Wharton. The Edward Steichen photograph of Willa Cather is reprinted with permission from Joanna Steichen and the Museum of Modern Art; other photographs of Cather are reprinted with permission from the Nebraska State Historical Society, where I am particularly grateful to Chad Wall for his help. The photographs of Zona

Gale are reprinted with permission of the State Historical Society of Wisconsin. A portion of Chapter Three was published in the *Willa Cather Pioneer Newsletter and Review,* and Chapter One appeared in slightly different form in *Studies in American Fiction;* I thank both journals for permission to reprint these materials. Finally excepts from Charlotte Perkins Gilman are reprinted with permission, courtesy of the Schlesinger Library, Radcliffe Institute, Harvard University.

INTRODUCTION

"STRANGLED WITH A PETTICOAT"

I t is a serious disadvantage to be a lady author, wrote Willa Cather to a friend in 1931, and anyone who thinks otherwise is just foolish.[1] Surprisingly, Cather was at the peak of her literary career when she wrote this: a best-selling, highly paid, well-respected author who had been awarded a Pulitzer prize, several honorary degrees from prestigious universities, and membership in the National Institute of Arts and Letters. But these successes did not alter her belief that being a woman writer presented significant difficulties, a belief she shared with her contemporary Edith Wharton. Like Cather, Wharton tended to dismiss other women writers as unrealistic romantics, shrill social activists, or followers of literary fads: Wharton characterized Mary Wilkins Freeman and Sarah Orne Jewett as the wearers of "rose colored spectacles" (1002) and described Harriet Beecher Stowe and Mrs. Gaskell as the "pleaders of special causes" who produced "that unhappy hybrid, the novel with a purpose" (175). Wharton and Cather are commonly considered hostile to other women writers, an attitude that has come to be seen as an integral aspect of each writer's personality.

One of my primary aims is to examine their hostility, which I argue is a deliberate strategy, a professional decision that had profound implications for both writers' careers and for their status in literary history. Wharton's and Cather's choice to remain publicly aloof from their female peers—a shared refusal that ironically yokes them together—becomes apparent when their careers are juxtaposed with the career of their literary friend and peer, Zona Gale. Gale's feminism, and her strong sense of female literary community, demonstrates that literary power and cultural authority could be achieved with strategies very different from those used by Wharton and Cather. Gale—herself a Pulitzer-prize winner, and a popular and critical success—did not find being a "lady author" a disadvantage, but her feminist fictions have not preserved a place for her in literary history.

The careers of these three writers highlight a transitional moment in the history of female authorship and the literary marketplace in the United States: the uneasy shift from nineteenth-century models of female authorship to some new but as-yet undefined twentieth-century alternative. Nineteenth-century writers such as Harriet Beecher Stowe, Fanny Fern, and Mrs. E.D.E.N. Southworth had wielded tremendous cultural authority at the peak of their careers, but by the turn of the century they were seen as gentle and genteel amateurs writing flowery and repetitive fictions that could be of only passing interest to a modern audience. [2] Cather, Wharton, and Gale were interested in distancing themselves from this tradition, which they all perceived as limiting the possibilities for female literary achievement. While these nineteenth-century women writers were commercially successful, their popularity made them suspect; they were not regarded seriously as artists and were not accorded the same respect in the marketplace as their male counterparts.

As Wharton, Cather, and Gale moved into the literary marketplace, they were working against what they saw as a tradition of women's writing that itself made no claim to be "art" and that was taken less seriously than men's writing. Elsa Nettels points out that between 1880 and 1889, *Harper's Magazine* published 263 works of fiction, including nineteen serialized novels, and that half—132—were known to be by women, or to appear under a woman's name (1). From similar figures in *Scribner's* and *Century,* Nettels concludes that "women writers enjoyed equal opportunity, even an advantage, in the world of commercial publishing." This commercial "equal opportunity" is contradicted, however, by the articles, reviews, and essays that ran alongside this fiction, which expressed opinions "that cast women as inferior to men, defined their difference from male writers as deviations from an approved standard, and satirized or belittled qualities labeled 'feminine'" (2). Nettels claims that individually none of this misogynistic writing made an impact, but that all together, "the mass of articles and reviews is important; the magazines, described by one observer as 'the recognized gateway to the literary public,' disseminated ideas and shaped and reflected public taste and belief" (2).[3] Thus by the time that Wharton, Cather, and Gale began their careers the role of moral guide and inspirational leader played by many nineteenth-century women writers—even those who conducted their literary business with consummate professionalism—was neither marketable nor desirable.

Wharton, Cather, and Gale considered themselves professional writers, but they also wanted to be seen—and wanted others to see them—as literary artists. Claiming the role of artist for themselves marks a significant departure from the tradition of nineteenth-century female authorship and contributes to their individual conceptions of literary authority. A writer can be considered a "professional," according to William Charvat, when her writing "provides a living for the author, like any other job; that it is a main and prolonged, rather than intermittent or sporadic, resource for the writer; that it is produced with the hope of extended sale in the open market, like any article of commerce; and that it is written with reference to buyers' taste and habits." Charvat goes on to explain that "the problem of the professional writer is not identical with that of the literary artist; but when a literary artist is also a professional writer, he cannot solve the problems of the one function without reference to the other" (3).[4] Wharton, Cather, and Gale used different methods to achieve their commercial and critical successes, but all three writers believed that women should be taken seriously as artists.

As these writers were creating new models for female literary authority, the publishing business was changing from a genteel occupation in which agreements were sealed with handshakes to a consumer-driven professional industry in which both the book and the author's own image became products. This transformation alarmed the publishing world's old guard, as Henry Holt makes clear in *The Atlantic Monthly* (1905): "Books are not bricks . . . the more authors seek publishers solely with reference to what they will pay in the day's market, the more publishers bid against one another . . . and the more they market their wares as the soulless articles of ordinary commerce are marketed, the more books tend to become soulless things" (578). Holt's fears notwithstanding, books did become more like bricks as the century progressed, and writers like Wharton, Cather, and Gale had to participate in this "soulless" endeavor if they wanted their work to be read.

Surviving and succeeding as women writers, however, presented another set of difficulties. Even as women writers created huge profits for editors, publishers, literary agents—and themselves—the literary marketplace, dominated by men, was at best ambivalent, if not hostile, about the presence of women. The novelist Joseph Hergesheimer, speaking for many male writers, complained in *The Yale Review* (1921) that literature in the United States was "being strangled with a petticoat" (718). Robert Herrick's 1929 essay, "A Feline World," echoes Hergesheimer's ideas in a subtler manner, claiming that "we have moved further along toward feminization. . . . Women know the neurotic sides of sex, which do not eventuate in either marriage or maternity, as well as what was once called (with a hush) the perverted side, the wooing of one's own sex. A disturbing number of recent stories by women deal with this taboo topic . . . [which] we must assume interests many of their readers" (3,4). The woman writer has "dared . . . to paint the slut to life," which she does very well, in Herrick's opinion, because she "understands her heroine . . . and is not crudely denunciatory of a character that . . . she perhaps realizes [that] many of her sisters share with her" (4). Women, according to Herrick, share a sororal relationship with sluts, which is why they portray them so vividly in their novels. Hergesheimer fears that women writers will silence men, and Herrick worries that they will create a perverse and sluttish literary world that ignores men altogether: "now [man] must give up the delusion that women are really interested in the things he cares about most, hunting and sporting, money-making and love-making" (2). These comments by Holt, Hergesheimer, and Herrick represent the upheavals about commercialization and feminization (which is really an anxiety about feminism) roiling the literary marketplace during the years that Wharton, Cather, and Gale established themselves as professional literary artists: both commercial success and female authorship are suspect, dangerous. The tactics used by Wharton, Cather, and Gale to negotiate the complex terrain of the marketplace and to establish their literary authority reveal the intricate intersections of literary and social politics that shaped their world.

In bringing Wharton, Cather, and Gale together, I have several concerns, including reassessing Gale's place in literary history. This book examines the ways in which gender and marketplace considerations shaped the literary careers of these three writers, all of whom were successful businesswomen who manipulated the market to their advantage, even when reviewers refused to recognize their achievements. Their similar perceptions of the marketplace led Wharton and Cather to separate themselves from other women writers, but Gale's career illustrates that literary success and wide readership did not depend on such a separation. Ultimately, however, Wharton's and Cather's rejection of public literary sisterhood was instrumental in their achieving canonical status, while Gale, who celebrated community, collaboration, and sisterhood, has been forgotten. Wharton and Cather appropriated the model of the Romantic artist—isolated, independent, solitary—developed in Europe and England a century earlier by Keats, Shelley, Goethe, and others. In *The American Adam* (1955), R.W.B. Lewis recontextualizes this image in the American grain, drawing on such writers as Cooper, Thoreau, and Hawthorne to make his point. Andreas Huyssen points out that this same model of the artist can be seen in the writings of Nietzsche, who situates the "artist-philosopher-hero, the suffering loner . . . in irreconcilable opposition to modern democracy and its inauthentic culture" (51). For Nietzsche and other turn-of-the-century male intellectuals, women were identified with the inauthenticities of mass culture, an association that Wharton and Cather were—to some degree—able to defy by inscribing themselves within the culturally ingrained and masculinized vision of the artist. As a result, I argue, Wharton and Cather were "safe" choices for feminist revision in the early 1970s and 1980s, while Gale remained obscure. Thus feminist literary critics have, perhaps subconsciously, replicated Wharton's and Cather's belief that literary authority is at odds with literary sisterhood.[5]

Gale's outspoken opinions about progressive politics and feminism are quite different from Wharton's and Cather's less vocal attitudes, but their three careers are quite similar. Like Cather, Gale was formally educated at a large university, and both were part of the New York publishing world for a number of years, Gale as a journalist and freelance reporter, Cather as managing editor of *McClure's Magazine*. Like Wharton, Gale had a lifelong interest in writing for the stage, and both lived most of their adult lives outside the American mainstream—Wharton in France and Gale in Portage, Wisconsin. They all published in the same magazines, won the same prizes and awards in consecutive years, and shared publishers, editors, and literary agents. Wharton won the Pulitzer in 1920 for *The Age of Innocence;* Gale for her stage adaptation of *Miss Lulu Bett* in 1921; Cather in 1922 for *One of Ours*. Wharton and Cather were admitted to the National Institute of Arts and Letters and were awarded gold medals from that institution; Wharton published with Appleton and was friends with Appleton's editor, Rutger Jewett, who also published and was friends with Gale. In 1929, Gale switched from Appleton to Knopf, which had been publishing Cather's work since 1920.

In addition to the parallels in their careers, the three writers shared a long correspondence: Gale corresponded with both Wharton and Cather for many years. Gale met with Cather whenever they were both in New York, and she was repeatedly invited by Wharton to join her in France. Long overlooked in studies of all three writers, these letters shed light on how the writers viewed themselves and their literary worlds. The letters between Gale and Wharton, and Gale and Cather, reveal that Wharton's and Cather's disdain for literary female companionship had more to do with their public postures than with their private desires. In their private letters to Gale, both Wharton and Cather claim her as a literary sister who shares what Wharton calls the "community of spirit," which can be inhabited only by women of letters. This correspondence demonstrates that Wharton and Cather wanted privately what they refused publicly—literary sisterhood—and highlights the fact that Wharton's and Cather's detachment from their female contemporaries did not happen incidentally but deliberately, as a plan for survival and success in the literary world.[6]

Wharton's and Cather's public refusal of sisterhood—and any other form of affiliative politics—is central to their creation of public authorial personae, images that emerged in response to the increasing demand for celebrity as a way to sell books. Literary history has followed their "spin": the two authors are almost never studied in conjunction with other women writers and are rarely contextualized within the literary marketplace where each experienced critical and financial success.[7] Gale also created a public persona for herself, but she did not separate her public from her private life as rigidly as did Wharton and Cather.

I am interested in how both their work and their public images participate in the cultural and political conflicts that mark the first decades of the twentieth century: arguments about women's roles in the public arena, about militarism and globalization, about an increasingly professionalized and technologized marketplace, about the growing gap between rich and poor. The attempts to resolve these conflicts through government intervention set the tone of the Progressive Era, from 1890 to 1924, the year that Robert La Follette, a close friend of Gale's, was defeated in his presidential bid on the Progressive ticket. Gale's lifelong involvement with social politics makes her career both the most similar to the model of nineteenth-century lady authorship and the most radical departure from it. Like her female predecessors, Gale merged her moral views with her fiction, hoping that her work would contribute to positive social change: she fought for pacifism, labor rights, racial equality, and ethnic tolerance. Unlike these earlier writers, however, Gale sought political parity for women and was not content to be thought of as just a "good influence." Moreover, Gale, like Wharton and Cather, thought of and presented herself as a literary artist. Gale's art directly engages almost all of the political and social issues of her day, but she was first and foremost a feminist.

The struggle over women's suffrage was a profound and pervasive debate in the United States from the turn of the century until the passage of the Nineteenth Amendment in 1920, and even then, the discussion about women's roles continued, albeit in different terms.[8] The fact that Wharton and Cather are seldom examined in the context of the suffrage debate demonstrates how powerfully Wharton's and Cather's own self-presentations have shaped critical understanding of their careers.[9] The struggle over suffrage was so much a part the culture of the early twentieth century that ignoring it would have been almost impossible; it was something about which everyone, particularly public figures, were expected to take a stand. Through such organizations as the International Council of Women and the more aggressive International Woman Suffrage Alliance, suffrage became a global struggle; they helped labor organizers to plan strikes (like the 1909 strike of women workers organized in New York by the Women's Trade Union League) and held rallies, parades, and pageants to promote their cause. Cather's silence about suffrage seems particularly suspect, given the strength of the New York state suffrage organization and the fact that New York was the first eastern state to enfranchise women. Several of the largest suffrage parades, in fact, marched only a few blocks from Cather's Bank Street apartment.

Given the intensity of the national debate over women's roles, the fact that Cather, Wharton, and Gale were *women* writers had a decisive influence on the shape of their careers, in terms of both the critical reception of their work and their own presentation of self to the marketplace. Although neither Wharton nor Cather made any public statement about suffrage, their silence should not be read as a lack of awareness or interest in the issue. After all, if critics and reviewers agreed that literature was being "strangled by petticoats," then someone who *wore* a petticoat needed to think about how her petticoats might influence her readers, editors, publishers, reviewers, and peers.

Not in Sisterhood begins with a discussion of the Gale-Wharton-Cather correspondence in order to establish each writer's ideas about the literary marketplace and her position within that world, particularly her attitudes about literary sisterhood and literary authority. Although Wharton never mentioned Cather in her letters or essays, and Cather publicly mentioned Wharton only once, their letters to Gale make clear that they saw the literary world in similar terms. In Chapter Two, I examine the trajectory of Gale's career, which demonstrates that success as a "serious" literary figure could be linked to working within a communal, political network composed almost entirely of women. In Chapters Three and Four, I consider these writers in the context of the two central conflicts of the early twentieth century: World War I and the struggle for woman suffrage. Because the fight for suffrage overlapped with World War I, there is not a neat chronological ordering to the work that I discuss in these chapters; instead I move back and forth along the span of each writer's career to examine how these conflicts are synthesized by the fiction. Using the suffrage debates as a context for all three writers, I examine the ways that their work intersects with pervasive questions about women's roles. Never as outspoken as Gale, Cather and Wharton nevertheless demonstrate their interest in questions of female autonomy and female authority throughout their careers, even in work that appears to be, on the surface, either utterly removed from such issues or highly pessimistic about the possibility of change. Despite Wharton's and Cather's pessimism, however, their novels do offer the possibility of escape from patriarchal society.

I discuss these alternatives in Chapter Three, which argues that in *The House of Mirth* (1905) and *My Ántonia* (1918), powerful feminist alternatives are deliberately positioned at the margins of both novels, rather than at center stage, thus allowing the writers to challenge social hierarchies without being labeled as feminists. Both novels were successful, but these "breakthrough" successes were more than matched by Gale's outspoken feminist parable, *Miss Lulu Bett* (1920), which was a smash hit as both a novel and a play and demonstrates that feminist politics and literary success are not necessarily at odds. These three novels, with their very different portrayals of feminist alternatives to traditional feminine domesticity, thus link feminism with the instantiation of female literary authority.

In addition to her belief in feminism, Gale was a devout pacifist, and both beliefs fueled the writing she did about World War I, which Wharton and Cather addressed in a more conventional manner. Drawing on previous critical successes, each writer felt compelled to tackle the subject of World War I and, as a result, collided with the rigidly gendered expectations about what "war writing" should be and who had the authority to write about it. In Chapter Four, I discuss the questions about gender and authority that arise when women write about war and the consequences of Wharton's, Cather's, and Gale's traversing the gender–genre boundary, a boundary that was being patrolled ever more vigilantly by the (mostly male) critical establishment. Although Gale writes about pacifism, and Wharton and Cather write about the war itself, all three received mostly poor reviews for their war fiction, reviews that either explicitly or implicitly blame the failure of the work on the fact that the writers are women, as if to suggest that when it comes to war it is impossible to escape gendered perspectives. Whether writing about pacifism at home or soldiers on the front lines, however, writing about the war fueled each writer's postwar career and enabled her to move into new areas.

The concluding chapter examines how the institutionalization of American modernism shaped Wharton's and Cather's careers and helped to "disappear" Gale altogether. This chapter also ties together a thread that runs through the entire book: the ongoing problem of popularity. Writing popular fiction implied a lack of seriousness, an absence of artistic integrity, particularly if the writer was a woman. A 1921 *Vanity Fair* photo spread, for instance, included Cather and Wharton as examples of "American novelists who have set art above popularity . . . authors who have consistently stood out against philistia" (55). Wharton and Cather are the only two women writers in the article, which also includes Sherwood Anderson, Theodore Dreiser, James Branch Cabell, and Joseph Hergesheimer, who one imagines would have been furious at being included with two members of the "feminine nuisance." Ironically, *Vanity Fair* accused popular writers of pandering, but it was from magazines such as *Vanity Fair,* and their primarily female readership, that writers derived their popularity. Because women were often associated with mass culture and the erosion of aesthetic standards, however, it was particularly difficult for a woman writer to be both commercially and critically successful.[10] In a 1921 journal entry, Virginia Woolf discussed the tension between art and popularity: "This question of praise and fame must be faced. . . . How much difference does popularity make. . . . One does not want an established reputation, such as I think I was getting, as one of our leading female novelists" (Marcus 142). This is the same problem that faced Wharton, Cather, and Gale: what does it mean to be a "leading female novelist" in the United States? Their different answers to this question form the crux of this book.

CHAPTER ONE

THREATS OF CORRESPONDENCE: THE LETTERS OF WILLA CATHER, ZONA GALE, AND EDITH WHARTON

Gale's friendship with Wharton started when they were both being published by Appleton; Rutger Jewett, the chief editor at Appleton, was a friend to both writers and forwarded to Wharton a letter that Gale had written him praising Wharton's *Glimpses of the Moon* (1922). In response, Wharton wrote to Jewett:

> I would give all the reviews, I mean all the most favourable ones, for such a letter as Miss Gale's, not only because I admire her work so much and consequently value her approval in proportion to my admiration, but also because she has put her finger on the very central nerve of my book. This does not happen more than once or twice, even in a long career. (August 29, 1922, State Historical Society of Wisconsin [SHSW])[1]

Gale's ability to read intimately, "touching the central nerve," establishes her in Wharton's mind as a sympathetic and intuitive critic, a reader who might be able to fill the gap created by the death of Sara Norton, Wharton's dear friend and longtime correspondent. Norton, who died in the summer of 1922, never achieved the literary success that Wharton did, but she often sent her writing to Wharton, who was both encouraging and complimentary about it.[2] Several days after she wrote this letter to Jewett, Wharton wrote to Gale, thanking her for her kind words about *Glimpses* and initiating a correspondence that would last for more than ten years.

The long correspondence that Wharton and Gale shared is rarely noted in Wharton studies, however, just as Cather studies has overlooked

the friendship between Cather and Gale, oversights fueled in part by
Cather's and Wharton's stern public silence about one another and about
Gale. Critics have been hypnotized by this silence: neither Wharton nor
Cather appears in studies of the other, although as the letters discussed
here make clear, their ideas about both the literary world and their own
literary status resemble one another's to such a degree that simple coinci-
dence is not sufficient explanation. When reexamined through the lens of
their correspondences with Gale, the silence between Wharton and
Cather testifies to the difficulty of forming a community of literary
women.[3] Their letters reveal a desire for sisterhood that is not ever expressed publicly: sisterhood, for Wharton and Cather, exists as a private
bond, not as a public affiliation. In the world of the letter there is a private community within which the two correspondents exist, but in public both Wharton and Cather are silent about Gale, their friend and peer.

Gale spoke and wrote about both Wharton and Cather in public, and
certainly the three writers were linked in the publishing world, Wharton's
and Cather's efforts to distance themselves from other women notwithstanding. Shortly after Wharton's letter to Jewett, in fact, an advertisement trumpeting the praises of *Glimpses of the Moon* appeared in the *New
York Times Book Review,* with Gale's name and words of praise promi-
nently displayed: "I spent a great half night with [the book] a week ago.
What a phenomenon she is and how much she has done and is doing for
American letters!" The ad raves about the popularity of the novel, claiming that "FIVE gigantic editions have not been sufficient to meet the demand for Mrs. Wharton's novel in the first month of its publication." The
hyberbolic praise of *Glimpses* is markedly different from the measured, although ultimately positive, review of Cather's *One of Ours* that appears on
the facing page, written by Fisher. A casual reader of the *Times* would
thus see Wharton, Cather, Gale, and Fisher on equal terms with one another, with Wharton, in fact, seeming like the least "serious" of the four.
Gale and Fisher frequently reviewed and "blurbed" other writers, but
Wharton and Cather seldom spoke publicly about others' work; their silences about other authors (both male and female) speak to their unwillingness to be seen as part of a literary community of any sort.[4]

Wharton's and Cather's public silences about their female peers negate
their privately expressed desire for sisterhood. Their relationships to Gale,
and to each other, manifest what Helena Michie has called "sororophobia," a relationship that "encompass[es] both the desire for and recoil from
identification with other women" (9). Sororophobia, according to Michie,
is not a static model but is "about negotiat[ing] sameness and difference,
identity and separation between women of the same generation. . . . [It is]
a matrix against and through which women work out—or fail to work

out—their differences" (9). Desire and recoil are the two movements of these letters; Wharton and Cather are drawn to Gale because she is, like them, a woman writer, and yet they distance themselves from her (and from one another) for the same reason. These letters are about fending off that threatening, scribbling Other, who is also, in some ways, the Self.

Both Wharton and Cather seek friendship and literary discussions with Gale, yet create boundaries that prevent intimacy. Wharton insists that she belongs to an older (and wiser) generation than Gale's; their letters collude in creating a relationship that establishes Wharton as mentor and literary mother, Gale as novitiate and daughter. Cather structures her relationship with Gale using geographical markers rather than generational lines; in her letters to Gale, Cather continually marks the physical distance between them, even as she professes hope for future meetings. Wharton's and Cather's correspondence with Gale creates a triangle that links Wharton and Cather despite their desire to be separate from their female literary peers, a desire that yokes them together even as it drives them apart.

I

A correspondence is a communication by letters between people who are separated, but a correspondence is also a point of similarity, a likeness. The very word itself incorporates the dynamic of the relationships discussed here: similarity and difference, distance and an attempt to bridge that distance through the establishment of similarity. Wharton and Cather find in Gale a correspondent who is in fact a co-respondent to a literary world hostile to women's attempts to wrest literary, artistic authority for themselves. Gale too must answer to the public's expectations of a woman writer, but unlike Wharton and Cather, Gale is unthreatened by correspondences between herself and other women writers.

In one of her first letters to Gale, Wharton uses the phrase "community of spirit" to describe her sense of connection to the other writer, a phrase that sounds as if Wharton had resolved her ambivalence about friendships with other women writers. She writes to Gale that "when one greatly enjoys and admires a book, one always (I find) takes for granted such a community of spirit between the writer and one's self" (October 22, 1922, SHSW). The relationship described by this phrase is far more complex than Wharton herself realizes: participating fully in a "community of spirit," for both Wharton and Cather, opposes many of their decisions about their public representations of self as well as complicates their perceptions of both the literary world and their female literary peers.

Communities form because people share a set of values or ideals; the boundaries of the group are created by what is shared.[5] Within these borders, then, one can reasonably assume a measure of understanding, of sympathy. At the same time, though, placing oneself inside the boundaries of a community carries with it the possibility that those on the outside will see only the group identity. Individual identity may appear to be erased because the communal identity becomes larger than the individual's. It is this difficulty that gives rise to xenophobic attitudes of all sorts—depending on one's position, the people either inside or outside the boundary are strange, or inferior, or dangerous, or interchangeable. In a community bound together by a shared set of ideals, however, one risks having the communal ideal become more important than individual achievement; individual ideals are subordinate to the good of the cause. One could argue that this is, in miniature, the ongoing struggle in the United States: Which should, or does, take precedence, the group or the individual? I am interested in how the struggle between group and individual identity gets played out along gender lines, particularly given that Wharton and Cather's model of the artist is that of the solitary hero, a figure coded "male," particularly in America. Defining themselves as artists presents a dual problem for both Wharton and Cather: they are assuming a role that is, implicitly, male, as well as a role that, while not necessarily precluding communal feeling, certainly precludes communal participation.[6] It seems unsurprising, then, that several of the women writers of this period (including Wharton) who wanted to challenge this definition of artist did so from Europe, separating themselves from the national community that they found so limiting. Gertrude Stein, for example, resolutely separated herself from the United States, and from other women writers, for many of the same reasons that Wharton and Cather did. Shari Benstock argues that Stein "would be furious at being grouped with . . . women writers" (9) because she thought that to do so would diminish her authorial power.

Wharton, Cather, and Gale sought to define themselves as artists and wanted to be perceived as such by the literary world. To Cather and Wharton, "artist" meant autonomous and celebrated, while "woman writer" automatically enrolled one in a community that was limiting and belittled. Artists needed to abstain from public politics, social action, and reform; involvement in social issues was too similar to the model of the nineteenth-century woman writer. These nineteenth-century writers presented themselves as professionals, not as artists: they spoke publicly about the fact that they wrote to support their families, or to offer moral instruction, or to speak for social change. Wharton and Cather used their definition of artist to reject this tradition, although as Gale's successes make clear, literary authority could be established without completely rejecting this tradition.

For Gale, community was both public and practical; she assumed that any community of spirit would eventually put itself into action for the greater good. Gale's writing—both fiction and nonfiction—engages with social and political causes, as does the writing of many of her female contemporaries, but in their work Wharton and Cather steadfastly resist such engagements.[7] While their letters express a desire for community, both Wharton and Cather shy away from public affiliations, from publicly defining themselves in any particular way. The community of spirit to which Wharton and Cather aspired is an exclusive and private realm that would cease to be ideal if it entered the public domain; it is a private bond that need not be physicalized any further than the pages of a book—or a letter. A community of spirit becomes the ideal for Wharton and Cather because it depends only on states of mind; it is something to think about, feel, and imagine, but not to enact in any public way.

The letters that Wharton and Cather wrote to Gale are marked by an awareness of shared experiences, ideas, and attitudes about the world and writing. These shared experiences create the community of spirit but also threaten Wharton's and Cather's self-created identities as individual artists who wanted to be free from considerations of gender, age, nationality, or class. The correspondence between Gale and Wharton, and Cather and Gale, make apparent that public resistance to community was difficult to maintain and yet central to Wharton's and Cather's conceptions of themselves as artists: their privately expressed desire for community conflicts with their public separation of "artist" from "woman." The contradictory dynamic of these letters thus reflects the shift from private expression to public silence, and from the idealized vision of a "community of spirit" to the reality of individual achievements, hard-won and jealously preserved.

II

Given Wharton's tendency to keep her distance from other women writers, particularly those who could be considered her peers, it seems likely that the loss of Sara Norton spurred her to initiate the correspondence with Gale. Wharton's letter to Gale, thanking her for the kind words about *Glimpses of the Moon*, seems, subtly, to ask for a response:

> "Miss Lulu Bett" and "Main Street" seem to me the two significant books
> in recent American fiction; the turning of a pretty long lane—and I am

very proud to think that in the new generation which you and Mr. Lewis seem to me to lead, there is so kindly and sympathetic an understanding for what I have always been trying to do. So often, when the form of expression, the manner of doing a thing, changes, the purpose seems to change too; but I think you and I have the same end in view, and that is to extract all possible significance and beauty out of plain things As They Are.

I cheer you with sympathy and admiration—and await with impatience the "little book" over which you are now hanging. (September 1, 1922, SHSW)

This is one of the few letters between Wharton and Gale that mentions a male writer, but in her comparison of *Miss Lulu Bett* with *Main Street,* Wharton is following a trend: when Gale's novel was published, critics argued about which of the two novels was more important.[8]

Wharton's letter accurately suggests that she and Gale are equals, writers who share a realist aesthetic that enables them to find beauty in everyday material and to imbue significance in "things As They Are." Wharton affiliates herself with Gale by initiating their correspondence and establishing their "community of spirit," but at the same time she distances herself from Gale by asserting that Gale is a member of the "new generation." Lest Gale be put off by this generation gap, however, Wharton ends the letter with the implicit request for a copy of Gale's next book, a request that is sure to flatter Gale and to ensure a response.

When Wharton wrote to Gale, she was in fact writing to someone who, in the literary world, would have been regarded as her equal for a number of reasons, not the least of which was that Gale was the only other woman who had ever been awarded a Pulitzer prize. Wharton was awarded the prize two years before the date of this letter, in 1920, for *The Age of Innocence;* Gale won in 1921 for the dramatic version of *Miss Lulu Bett.* Wharton earned more money than Gale, but Gale achieved success in the one arena that would continue to defeat the other writer—the stage. Their work appeared in the same magazines and was reviewed by the same people; they were being published by the same publishing house. Wharton's implication that her own work was passé seems like false modesty, considering that only two years earlier she had been awarded a Pulitzer and that *Glimpses of the Moon* sold over 100,000 copies in its first six months of publication. Moreover, the movie rights for *Glimpses* were purchased for $13,500, and F. Scott Fitzgerald wrote the screenplay. Presenting herself as someone who was past her prime, when in fact she was writing and publishing at a prodigious rate, suggests that what Wharton wants from Gale is cheerleading, admiration, and praise. The postscript to her first letter further suggests the type of relationship

Wharton wants to establish with Gale: "that you should have felt the bracelet scene—which nobody notices—is balm to me!" By praising Gale's abilities as an intuitive and sympathetic reader, Wharton does two things: she affiliates herself with Gale by virtue of their shared emotions, and she attempts to ensure that this is the type of response she will get from Gale in the future.

Gale's sympathetic reading ability makes her Wharton's ideal reader, a figure whom Wharton described in "The Vice of Reading" (1903), an early essay published in the *North American Review*. In her essay, Wharton asks, "What is reading, in the last analysis, but an interchange of thought between writer and reader?" She goes on to oppose the "born reader" with the "mechanical reader," whom Wharton blames for much of what she finds troubling about the contemporary literary world: a preponderance of "mediocre writing," a tendency to confuse "moral and intellectual judgments," and, worst of all, the "mechanical critic," who offers "pseudo-reviews" (*Uncollected Writing* 104–105). Gale, on the other hand, with her sympathy and intuition, possesses the skill that Wharton says "is an art, and an art that only the born reader can acquire" (*Uncollected Writing* 100). In her letters to Wharton, Gale lives up to these expectations by consistently seeking Wharton's advice, praising her work, and insisting on her literary importance.

Gale's first letter directly to Wharton makes no mention of Gale's own successes but instead characterizes Wharton as a mother, a queen, almost a god. She has no ambivalence about Wharton's presence in the literary world, only eagerness to establish a connection:

> I shall always be in the spell of your letter—the surprise of it, the incredibility of it, the gift of it. I must not try to tell you because I cannot. How since *Crucial Instances* [1901], in my first year in New York you have been to me cloud and fire. Not only in your own but in that you were taking us all, writers and readers, with you to new places. Because of you we could not stay where we were. I have known this from the first line of yours that I read. I recall the pang of the very passage. This emotion inevitably held a personal feeling—I have your photograph!—the one of you cloaked and reading a letter—by way of a magazine to which your publishers had furnished it. And now to have Her write to me in these words is the final emblem. It is like being knighted and as if I might now at last begin the long quest. (October 4, 1922, SHSW)

Wharton's letter to Gale praises Gale for her sense of aesthetic; Gale's response, in turn, makes clear that, for her and others, Wharton pioneered the role of female literary artist. Given Gale's feminism, the "us" who will be led by Wharton to "new places" should be read as women who seek a promised land where they can redefine the role of woman writer; Wharton becomes a literary Moses whose "cloud and fire" enables others to imagine new possibilities. Different from the reviewers who continued to see Wharton as merely a follower of James, Gale positions her as an unquestionably original presence.[9] Wharton is "Her," as if she were a goddess whose letters consecrate Gale in the sacred cause of Literature, but at the same time, Gale establishes an emotional bond with her idol by asserting that through reading Wharton's words, she knows what Wharton herself must have been feeling. From that connection it is a short step to link the words with the image; Wharton's photograph is for Gale the very type of the woman writer, someone to emulate and adore.

Wharton's response to this letter reveals her understanding of the literary world, although her characterization carefully leaves room for Gale to continue to offer flattering descriptions of Wharton:

> How could you think I hadn't felt the importance of Lulu, supposing you'd thought at all about my possible opinion of her?—I'm always, watchfully and patiently, on the look-out for what you young people are doing, and exulting and triumphing when a Lulu or a Babbitt emerges—the real surprise is that any of you should care about my work and my point of view. I thought you all regarded me as the Mrs.—well, fill in a respectable deceased Victorian name—of America, for, having all through my early career been condemned by the reviewers of my native land for "not knowing how to construct" a novel, I am now far more utterly banned by their descendants for "constructing."
>
> It all comes to the same thing in the end—but the praise of your generation consoles me as nothing else could for being so long and invariably criticized and approved for the [same] things!
>
> Thank you again for your letter—and do come see me someday, won't you? Yours ever sincerely . . .
>
> [Postscript] Please suppress the retired Prima Donna in the (appropriated) Opera Cloak! This is what I really look like—or did one day during the wars, seeing off an American ambulance—(October 22, 1922, SHSW, last long dash in original)

By using the word "felt" to describe her understanding of *Miss Lulu Bett,* Wharton links her reading style to Gale's—they are both "feeling" readers. Having established their similarity in that way, Wharton then distances herself from Gale by claiming that Gale is one of those "young people" who isn't interested in Wharton's opinion. Wharton continually asserts a generational split between herself and Gale, although in fact Gale was only about twelve years younger, and like Wharton, did not start her career as a fiction writer until her late thirties.[10] While Wharton's letter attempts to present her as a dispassionate observer who is "watchfully and patiently" surveying the literary world, she undercuts her detachment by admitting that Gale's praise "consoles" her for the inconsistencies of earlier critics.

The photograph that Wharton sends to Gale reveals Wharton's struggle to balance herself between generations, and between public and private selves. The photo to which Gale refers was published in a magazine, a public forum about which Wharton was ambivalent (wanting the money and yet feeling disdainful of the fiction published alongside her own). Gale responds to the photo precisely as publishers had hoped: the picture created a bond between writer and reader that facilitated sales. The magazine photo of Wharton presents her as an elegant woman, draped in an elaborate cloak, reading a letter—an emblem of private, personal communication. There is no indication in the picture that Wharton is a novelist or even a writer at all; she is a reader caught at a private moment. The photo creates a separation between "woman" and "novelist" by highlighting what Jane Gallop points out in her essay, "Annie Leclerc Writing a Letter, With Vermeer" (1986): that the difference between books and letters illustrates "writing and sexual difference. . . . Women write letters—personal, intimate, in relation; men write books—universal, public, in general circulation" (139). Nothing in the photo suggests that Wharton is a novelist; instead, she looks like a lady of luxurious leisure. Wharton replaces that photo with one that represents her as actively involved in the war effort, a photo also removed from writing, but one that Wharton insists is truly representative of her. The cloaked letter-reader is to be "suppressed" by an active woman; the two photos span the movement of generations: from genteel turn-of-the-century "prima donna" to a New Woman helping the ambulance corps in France.

Wharton tells Gale that this active figure is what she "really" looks like, a curious statement given that in the same letter she describes herself as a dead Victorian. How can she be both a dead Victorian and an active participant in the defining event of the "younger generation"? Despite her disparaging comments about her diminished status, Wharton seems to want it both ways: the status of an elder and the collegiality of a peer, to be both mother and sister, as it were. In both cases, however, Wharton attempts to control public perception of herself; she does not want her image in circulation without proper context. The two photographs represent two of Wharton's fictional modes, as well: the society woman writing a contemporary novel of manners like *Glimpses of the Moon* and the woman who asserts her literary authority by tackling that most masculine of subjects, the war, in such work as *The Marne* (1918) and *A Son at the Front* (1923).

Photo 1   "Please suppress the retired Prima Donna in the (appropriated) Opera Cloak!"
Edith Wharton to Zona Gale (October 22, 1922, SHSW). Reprinted by permission of the
estate of Edith Wharton and the Watkins/Loomis Agency and by the courtesy of the Lilly
Library, Indiana University, Bloomington, IN.

Wharton's struggle to define herself also occurs in her dealings with
publishers. At about the same time she began writing to Gale, Wharton
wrote to Scribner's, asking: "Will you please tell your advertising agent
once and for all that my name in private life is Mrs. Wharton, and in lit-

Photo 2   Edith Wharton at the front in France during World War I. Reprinted by permission of the estate of Edith Wharton and the Watkins/Loomis Agency and by the courtesy of the Lilly Library, Indiana University, Bloomington, IN.

erature 'Edith Wharton.' The coupling of the Mrs and my Christian name is very disagreeable to me" (September 13, 1922, Fales Library Collection). Interestingly, Gale's letters to Wharton are addressed to Mrs. Wharton, and Wharton signs her letters to Gale as Edith Wharton, often running the two words together as one. Gale writes to the private woman, but Wharton responds as a writer, as her literary self.

Wharton's letter implies that Gale's praise can counterbalance the critics who dismiss Wharton no matter what she writes. An earlier letter of Wharton's, to her friend Robert Grant, sheds light on Wharton's real quarrel with her critics—a quarrel that has to do with Wharton's own assumptions about the connections between writing and gender. Her difficulty in writing novels, she says to Grant, occurs because

> I conceive my subjects like a man—that is, rather more architectonically and dramatically than most women—and then execute them like a woman; or rather I sacrifice, to my desire for construction and breadth, the small incidental effects that women have always excelled in, the episodical characterization, I mean. The worst of it is that this fault is congenital, and not the result of an ambition to do big things. As soon as I look at a subject from a novel-angle I see it in its relation to a larger whole . . . and I can't help trying to take them in, at the cost of the smaller realism that I arrive at, I think, better in my short stories. This is the reason I have always obscurely felt that I didn't know how to write a novel. . . . [which is] such a sharp contrast to the sense of authority with which I take hold of a short story—I think it ought to be a warning to stop; but alas, I see things more and more from the novel-angle, so that I'm enclosed in a vicious circle from which I suspect silence to be the only escape. (*Letters* 124)

A "constructed" novel with breadth and scope is male; the short story, with its "small incidental effects" is female, her genre through an accident of birth, "congenital," rather than a deliberate choice.[11] Wharton's protestations at having no ambition for "big things" sounds disingenuous here, given that she had just published *The Fruit of the Tree* (1907), a 633-page novel that discussed, among its other issues, euthanasia, industrial reform, and female employment. Wharton's early critics, according to her letter to Gale, followed this same gendered reasoning: at first they dismissed her because she did *not* write like a man, and now, in this era of the "New Woman" critics dismiss her because she *does* writes like a man.[12] Although she does not say so directly, one of the assumptions underlying Wharton's narrative of frustration must be that Gale will understand her quandary because she too is subject to the same constraints. Because Gale praises both short stories and novels equally, her letters assure Wharton that she should not "escape" into silence.

Wharton begins writing to Gale just after publishing *Glimpses of the Moon,* one of Wharton's most "Gale-like" novels. Wharton's heroine, Susy Lansing, like so many of Gale's heroines, must work for a living, which ultimately she finds deeply satisfying because it allows her to be independent. Having rejected a rich suitor, Susy is forced to become the governess to the five Fulmer children, whose parents are traveling in Italy.

It is a job she learns to love, although she realizes that "'mothering' on a large scale would never, she perceived, be her job" (243). Managing this large and not-wealthy household gives her "the sense of being herself mothered, of taking her first steps in the life of immaterial values which had begun to seem so much more substantial than any she had known" (243–44). Susy's life with the Fulmer children, which looks hectic and unimportant on the outside, feels to her "wide and deep and crowded!" (247). The fact that Gale chose to write Jewett about *Glimpses* suggests that in the story of Susy's maturation Gale saw Wharton working with themes from her own work, particularly Susy's realization that "she could not bear . . . the thought of giving up this mystic relation to the life she had missed" (247). Like many Gale protagonists, Susy experiences an almost-spiritual awakening; and unlike many Wharton protagonists, Susy is rewarded for her independence by being reunited with her estranged husband, whom she has almost divorced. Taking care of others, and earning a living in the process, enables Susy to become an independent, self-sufficient woman.

Glimpses of the Moon marks the beginning of Wharton's increasing focus on the parent–child relationship, an interest that Wharton reveals in a comment to Gale that broke one of Wharton's own cardinal rules of criticism. In her memoir, Wharton writes that "there could be no greater critical ineptitude than to judge a novel according to *what it ought to have been about*" (939). But in writing to Gale about *Faint Perfume* (1923), Wharton does precisely that. Gale's novel, which was both a critical and popular success, tells the story of Leda Perrin, a writer and journalist who must return to her small-town home when she is stricken with neuritis in her writing arm.[13] When her father dies suddenly, Leda must move in with her ghastly cousins, the Crumbs, where she meets and falls in love with her cousin Richmiel's estranged husband, Barnaby. Richmiel is en route to California to get a divorce and wants to leave Oliver, their son, with her husband—until she realizes that Barnaby and Leda are in love. Although Richmiel doesn't want the child, she tells Barnaby that he must choose between Leda and Oliver. Barnaby first chooses Leda, but then the two of them realize that their love is strong enough to allow them to separate, so Barnaby renounces her and rescues his son from his venal ex-wife. The novel ends with Richmiel telling Leda maliciously, "You know, I'm doing you a favor, Leda, really—saving you from Barnaby. It'll work out so, you'll see" (218). Wharton tells Gale,

> The real subject [of the novel], then, seems to me to be the wife's retrospective jealousy, and the fact that she discovers that she can twist the screw by means of the child. That, I think, ought to have been your "front center"—

whereas it happens rather incidentally, as the book goes along, and you do not seem to me to get the ultimate extract out of it. (April 14, 1923, SHSW)

Wharton's letter to Gale suggests the book that Wharton would have written with the same material, and she may have been right: a novel about the vindictive Richmiel and her manipulations of husband and child may well have been more interesting. After this critique, Wharton goes on to criticize "new fiction" in general, saying that it "leaps across those silent depths over which I still think the great novelist will always have to lean patiently and quietly to attain his result." It is not clear whether Wharton includes Gale's work in this category. Should Gale be insulted or heartened by Wharton's frank assessment?

Wharton's letter about *Faint Perfume*, which moves between criticism and praise, enacts in miniature the dynamic of the entire Wharton–Gale correspondence. Most of the letter to Gale tells her that, essentially, she had missed the point of her own novel—hadn't gotten the "ultimate extract" from her ideas. But the letter begins by saying, "As I look across the room at that charming photograph [of Gale] . . . I feel I could say to it in five minutes just what I think . . . the book is full of good things, of delicious touches." Echoing her self-deprecating comment to Robert Grant about her own feminine knack for "small episodic touches," Wharton's use of the phrases "good things" and "delicious touches" here seems implicitly to compliment Gale for her feminine qualities. Wharton's letter to Gale thus damns with faint praise: she denigrates the novel's overall accomplishment but lauds its incidental moments. Then, as if to forestall Gale's protests, Wharton adds a handwritten note to the typed letter, apologizing for her comments: "[I] await your pardon with compunction, and your reply with the most sympathetic interest. Thank you again for your thought in sending me the book, and for making me believe that my comments on it can be of interest or use to you. That is a real pleasure to me." This handwritten touch adds a personal note of pleasure and makes the relationship sound curiously sadomasochistic: Gale has made Wharton believe that her opinions matter, and the price of establishing that idea is to suffer at the hands of her mentor. Wharton cleverly structures her letter in such a way that if Gale were to disregard Wharton's comments, she would in effect dismantle their relationship.

From the beginning of their friendship, in fact, Wharton has been both supporter and critic. In her first letter to Gale, about *Miss Lulu Bett*, Wharton tells her that "the very felicity of your choice of words, or rather, perhaps its *justness*, the way they unerringly fit your case, makes me somehow feel, that perhaps, in this instance, your style does *not*. And I feel that a book like 'Lulu' and books like those you may and must give us hereafter, are too much of a turning-point in our fiction for anything about them to be negligible—least of all the language in which they are written" (September 26, 1922, SHSW).[14] So on the one hand, Gale's novel is a brilliant success—if, that is, one can manage to overlook the very language with which the novel is written. Wharton always surrounds her tough critiques with affectionate praise, as we see with both *Faint Perfume* and *Miss Lulu Bett*. The letter in which she criticizes Gale's prose style closes with a request: "Forgive all this, please! and take it as the expression of an elder's warm admiration and interest."

In each case, Gale accepts Wharton's critiques gladly, almost joyfully, seeing their discussion as a manifestation of the "community of spirit" that she and Wharton share. Even when Wharton suggests that Gale should have completely restructured the plot of *Faint Perfume*, Gale offers only one small protest about her intentions, saying that she wanted the novel to be about "that moment when [the lovers] knew that concerning love, we do not divine the height or the depth thereof" (May 7, 1923, SHSW). Gale seizes Wharton's description of novelists leaning over silent depths (conveniently ignoring the dig at the shortcomings of "new fiction"), claiming that her letter is the "bread and wine of criticism, surely, your 'silent depths over which the great novelists will always have to lean patiently and quietly.' . . . How unerringly you touch [my] handling." Just as Gale's comments about *Glimpses of the Moon* touched a nerve with Wharton, Wharton's comments about this novel have touched a similar nerve. She is "impatient at much praise of this book," Gale writes, because critics seem to be praising things other than what she had intended, and she sees in the novel the same flaws that Wharton does: "the wife's jealousy bulks so surprisingly—I meant her to be only one obstacle . . . [but she] is as definite as an apple . . . and the 'character parts' do overshadow the two whom I wanted to tower." Despite these problems, Gale asserts that "I've learned a great deal from writing the book—and a great deal from your letter. This look of yours toward me is very dear to me, the wise word, the friendly hand, and over all a certain brooding hope which leaves one quite breathless. From my heart thank you for these." These last comments demonstrate Gale's balancing act between asserting her own development as a writer and maintaining her position as Wharton's student, a good daughter, who sees that Wharton's tough critique is good for her. Far from intimidating her, Wharton's presence in the literary landscape—hovering like some benevolent spirit—creates a sense of collaboration and community that will lead to new and better work.

Future letters to Wharton reflect Gale's increasing confidence about her own position in the literary world, although she always maintains a deferential attitude toward the other writer. She commiserates with

26

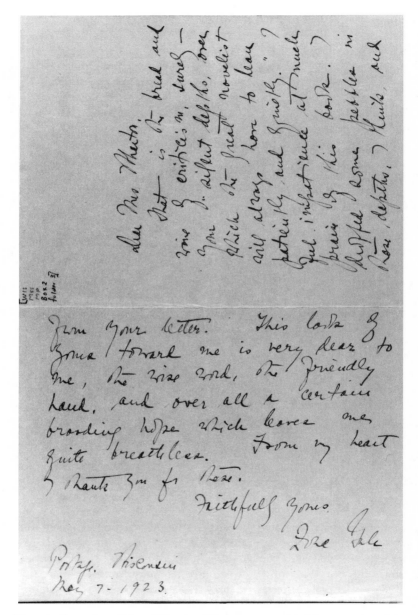

Photo 3   Letter from Gale to Wharton. Gale letter is reproduced by permission of the State Historical Society of Wisconsin.

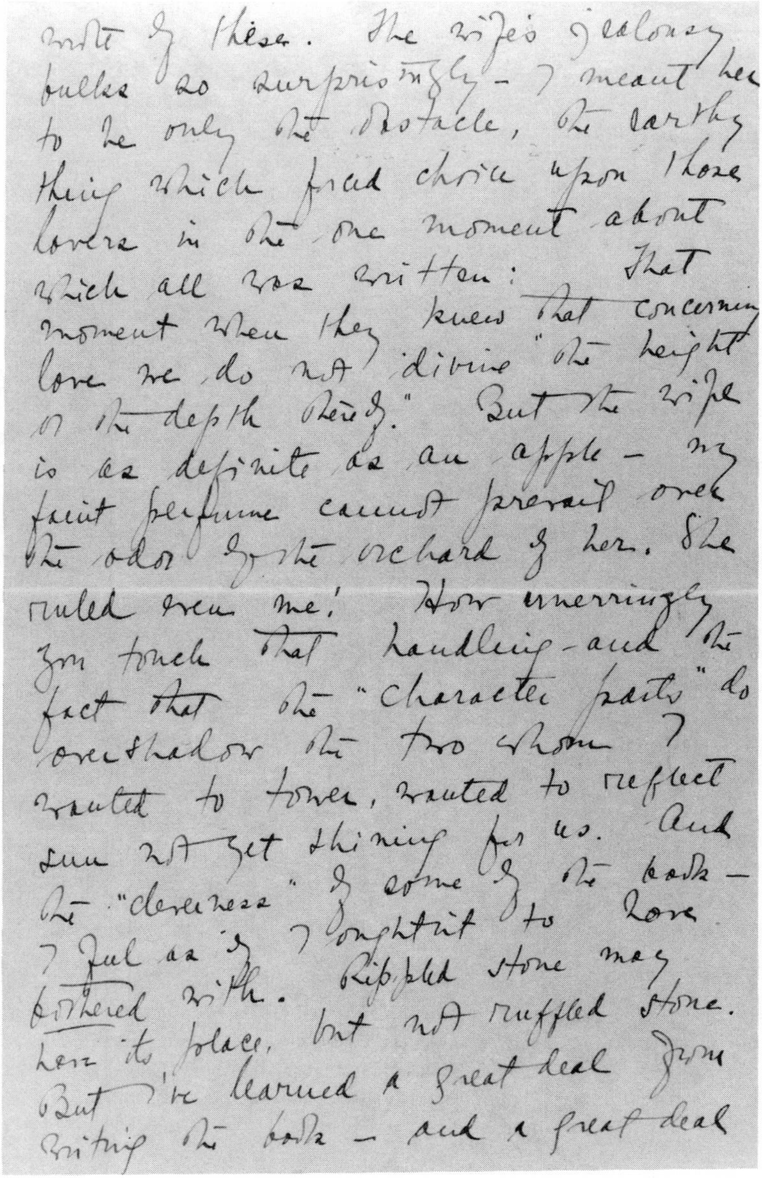

most of these. The wife's jealousy bulks so surprisingly — I meant her to be only the obstacle, the earthy thing which fixed choice upon those lovers in the one moment about which all was written: that moment when they knew that concerning love we do not "divine the height or the depth Verily." But the wife is as definite as an apple — my faint perfume cannot prevail over the odor of the orchard of her. She ruled even me! How unerringly you touch that handling — and the fact that the "character parts" do overshadow the two whom I wanted to tower, wanted to reflect sun not yet shining for us. And the "cleverness" of some of the book — I feel as if I ought it to have bothered with. Rippled stone may have its solace, but not ruffled stone. But I've learned a great deal from writing the book — and a great deal

Photo 3   Continued.

Wharton over the negative reviews that Wharton got for *The Writing of Fiction* (1925) but then consoles her with the fact that Gale chose to use it as an exemplar in a series of lectures she gave at Pennsylvania State College: "I was miserable over the notice of your book—I had so much from it . . . these problems and effects are for us, here, now in America. . . . In July, I am to give six lectures, for credit! at Pennsylvania State College and I shall be indebted to you once more, for this is the only text I shall use" (March 22, 1926, SHSW). Gale's status is such that she can extend her own literary authority to help publicize and popularize Wharton's work. In another letter, she asks Wharton her opinion about how to arrange dialogue on the printed page: in *Preface to a Life* (1926), she integrated the "necessary talk" into one paragraph without beginning new paragraphs for each speaker. The "vital talk" is paragraphed as usual, she explains, which creates what she thinks is "the logical page for the adult eye."[15] Teasingly, she notes that Wharton would of course tell her to "have only vital talk!" This structural rearranging will, she knows, "take close reading. They ought to give close reading! But will they?" This disparaging reference to "them" illustrates her sense that she and Wharton share a less-than-ideal audience and that they are equals in their attempts to make themselves understood to this group.

In response to Gale's question about formalist experimentation, Wharton seems more fully to accept Gale as an equal than as a promising member of the "younger generation"; she extends to Gale her highest compliment, calling her an "artist" and praising *Preface to a Life,* Gale's mystical and structurally experimental novel:

> Your new book has such a beautiful title that for a long time my imagination caressed it before I began to read. . . .
>
> This is the saddest book you have written, I think—and the greatest unconscious denunciation of the standardized and the immediate as against the haphazard and the gradual and the hidden spring underground.
>
> I say "unconscious" in the sense of simply painting a picture, and not seeking to enforce a moral—because the artist is always so acutely conscious that to state is enough; and this is particularly true of you.
>
> I am trying to say some of this more lucidly and explicitly in the "Yale Review," some time next year; and meanwhile will only tell you again how much I admired your manner, and your fresh eye and so reverent use of your language (occurs so little nowadays!), and that deep undertone of emotion which the hollow and tinny fictions of today so signally fails to give forth. (November 29, 1926, SHSW)

This image of Wharton "caressing" Gale's novel before she reads it marks a significant shift in tone: Wharton is both more affectionate toward

Gale herself and more unequivocally respectful of Gale's work. No longer does Gale's prose have the problems with tone and style that Wharton found in *Miss Lulu Bett;* instead, Gale's voice rises above the "tinny" sounds produced by other writers.

Wharton refers to the *Yale Review* essay again, a few months later, in a letter that positions herself and Gale as two artists who want to preserve the craft of fiction against its less accomplished practitioners. "You know how glad I am," she writes, "when any one of *our trade* condescends to take an interest in Technique and to assert that it cannot be practiced without thought and preparation" (March 11, 1927, SHSW, emphasis added). When she addresses Gale's query about the arrangement of dialogue, however, Wharton sounds more ambivalent—and a little condescending—about her friend's ideas: "I am inclined to think that there is some little confusion in your argument between book-writing and book-making . . . all problems of dialogue-spacing and the look on paper seem to me to matter nothing at all if the dialogue is properly used and contains the gist of the matter." Gale's letter accurately predicted Wharton's response, which essentially tells Gale that she should have nothing other than "vital talk." But Wharton's comment also ignores much of the modernist experimentation with words on the page—with book-making—and with the idea that the arrangement of words on the page could in fact influence "the gist of the matter." Wharton goes on to say that

> our writers are concerning themselves too much with such purely decorative questions through the lack of a richer life-substance to work in. But I won't develop this theory any further here because you will find it set out in the "Yale Review," probably in the July number to which I have sent an article called "The Great American Novel."—You know how hard it is to make a good fire in a hearth from which all the ashes have been cleared away—that is what America has done with all her great inheritance of culture and manners—and our fires do not burn long.

These letters illustrate Gale's worth as a sounding board, as a sympathetic audience with whom Wharton shares an essential understanding not only about contemporary fiction but also about the literary world in which they have made their careers. Gale is an artist, Wharton's highest accolade for a writer, but she is also a woman who understands the domestic rituals of housekeeping: their shared experiences with the difficulties of both writing and housekeeping help to establish the "community of spirit." Sarah Luria has argued that Wharton considered "housekeeping [to] be the very best training for the would-be novelist" (315), and this letter demonstrates Wharton's sense of the relationship between houses

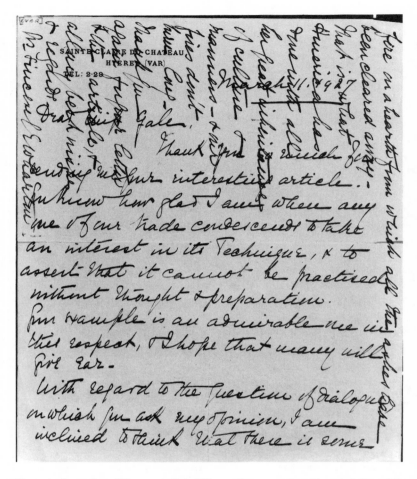

Photo 4   Letter from Wharton to Gale. Wharton letter reproduced by permission of the Estate of Edith Wharton and the Watkins/Loomis Agency and by the courtesy of the State Historical Society of Wisconsin.

and writing. Given Wharton's opinion of Gale, however, it comes as a surprise that she never refers to Gale in the *Yale Review* essay that Wharton has twice described to her.

In the privacy of their letters, Wharton shares ideas with Gale as if they were equals, but in public, Wharton is adamantly silent about her friend's work. "The Great American Novel" holds up Sinclair Lewis's *Main Street* as "epoch-making" and then cites three other American little confusion in your argument between book-writing + book-making. Important as the latter is, it is inexistent compared to the other, + all problems of dialogue-spacing + the look of a page seem to me to matter just nothing at all if the dialogue is properly used, + contains the gist of the matter.

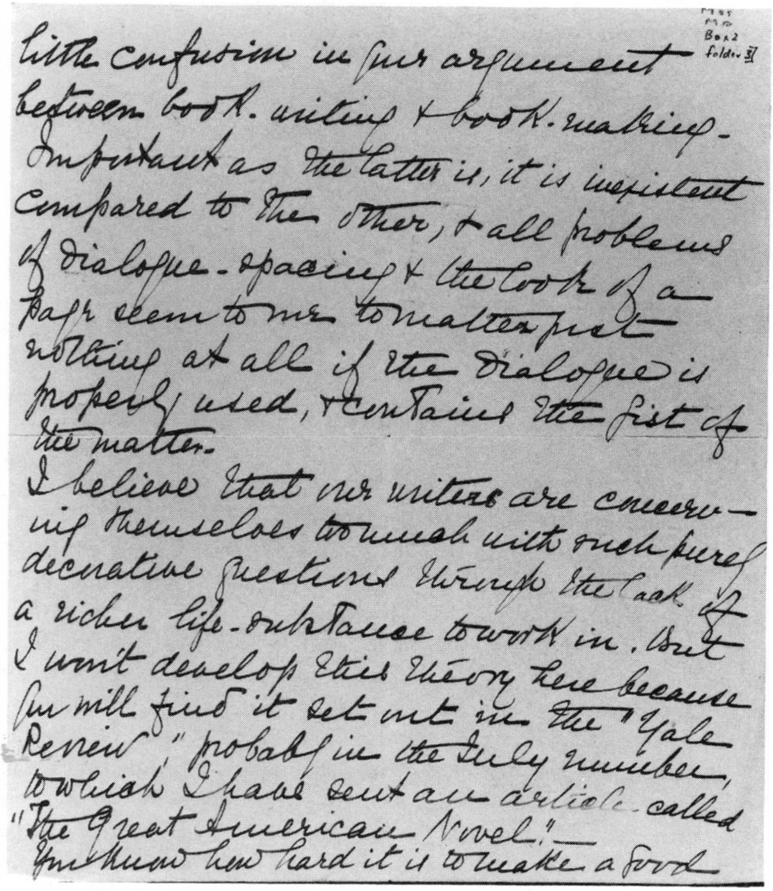

I believe that our writers are concerning themselves too much with such purely decorative questions through the lack of a richer life-substance to work in. But I won't develop this theory here because you will find it set out in the "Yale Review," probably in the July number, to which I have sent an article called "The Great American Novel."—

You know how hard it is to make a good

Photo 4   Continued.

writers whose novels were situated in "the same thorough-fare [as *Main Street*] . . . Robert Grant . . . Frank Norris . . . [and] Graham Phillips" (648). She does not mention Gale's work at all in this essay, although as her early letters to Gale demonstrate, Wharton thought of *Miss Lulu Bett* and *Main Street* as equally important novels. Omitting Gale from the *Yale Review* essay looks like a deliberate oversight on Wharton's part, an indication that even at this point in her career, public affiliation (correspondence) with another woman writer is not something that she can accept.[16]

In contrast to Wharton's public silence, Gale published essays about both Wharton and Cather that praised their literary achievements. She wrote in *The Bookman* that her current "favorite character in fiction" was Tom Outland, from Cather's *The Professor's House* (1925). In this character, Gale claims, "Miss Cather creates a living being, passionately pursuing an objective that has no personal taint" (323). And in a *Yale Review* essay published the year before Wharton's "The Great American Novel," Gale wrote that *Ethan Frome* was a novel in which "without a comment the horror [of the novel] . . . is hurled before you in a page, and . . . you are shaken by the experience" (283). Wharton had discovered a "new substance . . . rearrang[ed] the molecules of the novel" (283), a discovery that Gale likens to the scientific term *allotrope*. As she describes it, an allotrope is something "whose constituents, identical with those of something else, yet have a different molecular arrangement, so that the two present quite different aspects. . . . [A] diamond is loosely spoken of as the allotrope of coal, both carbon" (282). Using this term as her guide, Gale goes on to discuss both the current state of fiction and its future direction, praising not only Wharton but also Nathaniel Hawthorne, Joseph Conrad, and Anne Douglas Sedgwick. Drawing on a typically wide range of examples—from Walter Pater and George Santayana to Marie Curie and A. R. Orage—Gale compares art to such other disciplines as physics and philosophy: art "does not invent," she writes, "it reveals." Art's revelatory quality comes from the power that artists have to see a "lovelier and stranger world than you and I see" (294). She concludes by asserting that we must be open to "allotropic" possibilities, even though they may seem "to deny the scholarship of to-day or transcend [today's] art." Crediting Wharton with one of these "allotropic" discoveries in prose reiterates Gale's opinion of Wharton as a kind of Moses figure, leading "us" to some new land. Gale praises both Wharton and Cather in print, but they both are publicly silent about Gale. Even as Wharton moves toward Gale by sharing ideas and praising her work, she moves away from Gale by not publicly acknowledging the "community of spirit."[17]

Wharton's public silence suggests how jealously she watched over her position in the literary landscape. It is easier for her to share the public terrain of writerly achievement with someone who will not be readily equated with her (like Lewis, for example), than with someone like Gale, whom critics might see as similar on the basis of gender alone. An example of this sort of conflation is William Lyon Phelps's *New York Times Book Review* piece on *The Age of Innocence:* "In the present year of emancipation it is pleasant to record that in the front rank of American living novelists we find four women . . . Dorothy Canfield Fisher, Zona

Gale, Anne Sedgwick, [and] Edith Wharton" (qtd. in Madigan 5). Although Wharton makes it to the "front rank," she is in a list of other women in the year of "emancipation," something about which she publicly professed to care nothing about. Wharton can act as literary mother and mentor for Gale; she can ask Gale to reflect back Wharton's literary successes, but she is ultimately ambivalent about having a female literary companion. The threat of being publicly linked with other women writers and becoming merely one of a group is too great. Wharton and Cather see the artist as a solitary, almost alienated figure; in their understanding, the female literary artist has no choice but to emulate this model. Gale, on the other hand, can imagine the woman artist in relation to other women artists. Sisterhood is an unthreatening actuality for Gale in both her life and her fiction: Richmiel drives Barnaby and Leda apart, a rather unsisterly act; but another woman, an artist named Alice Lebanon, offers Leda her apartment in Chicago as a temporary refuge from the Crumbs. Additional acts of sisterhood and support run through all of Gale's writing, from her earliest short stories to her final novel, *Magna* (1938).

Although Wharton does not publicly affiliate herself with women writers in general or Gale in particular, her later letters to Gale suggest a need for sympathy in ways that have nothing to do with reading or writing. The letters between both writers in the late 1920s and early 1930s are filled with apologies and confusion over lost letters or letters imagined but not sent. Both Gale and Wharton suffered severe losses during this time, and their households were in a state of some tumult—Gale lost her father, and Wharton lost Walter Berry, as well as her beloved housekeeper and her personal maid; Gale got married in 1928 and became a mother to her husband's teenage daughter in addition to the young child she had adopted herself a few years prior to her marriage. Despite these upheavals and sorrows, the two women managed to stay in touch and mention repeatedly how much they would like to have a chance to visit with one another, to bring the "community of spirit" into physical reality.

Loss and a desire for intimacy pervade a letter Wharton wrote to Gale in 1933, the same year she published *A Backward Glance:*

Your letter makes me really unhappy; both because I am distressed to think that you should have imagined there was any sort of a chill between us and also because I am dismayed that the admiring letter written to you months ago in my head should (it would appear) never to have been put on paper.—I do not believe much in "lost letters," or else I should swear that mine had been written and sent; but the fact is that I have had a distracted and incoherent life for the last few months, and the probability is that all the appreciative things I had to say to you—and did say, as I read—remained embedded in their native gray matter. . . . Within the last few months I have lost the two mainstays of my household, a wonderful old Alsatian, who had been with me, first as maid then as housekeeper for 48 years, and my own personal maid, a much younger woman who had been with me 20 years and died harrowingly of pernicious anemia, against which all the most modern medical science battled in vain. (November 6, 1933, SHSW)

Wharton's affection for the women who ran her household reflects Gallop's assertion that professional women of any sort "must know the women of another class whose labor we rely on so that we can write: the women who clean our houses, care for our children, type our manuscripts, cleaning women and secretaries" (146). The deep bonds that Wharton formed with her housekeeper, Catherine Gross, whom she had known since 1884, illustrate that while Wharton was capable of and relied on her friendships with other women, none of these women were professional writers. Wharton can afford to hire people to "mother" her, thus giving herself time to write; her writing, in turn, enables her to afford this web of relationships. Wharton's earnings finance "a room of her own," but when the caretakers are gone, the house collapses, leaving Wharton sounding rootless and alone: "my house [is] so strange and empty to me," she writes, "that I have been making little trips here and there."

To combat her sense of loneliness, Wharton turns to Gale, hoping that Gale's unwavering admiration will establish stability:

I yet hope that you, the one immoveable figure in a shifting universe, may pull up anchor long enough, some day, to sail my way. What a lot of things we should have to say about the world of letters, which is a sacred grove to us, but to our successors: what?

How kind of you to remember me, and to quote me when you talk of the writing of books [Gale again used Wharton's *The Writing of Fiction* as a central text in a seminar she gave at the University of Colorado in 1931]. I wish I could be there to listen. Thank you so much for writing, and do come and see me some day. Yours ever—(November 6, 1933, SHSW)

Gale's role in this letter is still to be the keeper of the flame, the messenger who will bring Wharton's words to the masses in her lectures and seminars. At the same time, though, there is a marked shift in Wharton's reference, for the first time, to herself and Gale as members of the same generation: she talks about "our" successors rather than "her" successors, which suggests either that Gale is no longer a member of the "younger generation" or that Wharton hopes to shave ten years off her career by inserting herself among those whom she had previously only observed. In her efforts to still the "shifting universe," Wharton places herself alongside a writer whose presence in the world remains constant. But almost in spite of herself, Wharton does not allow a full connection: even as Wharton admires Gale's immovability (Gale rarely left Portage, Wisconsin), she proffers an invitation for Gale to visit her in France, the acceptance of which would undermine the very quality that Wharton admires. Wharton won't leave France to come to Wisconsin, so until Gale journeys to France, they visit only in their letters, which create the "sacred grove" and limit its growth. Wharton wishes for the geographic distance between them to vanish, but senses it will not, or cannot; the vague "some day" accepts that Gale's visit to France will always be deferred. Both sacred grove and community of spirit thus stay safely epistolary; Wharton will not be presented with a flesh-and-blood literary "sister" as a houseguest. The world of the letter is the only place where Wharton can have her "community of spirit"; Gale's physical presence—the presence of any literary sister—would overwhelm Wharton's sense of artistic individualism.

Gale's full-scale acceptance of an almost overwhelming foremother is different from Wharton's own, more tempered relationship with those writers who came before her. For instance, in a 1902 review of Leslie Stephen's biography of George Eliot, Wharton both praises her literary foremother and gently distances herself from her (in much the same way, actually, that Cather will distance herself from Wharton, thirty years later). Wharton says that Eliot is a "genius" but that her novels suffer from "cumbersome construction." She also makes claims about the connections between Eliot's life and her work that are not entirely flattering: "If George Eliot had been what the parish calls 'respectable' her books would have been a less continuous hymn to respectability. . . . The novelist of manners needs a clear eye and normal range of vision to keep his picture in perspective; and the loss of perspective is the central defect of George Eliot's later books" (250). Wharton, even at this early point in her career, sees peril (literary and otherwise) in stepping outside the bounds of "respectable": only within the safe confines of convention can one write critical fictions. Keeping the self (the woman) within bounds will allow the novelist to move beyond those boundaries. If a writer becomes an object of the public eye, her own eye on the public may lose its focus.

The responses that Wharton, Cather, and Gale had to Eliot demonstrate their different attitudes toward the female literary tradition. Wharton saw Eliot as a "cultivated reader . . . [with] great intellectual curiosity" who freed her spirit "from the bonds of ethical pedantry" (251). This description of Eliot turns her into another of the "born readers" to whom Wharton refers in "The Vice of Reading," written a year later. Looking at Eliot helps Wharton to see that the female creative spirit can be freed from socially imposed constraints, which in turn gives license to Wharton's own intellectual curiosity. Wharton affiliates herself with Eliot through her intellect and abilities as a reader, however, rather than through her achievements as a fiction writer. Cather had a similarly ambivalent response to Eliot and to her other female predecessors, as she demonstrates in "The Demands of Art" (1895), written for the Nebraska *Courier* while she was still in college. She writes that "They [women writers] are so few, the ones who really did anything worthwhile; there were the great Georges, George Eliot and George Sand, and *they were anything but women*" (Slote 409, emphasis added). Gale cites Eliot in "Allotropes" as an example of how literary tastes shift, but she does not attempt to diminish her in the same way that Wharton and Cather do: "Even with the humanity and poignancy of George Eliot . . . her long dissertations, her constant intrusions of authorship are no longer tolerated. Even with the story-telling power of Scott we know now that when we used to skip his 'fine writing,' his 'descriptive passages,' we were fundamentally right and that our sense of guilt was our literary taste, budding" (288). These remarks reflect each writer's ideas about the idea of the "woman writer." Gale's opinion, unsurprisingly, is the most egalitarian: gender does not enter into her account of why literary tastes change; all writers are equally susceptible to changing literary opinion. Wharton and Cather, on the other hand, disavow either the *woman* or the *writer* in their efforts to move away from the pejorative connotations that the phrase "woman writer" carried in their minds. Wharton admires Eliot's intellect but not her novels; Cather admires Eliot's novels but dismisses her as a woman. These essays about Eliot demonstrate that Wharton and Cather's sororophobia structures not only their relationships with female contemporaries, but also with their female precursors.

In her review about Eliot, as in her letters to Gale, the bond that Wharton creates between herself and another woman writer is always tempered by distance; the affiliation can exist on paper but not in the flesh, not in public. Wharton conceptualizes the role of artist as a solitary figure; an artist must remain unaffiliated, at least publicly, to anyone or anything. Yet as the letters to Gale demonstrate, Wharton's interest in the other woman's work and ideas seems far from perfunctory: the community of spirit is attractive, a sacred grove wherein like-minded artists can talk about the writing of fiction. Despite the pull of this imagined space, however, Wharton and Gale never actually met, although their correspondence spanned more than a decade.

III

Cather shares Wharton's ambivalence about literary mothers and sisters, which results in a similar impulse to distance herself from her female literary peers. In Cather's case, this means also distancing herself from Wharton. Wharton's essay about Eliot anticipates an essay that Cather will write almost thirty years later, in which she positions Wharton as an oppressive presence that has to be banished. In Wharton, Cather saw characteristics similar to her own, particularly a rejection of both nineteenth-century female conventions and public, sororal affiliations. But Wharton presents more of a problem for Cather than did Eliot for Wharton, because of the simple fact that Wharton was only ten years older than Cather and was prodigiously productive—she is both a predecessor and a contemporary. Cather's essay, "My First Novels [There Were Two]" (1931), denigrates Wharton's early influence on her and downplays Cather's efforts, in *Alexander's Bridge* (1911), to emulate both Wharton and Henry James.[18] *Alexander's Bridge* "was very like what painters call a studio picture," written from her youthful belief that "the new [was] more exciting than the familiar" (*Willa Cather on Writing* 91). When she started the book, she thought that "a book should be made out of '*interesting* material,'" which is why she followed the "conventional editorial point of view." The conventional perspective that produces *Alexander's Bridge,* she condemns as lifeless, unoriginal, and "very shallow." Several paragraphs later, she places Wharton and Henry James within this tradition of lifeless interiority, claiming that "Henry James and Mrs. Wharton were our most *interesting* novelists, and most of the younger writers followed their manner, without having their qualifications" (*On Writing* 91, 93, emphasis added). Although she does not explicitly connect herself with those "younger writers" who blindly emulated James and Wharton, her use of the word *interesting* to describe both her first novel and the work of James and Wharton reveals Cather as one of those "without qualifications." The rest of the essay, however, recovers Cather from this tradition and disparages both Wharton and James.

Cather goes on to say that her second novel, *O Pioneers!* (1913), was wholly her own creation—in fact, one might say she protests too much, saying: "I began to write a book entirely *for myself* . . . Since I wrote this book *for myself*. . . . the book I had written *for myself* would remain faithfully *with me* and continue to be exclusively *my property*" (*On Writing* 92–5, emphasis added). She cannot emphasize enough that *O Pioneers!* is hers alone, and that in writing it she broke with tradition and thus with Wharton: after *O Pioneers!* books like *Alexander's Bridge* seem stilted and

inorganic. The fact that Houghton Mifflin agreed to publish *O Pioneers!*
"truly astonished" her, she claims, because she thought that the literary
independence of her subject matter would preclude anyone ever being interested in it. The publication of *O Pioneers!* thus becomes a classic American success story of the iconoclastic outsider who bucks tradition and
triumphs, and Cather's essay creates a similar story about the author herself, feeding into her populist public persona as the independent, plain-
spoken Midwesterner. The essay is also an interestingly belated assertion
of aesthetic independence: why at this late date does Cather need to declare her independence from earlier traditions in general, and from
Wharton in particular? One possibility has to do with Cather's need to
define herself against sameness. Wharton as a literary mother needs to be
distanced; Cather needs to set herself apart from the tradition that Wharton appears to symbolize for her.

Cather's essay explicitly discusses the genesis of *O Pioneers!*, but it also
reveals the complicated relationship that Cather has with both her female
precursors and contemporaries. Dismissing Wharton as an influence allows her to establish her own myth of artistic origins: Cather becomes an
artist because of her own creative energy, not because of any "literary" influences. Her inspirations for *O Pioneers!* come from farm women and
their stories, from the landscape itself: "a story about some Scandinavians
and Bohemians who had been neighbors of ours. . . . Here [in *O Pioneers!*] there was no arranging or 'inventing'; everything was spontaneous
and took its own place . . . it had to do with the country I loved" (*On
Writing* 93). Cather's novel comes from stories about the land, a marked
difference from the interiors of Wharton novels and the conventions that
dictated "the drawing room [as] the proper setting for a novel" (*On Writing* 93). In an almost literal sense, Cather moves out of the novelist's traditional "house" into unexplored fictional territory. She wants to erase the
first novel, which betrays a connection to tradition, and begin her career
as a literary artist with a novel that—if her essay is to be believed—sprang
into her mind and formed itself spontaneously. Cather creates the illusion
that her creativity needs no technical arrangement, that she has no need
for craft, another shift away from Wharton's "constructed" novels. By setting her novel in Nebraska, which was "distinctly déclassé as a literary
background . . . [because] the 'novel of the soil' had not then come into
fashion," Cather sets herself apart from fashion (*On Writing* 93–94). She
can then dismiss as "unnecessary and superficial" (92) the traditions and
conventions that inspired *Alexander's Bridge*. Implicitly, then, Wharton's
novels are also "unnecessary and superficial," because it is Wharton's work
that Cather had taken as her first model. Cather thus installs multiple
levels of difference between herself and her slightly older literary "sister":

Cather is organic, original, exterior, American; Wharton is artificial, imitative, interior, European.

Curiously absent from Cather's essay is Sarah Orne Jewett, another of Cather's literary influences. Her absence is striking because Cather dedicated *O Pioneers!* to Jewett and thought of the novel as a continuing conversation with that writer. Several possibilities arise as explanation: one is that Cather wants to reject the tradition represented by Wharton and James, a tradition to which she does not connect Jewett. Second, by 1931, Cather's fame had exceeded Jewett's, which diminished Jewett as a threat and meant that Cather did not have to write herself out of Jewett's sphere of influence. Finally, whereas Jewett died in 1909, Wharton is still very much alive in 1931; Jewett can no longer compete with Cather, but Wharton often does and wins: first to win a Pulitzer, first to receive an honorary degree from an Ivy League institution, first to be made a member of the American Academy of Arts and Letters, first to receive a Gold Medal from that institution, and so on. Wharton is a mother who refuses, as it were, to act her age; she reaps the benefits on both sides: a venerable elder, and a postwar writing sister arguing, like Cather, against the dangers of technology and mechanization. In order to prevent comparisons with Wharton, Cather needs to create separation and distance between them.

Cather did, however, edit and write the introduction to *The Best Stories of Sarah Orne Jewett* (1925), an act of tribute to her mentor that also subtly points to Cather's own superior status in the literary world. Jewett's stories, particularly the *Pointed Fir* sketches, "are living things," writes Cather, "caught in the open, with light and freedom and air-spaces about them. They melt into the land and the life of the land until they are not stories at all, but life itself" (*On Writing* 49). Cather describes Jewett's work as being about "the people who grew out of the soil and the life of her country near her heart," which sounds similar to the descriptions that Cather will offer for the composition of *O Pioneers!* six years later. In further tribute to Jewett's greatness, Cather cites Pater's comment that "every truly great drama must, in the end linger in the reader's mind as a sort of ballad," which she extends to Jewett's work by saying that "the same thing might be said of every great story" (*On Writing* 49–50).[19] Despite the essay's overall admiring tone, Cather inserts small moments of criticism—some of the stories "fall a little short of being Miss Jewett's finest," and another story "is a little vague, lacks the last co-ordinating touch of the writer's hand" (*On Writing* 54–55). In articulating criteria for Jewett's greatness, Cather helps to establish her own, particularly in her closing comments about Jewett's *Country of Pointed Firs,* which she praises for being "so tightly yet so lightly built, so little encumbered with heavy materialism that deteriorates and grows old-fashioned." Jewett's book, along with *The Scarlet Letter* and *Huckleberry Finn,* are the "three American books which have the possibility of a long, long life [because they] confront time and change so serenely" (*On Writing* 58–59). Cather's homage to Jewett allows her to create a canon that will be receptive to her own work; the family she creates by marrying together Twain, Hawthorne, and Jewett offers her support because none of them are her contemporaries. When, in the course of their correspondence, Gale offers Cather a similar "family," Cather is much more resistant: a dead literary mother is easier to manage than a living literary sister.[20]

Cather's letters to Gale illustrate her ambivalence about establishing bonds with women writers as well as her anxiety about her own public image. This need for control extends even beyond the grave: Cather's will stipulates that none of her letters, or any other material unpublished in her lifetime, can be published in any form.[21] Cather's first letter to Gale, about Gale's book *Portage, Wisconsin, and Other Essays* (1928), illustrates Cather's idea of a kind of literary geography, in which there can be only one writer for each landscape—a kind of literary quota system. The essay collection was the first book that Gale published with Knopf, although Cather would have been aware of Gale's work prior to this because of their overlap in magazines and because, as she mentions in this letter, Gale came to visit Cather once, at her Bank Street apartment, in the company of William Allen White. Cather begins her letter by calling Gale "my dear" and then goes on to tell her that Gale's essay about her home town makes Cather want to live there, so that although she isn't fond of writing letters, Portage is haunting her, compelling her to write. The rest of the letter provides a contrast to the images presented in Gale's essay, which describes the beautiful view outside her study window and the ease of living in a small town. Cather tells Gale that her apartment on Bank Street, her home of fifteen years, has been torn down because the new subway is being built underneath it, and that as a result she is leading a wretched existence in hotels and hating her life in New York. (The letter is written on letterhead from the Grosvenor Hotel on lower Fifth Avenue.) Cather ends her letter with a joking threat, saying that if she were not a truly honorable woman, she would move to Portage, but she knows that would be the meanest thing one writer could do to another. If Gale were to move to her small Nebraska town, Cather claims, she would be furious—so she won't threaten Gale but will end her letter by saying that Portage must be lovely (October 23, 1928, SHSW).

Cather, like Wharton, is attracted to Gale's sense of place, but this attraction presents a threat to Cather in a way that it does not to Wharton— Portage is more similar to Red Cloud, Nebraska, than it is to Old New York (or even to new New York). Cather chooses to comment on Gale's book of essays because it is a genre in which Cather herself had not published extensively. (Individual essays had been printed in magazines, but in 1928 none had been collected.) Choosing to compliment Gale on her essays leaves the field open for Cather's short stories and novels; she needn't worry that Gale's success would cancel out work she herself is doing. The literary map she describes, on which each writer has her own town, suggests a limited vision on Cather's part. It is hard to know whether she really saw the world this way or whether she was merely reacting to the tendency of critics and reviewers to lump writers together, putting all the "middlewest" writers together, all the women writers together, all the war writers together, and so on. Cather's letter establishes the similarities between herself and Gale but then immediately creates boundaries between them; getting too close—sharing towns and thus literary inspirations—is the "meanest thing" that one writer can do to another. Certain areas are Cather's literary property, and for Gale and Cather to remain in contact as friends they need, in Cather's eyes, to remain separate. Despite the separation, however, Gale's town "haunts" Cather. Both Cather and Wharton seem moved to write Gale through some almost uncanny ability on Gale's part to touch them: she hits the "central nerve" of Wharton's book, she "haunts" Cather. Cather and Wharton are drawn to Gale, but they are afraid of being utterly pulled in; the threat of correspondence is too strong. The community of spirit, the correspondences they share within their letters, are written but not enacted.

Cather did have other women writer friends, but none were quite as famous as Gale—and none of them were particularly "midwestern." Whether coincidentally or not, they stayed out of Cather's territory. Dorothy Canfield set her novels in Vermont, and lived there herself, maintaining her long friendship with Cather through infrequent visits and many letters. Cather's old friend (and biographer) Elizabeth Sergeant was a successful journalist, although, as Sharon O'Brien observes, "Sergeant's transition from timid apprentice to accomplished journalist strained the friendship" (O'Brien 359). Zoë Akins, a California screenwriter and playwright (who won a Pulitzer for her dramatization of Wharton's "The Old Maid") was another "lifelong friend" who received "tough responses" when she sent Cather her books, although it was Cather who suggested that Akins try her hand at drama (Lee 69, 189). There were definite boundaries, physically and generically, between these women and Cather; the women with whom Cather was more intimate—Isabelle McClung, Mariel Gere, Edith Lewis—did not make their living as writers.

Gale attempts to create an actual community of spirit with both Wharton and Cather, but ultimately their ambivalence defeats her. In

October 1929, Gale invites Cather to come and live in her parents' empty house in Portage, the town that Cather has professed to admire so whole-heartedly. Gale lived with her parents for almost all of her adult life, moving out only when she married, in 1928, at the age of fifty-four.[22] She, her adopted daughter, her new husband, and his teenage daughter moved only a few blocks away, so that if Cather were to move to Portage she and Gale would truly be neighbors. Gale's invitation completes the literary "family" she created with Wharton, an utterly female literary family in which Wharton is the mother and Cather is the sister. Gale opens the house of American literature to women and sees her literary heritage in terms of what they offer her. Her attempts to create a community of women, to assume that an artist does not need to be alone in order to be independent, suggest a dramatic revision of artistic identity.

Cather also wants to redefine artistic identity, but she has more interest in exploring questions of genre and form than in establishing a new form of artistic community. Being installed in the "father's house" would seem to preclude such explorations, and may offer a symbolic reason why Cather ultimately refused Gale's invitation. Cather turns down the offer effusively, carefully detailing the pleasure the invitation gives her. Gale's invitation had been waiting for her in New York when she returned from a short motor trip, she writes, and she cannot remember when anything has been more pleasing to her than the thought that Gale would like to have her as a neighbor. She wishes that Portage were near enough that she could just hop on the next train (October 16, 1929, SHSW). Gale's invitation becomes tangible proof of her desire to erase boundaries, and for a moment Cather sounds delighted by such a communal existence. Despite her pleasure, however, in the next sentence, Cather insists that she must decline Gale's kind offer; no "community of spirit" will be established in Portage. Her mother has had a stroke, she explains, only a few weeks after Cather and Gale had dinner together in New York, and since then Cather has been in Pasadena tending to her and living chiefly on various transcontinental trains. So despite being wretched in New York, Cather cannot come to Wisconsin, because when her mother begins to fret, she simply must go to California to see her. The last time she left her was in June, Cather writes, in order to come back east and receive an honorary degree from Yale (October 16, 1929, SHSW). Cather was the second woman so honored by Yale; the first, not surprisingly, was Wharton. Cather's letter reflects the pull between dutiful daughter and famous writer: Willa tends to the family, and Cather receives honorary degrees. Cather's travels across the country in order to fulfill both roles simply concretize the ongoing struggle between woman and novelist.

After explaining why she cannot come see Gale, Cather launches into an odd homage to Gale's father's house—odd because it is both pleasured and plaintive. In fact, her outpouring is so flowery that it almost doesn't sound like Cather at all. She gushes that the picture Gale sent of her father's house looks superior and high-minded and very American, and that good American things are so good! It is a house, she says, that she would try to live up to, were she ever able to get to Portage. Given Cather's ambivalence toward America and American culture in the 1920s, her apostrophizing of the Gale house would seem almost tongue-in-cheek, although the rest of the letter sounds only delighted at the thought of Gale's friendship. The letter thanks Gale for her kindness and adds wistfully that a happy working winter is, at the moment, as beyond her reach as winter on another planet. She wants Gale to know, however, that her invitation gave Cather hope and cheer at a time when she was low in mind.

These letters to Gale, in which Cather sounds so ambivalent, rootless, and unsure of her place in the "house" of American fiction reverberate in the novel that Cather wrote during this period. *Shadows on the Rock* (1927) is set in seventeenth-century Quebec, an outpost for French colonists; one of the novel's central themes is how to make a home out of a wilderness. The heroine, Cecile Auclair, is an only child who keeps house for her father because her mother is dead (which describes exactly Gale's life until her father's death). The preservation of ritual and history—personal and cultural—is of great importance to Cecile's father, and to the novel itself, which suggests that in writing this novel Cather may have been constructing a stable, fixed world in response to her own life, which seemed fragmented and disorderly.

Cather's ambivalence about Gale, like Wharton's, creates a connection to Gale but carefully circumscribes the boundaries of their intimacy. Although Cather sounds rapturous at the idea of a small town, she immediately pulls away; there is only a deferred wish, a "someday," rather than any specifics. Instead of going to Portage, however, or inviting Gale to come west, Cather and Gale meet only in New York, a city to which neither woman had particular literary claim. Gale's strong sense of place intrigued both Wharton and Cather, as did the fact that Gale seemed so easily to unify the roles of woman and writer, to consider herself both daughter and artist without any apparent sense of conflict. Just as Gale wants to eradicate the boundaries that exist between women writers, so too does she break down the boundaries that the popular imagination has erected between feminism and familial responsibility; in her mind the two are not mutually exclusive.

Both Cather and Wharton cling to the image of the artist as a solitary figure; neither wants to risk losing her hard-won individuality. Cather is

particularly invested in her myth of self-creation, as an artist with no female American precursors. Being neighbors with Gale and living in the
house formerly occupied by Gale's parents would erase the boundaries of
Cather's hard-won literary territory; she would become another "midwestern writer" and lose her individual public reputation. Although place
and landscape are central concerns in many of Cather's novels, she herself
wants to be free to define and re-define both herself and the genres in
which she works. Many of Cather's letters to Gale, in fact, are written en
route from one place to another, signifying Cather's refusal to remain
fixed, categorized. Cather's refusal to consider the boundaries of genre
can be seen in many of the comments she made about her own work, perhaps most famously about *Death Comes for the Archbishop:* "I am amused
that so many of the reviews of this book begin with the statement: 'This
book is hard to classify.' Then why bother? Many more assert that it is not
a novel. Myself, I prefer to call it a narrative" (*On Writing* 12).

Cather neatly sums up her ambivalence in a letter written to Gale a
month later, in which she says that one cannot live in a test tube, but that
most contact is pernicious (November 25, 1929, SHSW). This is the
dilemma with which both Cather and Wharton wrestled throughout
their careers: a tug-of-war between their need for recognition as individual artists on the one hand and, on the other, their need for social contact, for community. Cather cannot live in a test tube, but contact is
pernicious—and the contact of literary influence is perhaps the most pernicious of all. It is in part to escape or avoid pernicious contact that
Cather developed a public persona that appeared to exist aloof from and
oblivious to contemporary politics, social reforms, and gender issues; it is
for this same reason that she attempted to create strong distinctions between herself and other writers, particularly her female contemporaries.
In this same letter, Cather also praises Gale's new book, *Borgia* (1929), a
novel in which Gale tells the story of Marfa Manchester, a woman who
believes she destroys everything and everyone she touches. She read the
novel with delight and grim amusement, Cather writes, and notes that we
are all "Borgias," or at least anyone who gets involved in other people's
lives, even with the best of intentions, is a Borgia. And then, despite her
warning about pernicious contact, she asks Gale if they could have dinner together the next time Gale is in New York, and she inquires after
Gale's daughter, whom she says she liked so much the last time she met
her (November 25, 1929). With this wish, Cather reverses her desire to
come to Portage; it is now Gale who must come to Cather. Cather thus
alleviates the threat of pernicious contact by arranging meetings on the
neutral ground of New York and by containing the community of spirit
within the space of a letter.

Gale conceives of a literary landscape that is very different from what Cather and Wharton saw, which was a literary world fiercely populated with male writers whose work celebrated the necessity of being an unencumbered individual.[23] Wharton and Cather both regarded their individual claims on literary mastery as something unshareable, or as something easily stolen by another. Virginia Woolf shared Cather and Wharton's ambivalence about female peers, her publicly feminist stance notwithstanding. In "Virginia Woolf and the Hogarth Press," Laura Marcus quotes an observation that Woolf made in her journals after she had refused to write a review of Dorothy Richardson's latest novel: "The truth is that when I looked at it, I felt myself looking for faults, hoping for them," Woolf wrote. "And they would have bent my pen, I know. There must be an instinct of self-preservation at work. *If she's good then I'm not*" (132, emphasis added). The literary world appeared to these writers too small to share the spotlight with one's same-sex competitors, and yet only through identification with other women writers could one find understanding and support. Gale, on the other hand, imagines that the woman artist does not have to accept the model of the solitary genius but could instead exist in a community created by women writers, family relationships, and political colleagues.

Gale's friendships with Wharton and Cather are typical of Gale's relationships with other women writers, which are equally sororal and affiliative. She funded scholarships at the University of Wisconsin, Madison, for example, that gave writers such as Margery Latimer and Anzia Yezierska a year of full support for their writing. Yezierska wrote to Gale that "her whole being has been recreated through this opportunity you've made possible for me—here in Madison I am changed and the whole world seems changed" (n.d. SHSW).[24] Meridel Le Sueur, the activist and novelist, referring to this scholarship, praised Gale for "nourish[ing] the creative spirit," and called her one of the "early prophets of America" (n.d., SHSW). Le Sueur also credited Gale with helping many younger writers, including Latimer and Le Sueur herself, to find an audience: without Gale, writes Le Sueur, Latimer "might not have written at all [and] I might have remained unpublished." The friendship between Le Sueur and Gale began when Le Sueur sent Gale one of her short stories, although the two writers had never met. Gale's response was supportive and enthusiastic: "I began your letter with an open mind," she writes, "read it with growing excitement, and finished it in awe." Then she asked Le Sueur if she might send the story to various editors for publication consideration (May 10, 1926, SHSW). Whether as mentor or peer, Gale attempted to establish a "community of spirit" that would foster and develop women writers.

Gale had an equally powerful effect on her old friend Charlotte Perkins Gilman, late in Gilman's life, when Gale helped the older woman to find a publisher for her autobiography, *The Living of Charlotte Perkins Gilman* (1935). Gilman had originally asked Gale to write the book, saying that "you have seen better than any one else what I have tried to do, and measured better than anyone else what I have done. If you could do this I feel it would stir an interest in my other books, now all out of print. . . . For the sake of the work, the scrappy, imperfect, desperately earnest work I have done, I hope you'll do this for me" (December 14, 1934, Schlesinger Library [SL]). Gale refused, insisting that she was in no way up to such a task and that the world needed to hear Gilman's own words about her life. The subsequent letters between the two women, as Gilman attempted both to battle breast cancer and to compose her memoirs, are a combination of pathos and practicality: Gale suggests various herbal remedies and a "nature-cure" doctor for Gilman's shingles, agrees to write an introduction to the memoir, and promises to make all the arrangements for the book's publication—finding photos, creating an index, and negotiating for higher royalties to be paid to Gilman.

In response to Gale's announcement that Appleton had agreed to publish her autobiography, and would give her an advance as soon as the contract was signed, Gilman called her a "witch-angel" and asked, "How can you find that dreary mass of data a good piece of work?" (June 17, 1935, SL). Gilman gave Gale a bound set of *The Forerunner*, the magazine that Gilman single-handedly published between 1909 and 1916, telling her, "I feel as if you were one of the few people in the world who would really enjoy having them." The only string attached to the gift, Gilman wrote, was that Gale had to promise to leave them to Gilman's grandchildren, "if they want them at all." In this same letter, Gilman says that she is "approaching the stepping-off place very closely. I see no reason whatever in prolonging an increasingly uncomfortable existence—as soon as I'm too weak to totter to the bathroom, off I go. I know what it means to be 'tired to death'" (August 5, 1935, SL). Twelve days later, Gilman killed herself. Gale's introduction, part of which also served as Gilman's obituary in the *Nation*, called Gilman "one of the great women of the two centuries" (xxxvii). Gilman's feminism, according to Gale, came from her sense of deep empathy: "She was intensely sad about women, about their lost opportunities, their lost advantage and for the millions who had gone down to the breast of the earth with no knowledge that they were not the inferiors of the men who had taught them so well that they were so" (xxiv). *Women and Economics* (1898), writes Gale, "lit to energy many thousands of the unaware, the indolent, the oblivious, and made of them socially-conscious beings" (xxxi). It is her own sense of social consciousness that spurs Gale to affiliate herself with Gilman and other women, as well as with feminist politics in general.

Elizabeth Ammons has suggested that the women literary artists of this period—including Wharton and Cather—who refused to partake of feminist rhetoric "play a dangerous game in their own survival" (*Conflicting* viii), but it is Gale who has disappeared from literary history, who seems not to have survived. Her disappearance suggests that to be affiliated with women writers, to attempt to make the "community of spirit" an actual place (perhaps with a Portage address?) is the more perilous course. Thus it seems that in fact Cather and Wharton were wise not to commit fully to the "community of spirit": their refusal means that their contributions and individual artistic identities are still acknowledged. They worked within existing models and survived; Gale attempted to create a new model and has been lost.

The shared ambivalence felt by Wharton and Cather toward Gale also explains why Wharton and Cather stayed away from one another. They could not share the same "house"; they could not negotiate a relationship. Cather looms too large in the literary landscape for Wharton to offer advice or act as 'mother'; Wharton is too present to be ignored and too overwhelming for Cather to do anything but ignore her. In their individual correspondence with Gale, each writer's particular vision becomes clear: Wharton's desire, cloaked with maternal advice and old-fashioned manners, to have a lasting impact on the literary world; Cather's profound commitment to self-definition, a commitment Wharton shared but did not write about as openly. Although both could believe in a community of *spirit* with another woman writer, neither could allow herself to become publicly a member of such a group. The private desire articulated in these letters gives voice to the public silence that Wharton and Cather used to maintain their artistic, authorial identities.

CHAPTER TWO

WOMEN WHO DID THINGS OPENLY: ZONA GALE'S UTOPIAN VISIONS

"Art is not a department by itself," wrote Gale in "The United States and the Artist" (1925). "Art is the imaginative interpretation of the life of the people, whatever that life may be."[1] The artist works alone and needs only "his four walls and his tools" (22), but when he emerges from his studio he "becomes again a social being" and may "sigh to think—if he does—of the disabilities of his country as a garden for his growth. It is then that he fears its effect—if he does fear—upon his exalted hours of creation." In this essay, first published in the *Nation* and then reprinted in *Portage, Wisconsin, and Other Essays* (1929), Gale argues that the artist has two central challenges: creating a new "American" artistic tradition and fighting against the "social disabilities" that plague the country. The two projects are inseparable, in her mind, precisely because the artist is always also a "social being." Unlike Wharton and Cather, who construct their authorial and artistic selves through public silence, Gale's artist defines herself as part of the public; ignoring social issues, in Gale's formulation, becomes detrimental to the making of art.

Gale's comment about an artist needing only his "four walls and his tools" sounds similar to what Cather wrote in "The Novel Démeublé" (1922), which concludes with the statement that "to make a drama, a man needed one passion and four walls" (*On Writing* 43). Gale's artist, however, emerges from her four walls and defines herself within a social context.[2] In "The United States and the Artist," Gale makes a distinction between art and social involvement, but it is not a permanent distinction, and ultimately, as the essay goes on to demonstrate, the two spheres merge. Her statement is very different from Cather's comment in "Escapism" (1931) that artists are valuable "like powerful stimulants, only when they [are] left out of the social and industrial routine which goes on every day all over the world. Industrial life has to work out its own problems" (*On Writing* 21). Cather's essay is a response to the leftist critics of the 1930s, particularly Granville Hicks, who accused her of being a "supine romantic" and of avoiding the "real" issues of life. Her ideas about activism notwithstanding, Gale's work suffered similar attacks because of its mysticism, which critics on both the left and right saw as naïve optimism rather than as a vehicle for social or cultural critique.

Gale contends that there is "no more challenging artistic adventure than waits in this land," and that in the United States she could "confidently expect to do [her] work." Her assertion digs at the expatriate writers who have sought the "decays of Italy and the fatigues of France and the deepening impassivities of Great Britain." As she argues for the recognition of an artistic tradition in the United States, she notes wryly that although the Pilgrims came to the new world "in search of liberty of expression," they did not bring with them any "effective revolutions in art." Artistic revolution had to wait for Whitman, whose experiments are being continued "now, in 1925." Recasting Emerson's famous admonition in "The American Scholar" (1837) that Americans have listened too long to the courtly muses of Europe, Gale urges artists to turn from the "flowered debris, the resonant footsteps, the delicate somnolence, the emanations of genius and of ruin" that characterize the old world. Unlike Emerson, however, Gale concedes that opportunity—artistic or otherwise—is not equally available. The United States is "long ridden by prejudice and standardization," she writes, and "if the artist is a Negro, his difficulties are needlessly greater in this country than in any other land in the civilized world." By integrating political and social problems with a discussion of aesthetics, Gale demonstrates how an artist is also a "social being," a view very different from the way that Cather and Wharton imagined the role of "the artist." In Gale's understanding, artistic, political, and social traditions cannot be divorced from one another.

All of Gale's fiction reflects her social awareness and her commitment to the reformist ethos that marks the Progressive Era.[3] Simply put, Progressive reform focused in two directions: regulating business and commerce, on the one hand, and enacting a program of humanitarian social reforms, on the other. These two directions, in Gale's view, were inextricably linked. She believed that social reform was good for business, because if people were healthier and had better living conditions, they would lead happier lives and be more productive workers. At the root of Progressive reform and Gale's own writing is a shared belief in the transformative power of *grassroots politics*, a term that came into use during this period. What remains constant in Gale's work, which sketches in microcosm the changes in U.S. literature between 1900 and 1930, is the representation of this transformative power as female or feminine. In her early regionalist fiction, women's organizations create improvements in their towns and communities, which lead in turn to women's increased sense of power in their own lives. The later fiction presents spiritualism and mysticism as solutions to the world's ills, with the spiritual power coming from an unnamed goddess rather than a patriarchal God. Whether through women's clubs and suffrage or through a transcendent mystical encounter, however, the emphasis always returns to the social well-being; it is never enough, in Gale's work, to improve only the self. The individual—like the literary artist—must always realize that she is a social being.

Gale's social conscience emerged when she moved from Milwaukee to New York in 1902, a move that transformed her from a small-town dutiful daughter to an urban radical feminist. She had gone to Milwaukee from Portage, Wisconsin, after she graduated from the University of Wisconsin at Madison in 1895. Followed by her doting parents, Gale spent almost six years in Milwaukee working as a journalist, but she decided that her chances of becoming a successful fiction writer were better if she lived in New York. In New York she became a staff reporter for the *World* and thus joined a growing industry: increasing numbers of newspapers and magazines were being published and increasing numbers of women were working in the publishing world.[4] Gale found work through sheer persistence: she went to the newspaper offices every day with lists of possible news stories that she could investigate. In both Milwaukee and New York, after several weeks, the editors gave in and hired her. She practiced her craft diligently and gained a reputation as a "model reporter" (Simonson 24).

After working for two years in New York as a staff reporter, Gale quit in order to work as a freelance writer and as secretary for Edmund Clarence Stedman, the poet and editor of one of the first anthologies of American literature, *American Anthology* (1900). Working for Stedman introduced Gale to a new circle of writers, including Harriet Monroe, who would go on to found *The Little Review*, and the poet Edward Arlington Robinson. Through Stedman, Gale also met Richard Le Gallienne, a writer and critic, and Ridgeley Torrence, poet and playwright. Both men were romantically interested in her, and she was briefly engaged to Torrence, but she broke off the engagement when her parents worried about whether a writer could support a family. In addition to her romances, Gale also began to *see* New York and regaled her parents, in her frequent letters home, with stories of theaters, nightclubs, parties, lectures, art galleries—and talk of suffrage, labor strikes, socialism, and "Negroes." Her parents were amazed that their sheltered only child was developing such apparently radical interests, particularly feminism, an idea that moved her mother to urge that she "leave that mess of women *alone!*" (qtd. in Simonson 47).

But Gale had no intention of leaving anything alone, and instead she became more and more involved with social reforms and radical causes. Through her work in Milwaukee, she had met Jane Addams, and in New York she met Charlotte Perkins Gilman; she became friends with both women, whose ideas deeply influenced her. Her work combines Addams's social progressivism with Gilman's clear awareness that without economic independence, women would never claim their lives as their own. Like many early feminists, Gale realized that putting women on a pedestal was only an excuse to exclude them from their own lives, and in no way prevented exploitation: "The pedestal does not seem to be high enough to prevent a husband from scaling it to collect his wife's earnings," she wrote in 1922. Gale found support for her views among the membership of Heterodoxy, a group of women committed to progressive politics, social reform, and woman's suffrage. Founded by Marie Jenney Howe, a suffragist, feminist, and Unitarian minister, Heterodoxy met regularly in Greenwich Village from 1912 until the beginning of World War II. At their meetings, the Heterodites, as they called themselves, discussed issues ranging from socialism, birth control, and militarism to child-care tips, broken hearts, and the latest gossip; their wide-ranging discussions anticipate the consciousness-raising groups of the post-Friedan "women's lib" era. Through her membership in Heterodoxy, Gale met and became friends with women who were among the most politically active in the city—perhaps the entire country. Mabel Dodge (later Luhan) described the Heterodites as "unorthodox women, that is to say, women who did things and did them openly . . . women whose names were *known:* Charlotte Perkins Gilman, Mary Fels, Inez Haynes Irwin, Edna Kenton, Mary Shaw, Mary Heaton Vorse, Daisy Thompson, Fola La Follette" (143). Although heterodox in their professional lives, what unified the Heterodites was their liberal outlook: all of them supported suffrage and many also supported labor organization, increased protections for immigrant women and children, and equal rights for African Americans.

In her unpublished autobiography, "The Adventures of Yesterday," Inez Haynes Irwin, a charter member of the group, wrote:

> Heterodoxy members came from many states of the Union. Most of them had traveled with amazing extensiveness. Among them were Democrats, Republicans, Socialists, anarchists, liberals and radicals of all opinions. They possessed minds startlingly free of prejudice. They were at home

with ideas. All could talk; all could argue; all could listen. . . . Our occupations and preoccupations ranged the world. Many of our members were
working for various reforms. A sizable proportion were always somewhere
else. During the First World War, when no Americans were supposed to
enter Russia . . . at least two members of Heterodoxy were there writing
articles. (414)

Although there is no recorded indication that the Heterodites used the
phrase "the personal is political," it is clear that the group recognized—
and often capitalized on—that linkage. Because so many of the Heterodites were well known—whether as actresses, writers, academics,
doctors, lawyers, or activists—any cause they chose to support gained a
great deal of exposure. They were also aware that personal decisions—like
the decision to keep one's own name after marriage—had political and
public repercussions.[5]

An alternative view of Heterodoxy is offered by Hutchins Hapgood, a
columnist and reviewer, who wrote in his memoirs that "this club was
comprised of women, many of them of force, character and intelligence,
but all of them shunted on the sliding path from the early suffrage movement into the passionate excesses of feminism in which the 'vital lie' was
developed, that men had consciously oppressed women since the beginning of time . . . [the club] had almost an insane atmosphere" (337).
Hapgood's attitude represents the sort of mainstream opinion of feminism that Wharton and Cather wanted scrupulously to avoid.

As its name implies, Heterodoxy drew on a diverse membership, particularly for an early-twentieth-century women's organization. Unlike
other women's clubs, which tended to be predominantly white, Protestant, and middle-class, among the Heterodites were Catholics and Jews,
recently emigrated Irish, Italian, and Eastern European women, at least
one African American woman, a number of openly gay women and their
partners, and several multiply divorced women. All of them were women
whose private lives and public politics made them startling figures in the
public eye. The diversity of membership reveals that the group was openly
committed to challenging social conventions and to arguing for legisla-
tive reforms. Although they supported suffrage, most Heterodites chose
to call themselves feminists rather than suffragists, a decision that placed
these women far to the left on the political spectrum. For Gale and her
sister Heterodites, feminism was not limited merely to the fight for suffrage but meant working for all sorts of reforms that affected women's
lives, nationally and internationally: birth control, divorce and child support laws, sanitation and disease prevention, wage stability, workplace
regulations, world peace.[6]

Gale's adventures in New York illustrate the possibilities available to the "New Woman," which Ann Ardis defines as a woman who "challenges not only bourgeois Victorian sexual ideology but also the related ideology of domesticity, the normalization/standardization of both the nuclear family and the independent middle-class household" (14). The New Woman was economically self-sufficient, interested in sex, and claimed "the right to self-definition" (27). Early in her career, however, Gale's fiction did not illustrate her New Woman freedoms. Her first novel, *Romance Island* (1906), is a utopian fantasy set on an island that can be found only by using a four-dimensional map. The novel was poorly reviewed, but it demonstrates Gale's interest in spirituality and the occult, as well as her belief in the possibility of a perfectible world. Gale's second book, *The Loves of Pelleas and Etarre* (1907), is a loosely connected series of stories in which the title characters, both seventy years old, reflect on the ways that love has helped them to survive lives marred by poverty and loss. The fantasy-like elements of both books ran counter to Gale's deepening engagement with questions about suffrage and social reform, both of which were often the subject of the freelance journalism she published during this period. Shortly after the publication of *Pelleas and Etarre*, however, Gale stopped writing fantasy stories, because she was having more success with a series of separately published short stories about a fictional town called "Friendship Village." Although these stories are much more realistic than her previous work, the seemingly conventional portraits of Friendship Village women appear to be at odds with Gale's feminist progressive politics. When these stories, and the work that follows them, are seen in the context of the twentieth-century suffrage movement, it becomes clear that Gale uses these traditional images in the service of her feminist message.

Early-twentieth-century suffrage politics borrowed heavily from traditional images of womanhood in order to present suffrage as a non-threatening means of improving the general well-being of the country. Mainstream suffragist organizations used the rhetoric of the "angel in the house" as a way to refurbish their public image, which was subject to contemptuous and hostile portrayal by the popular press. While she was a student at Radcliffe in the early 1900s, remembers Inez Irwin, the Boston papers ran cartoons featuring a suffragist named "Priscilla Jawbones, a tall, thin female of great strength and appalling ugliness . . . the figure at which all the jokes were hurled." Irwin points out that "to the man in the street, Woman's Rights was extremely comic" ("Adventures of Yesterday"). The National American Woman Suffrage Association (NAWSA), led by Carrie Chapman Catt, realized that the concepts of motherhood and "maternalism" could be used to combat public hostility; suffragists argued that suffrage was in keeping with a woman's "natural" inclinations to domesticity, child-rearing, and moral uplift.[7] Exemplifying the antisuffrage rhetoric that NAWSA suffragists attempted to subvert for their own purposes is a comment made in an early issue of the antisuffrage newspaper *The Remonstrance:* "Protection in the home and immunity from public service and labor, in order that her time and strength may be given to the supreme work of creating anew the human race . . . for a destiny of progress and brotherhood, is the most ancient, the most fundamental, right of women, and the one in which the future of the race is deeply involved" (qtd. in Burt 73). Suffragists used this idea—that the future of the race was the woman's responsibility—and expanded its purview, so that the domestic home became the domestic nation.[8] As Gale's sister Heterodite Rheta Childe Dorr wrote: "Woman's place is Home . . . But Home is not contained within the four walls of an individual house. Home is the community. The city full of people is the Family. The public school is the real Nursery. And badly do the Home and Family need their mother" (qtd. in Baker 632). In Dorr's configuration, the "mother" is not merely a good influence, but also has the potential for both political and social power, a potential that Gale wanted to call into action through her writing.

At the heart of Gale's feminist-progressivist thought is an idea articulated by Jane Addams: women are the housekeepers of America, and the nation should give them the vote as a means of making it possible for them to sweep the nation clean (Chafe 105). While on the one hand this idea seems to maintain women in their traditional role of housekeeper, it nevertheless presents a radical enlargement of the domestic sphere and gives women tremendous power within this "national domestic." Following this line of thought, NAWSA organized public lectures that linked domestic housekeeping with civic housekeeping, planned pageants and parades, and sponsored interviews with early suffrage activists that presented them as comforting old grannies.[9]

Linking domesticity and civic reform uses the rhetoric of the "angel in the house" to get the angel out of the house and into the streets, as it were. The domestic and maternalist rhetoric utilized by the suffragists to further their political agenda draws on essentialist beliefs about women in order to convince antisuffragists that the vote need not be a threat. This surface essentialism, which makes it seem as if all women are innately nurturing and compassionate, demonstrates what Gayatri Spivak calls a "*strategic* use of positivist essentialism in a scrupulously visible political interest" (205). In her commentary about Spivak's argument, Diana Fuss asserts that "essentialism can be powerfully displacing and disruptive. This . . . represents an approach which evaluates the motivations *behind* the deployment of essentialism rather than prematurely dismissing it as an unfortunate vestige of patriarchy (itself an essentialist category)" (32). Although many suffragists were white and came from privileged upper-class backgrounds, their political disenfranchisement placed them in a subordinate position, as did their willingness to ally themselves with working-class women. Their rhetoric of national domesticity should thus be seen as a tool with which to dismantle their subordinate status rather than as a failure to reimagine female possibility.

Enfranchising women was a terrifying thought to much of the country: suffragists were thought to be a threat to the natural order; they were going to destroy the family and the country itself through their disregard for convention.[10] In order to combat these powerful antisuffrage arguments, the angels of suffrage took to the streets and argued that voting was every mother's responsibility—for the well-being of the national child. Gale makes a clear distinction between "maternalism" and motherhood in *A Daughter of the Morning* (1917): her heroine, Cosma Wakely, is "the new factor . . . the mother-to-the-race woman. A woman whose passion for the race isn't necessarily to be confused with a passion for keeping their ears clean" (288). Most of the women in Gale's fiction have more facility for this conceptual motherhood than for actual parenting; few of her female characters, in fact, are mothers themselves, although they all adhere to the belief that women should be involved with local and national politics because of their innate abilities as caretakers.

I

Gale's 1911 novel, *Mothers to Men,* clearly illustrates her participation in the rhetoric of national housekeeping: the women in this novel are mothers to the world and thus particularly well-equipped to heal the social ills by treating the body politic as one of their own children. Written the year after Jane Addams published *Twenty Years at Hull House, Mothers to Men* featured characters and a setting that would have been familiar to Gale's readers from her two volumes of short stories, *Friendship Village* (1908) and *Friendship Village Love Stories* (1909). These stories, although not critically successful, established Gale as an author with a national reputation: the stories were tremendously popular and appeared regularly in such magazines as *The Woman's Home Companion, Everybody's, The Delineator,* and *Harper's Monthly Magazine.* Almost all the stories are narrated by Calliope Marsh, who is introduced in *Friendship Village* as "a little rosy wrinkled creature . . . mender of lace, seller of extracts, and music teacher, but of the three she thinks of the last as her true vocation" (7). Like many of the central female figures in regionalist fiction, Calliope is unmarried and plays a number of roles in the community—sage, confidante, mediator, goad, or even, as is the case in *Mothers to Men,* public conscience. Like the women whom Marjorie Pryse discusses in her essay "Reading Regionalism" (1994), who might be "conjure women, herbalists, [or] visionaries," Calliope serves a central function: "to critique so as to heal" (51).[11] Calliope's name serves as further indication of Gale's larger goals: Calliope is the muse of heroic poetry.

Mothers to Men is a change from Gale's first novel, the fanciful *Romance Island,* because she attempts here to merge her politics and her craft; Calliope becomes the vehicle for Gale's suffragist and reformist messages, albeit messages delivered in the language of small-town aphorisms and gentle wit. A heated exchange between Silas Sykes, a Friendship Village town councilman, and Mis' Toplady, one of the leaders of the Friendship Married Ladies Cemetery Improvement Sodality, provides a clue to the central idea behind the novel. The town council and the Ladies Sodality disagree about how the town should celebrate the Fourth of July: Sodality wants to arrange something patriotic and community oriented, while the men want the day to be a "business bringer." But when the council's scheduled speaker cancels his appearance, the women suddenly have an opportunity to put their plans in motion, which leads Silas Sykes to ask, "What are you goin' to *do* if the men decides to let you try?" Mis' Toplady responds, "It ain't for the men to *let us do* nothin'. It's for us all to do it together, yoke to yoke, just like everything else ought to be done by us both, an' no talk o' *'runnin'* by either side" (114). But ultimately, neither of them has it right: the council doesn't "let" Sodality take over; the women simply pitch in at the last minute. And although Sodality gets what it wants, the ideal of working "together, yoke to yoke" seems unattainable because they are only allowed to help when there is a crisis. *Mothers to Men* charts Sodality's growing dissatisfaction with this state of affairs and their gradual awareness that without suffrage, they will never have any direct power in the community. In this lighthearted tale of the small-town people already known to readers through her previous short-story collections, Gale embeds a conversion narrative: women becoming aware that they need the vote in order to create a better community for themselves, their children, and the town itself.

Feminist criticism has perceptively argued that the small communities depicted in regionalist writing and the emphasis on women-to-women relationships embody critiques of patriarchal capitalist structures and bring to light alternative social practices that allow for greater individual flexibility. In Friendship Village, the women of Sodality work together to improve their town, finding more fulfillment in their women's club than in their household tasks. By hook and by crook, Sodality manages to institute regular sanitation pickup, force shopkeepers to keep cleaner businesses, institute a lending library, and find a home for an orphaned child. Typical of the women's clubs that flourished at the turn of the century, Sodality offers its members a way to participate in the community outside their own homes, creating a bridge between private life and public government.[12] Sodality's deepening involvement with civic issues echoes a process that Gale wrote about in a 1906 report, "Civic Activities of Women's Clubs": "The initial steps usually include 'clean-up' days . . . prizes for backyard improvement . . . Next comes constructive work in beautifying . . . This leads *naturally* to work for sanitation . . . medical inspection of school children, the tuberculin testing of cattle . . . investigation of . . . child labor, of factory and shop conditions in general—hours, sanitation, wages, and so on, gradually to the whole underlying industrial situation and to the economic conditions which have begotten it" (qtd. in Scott, *Allies* 159, emphasis added). Gale's comment plays on the suffragist's rhetorical strategy that women are "naturally" inclined to community affairs, and that improving one's own backyard engenders an interest in the entire national socioeconomic structure: women start with flowers and decorative hedges and end up questioning the wages paid to factory workers.

Because they are prohibited from directly involving themselves in community affairs, the Sodality ladies must continually resort to subterfuge and trickery—even blackmail—to effect positive changes in Friendship Village. When Sodality offers to guest-edit a special issue of the town paper to raise money for the cemetery fund, for example, their ulterior motive is to get the male business owners to clean up their shops and institute progressive sanitation and hygiene practices. To accomplish this, they decide to "interview" all the men, all of whom also sit on the town council, and tell them that the women are "goin' to give [each man's business] . . . a nice, full printed description in to-night's *Daily*, just the way things are. If he wants it changed any, he can clean it all up, an' we'll write up the clean-up like a compliment" (141). The men can choose to reform themselves or to have their shortcomings written up for the entire town; and as Mis' Sykes points out, the men "can't very well sue us for libel, because they'd hev to pay it themselves. Nor they can't [sic] put us in prison for debt, because who'd get their three meals?" (143). The Sodality women, like Gale herself, will use their skill as writers to improve their community. Sodality also knows how to use the pressure of public opinion to force social changes: they decide to poll the townspeople to find out if they would be willing to pay for regular garbage pickup and for a shelf of lending library books in the grocery store, two things that Sodality had been lobbying the town council to institute for years to no avail. The women assume that if the council is faced with statements of public desire in the newspaper, the council will have no choice but to acquiesce. Sodality uses its powerlessness to an advantage—they cannot be sued or jailed—but their occasional successes blind them to the limits of their position. Because they accomplish some of their goals, none of them, except for Calliope, imagines that there might be other possibilities.

The only man who resists Sodality's reforms is the dairy farmer, Rob Henney, whose protests illustrate the arguments made by those who did not want reformers to tamper with the "natural order" of things. Henney's barns are so filthy that Calliope feels "squeamish" about ordering his milk but he won't change: "His cows had never been inspected because nothing of that kind had ever been necessary," he tells Sodality. "Folks had been drinking milk since milk begun, and if the Lord saw fit to call them home, why not through milk, or even through consumption, as well as through pneumonia and others?" (159). In Henney's mind, if the milk were contaminated with disease-carrying germs, well, that is just the way it is because that is how it always had been. He gets so angry at Sodality that he threatens the women with what Mis' Holcomb says are "injunctions—*is* that like handcuffs, do you know?" (163) The dairy farmer's protests echo the efforts of dairy farming cooperatives, in 1900, to resist mandatory tuberculin testing on their cows. In Milwaukee, for instance, dairy farmers withheld milk from urban markets to protest government testing of cows. They were more interested in "maintaining unfettered control over the sale of their milk" (Diner 105). Real-life reformers had to battle attitudes similar to Henney's, a social Darwinist outlook that saw the poor and sick as innately weak and inferior, which meant that their miserable lives were the result of their own weakness.

Jane Addams and other settlement house leaders pioneered the fight against these attitudes, arguing that environments shape people's lives, so that if the poor were unhealthy, it might be because they lived in unhealthy environments. Attempting to alter the living conditions for people in the cities and small towns led to concerted efforts at improving sanitation and hygiene—linchpins of social reform movements. Addams was so concerned about having regular garbage pickup in Chicago's Nineteenth Ward (where Hull House was located), that she got herself appointed garbage inspector and followed the garbage wagons on their routes to make sure they did a thorough job. Resistance to these changes, however, was widespread and emerged from surprising quarters—even health care workers were not exempt from the resistance to change. Dr. Sara Josephine Baker, head of New York's Bureau of Child Hygiene (and a Heterodite), wrote that after she opened a public health clinic for babies in Brooklyn,

"a petition was forwarded to my desk from the mayor's office, signed by
30-odd Brooklyn doctors, protesting bitterly against the Bureau of Child
Hygiene because it was ruining medical practice by its results in keeping
babies well, and demanding that it be abolished in the interests of the
medical profession" (qtd. in Diner 182).

The petition that Baker mentions echoes the sentiments of the aptly
named Alex Proudfit, who is Friendship Village's richest inhabitant as
well as one of its most conservative. Proudfit's views collide with those of
his fiancée, Robin Sidney, and her aunt, Mis' Eleanor Emmons. Mis' Emmons is a Sodality member and widow who, much to the confusion of the
other women, violates Friendship Village convention by using her own
first name when she introduces herself. The other married or widowed
women use either their husbands' first names or his occupations to identify themselves—Mis' Postmaster Sykes, for example, or Mis' Timothy
Toplady. "My land," says one woman, "was her husband a felon or a thief
or what that she don't use his name? What's she stick her own name in
front of his last name like that for? Sneaked out of usin' his Christian
name as soon as his back was turned, *I* call it . . . I'd use my dead husband's name if it was Nebuchadnezzar" (24). Mis' Emmons—Friendship
Village's version of a "Lucy Stoner"—shares her progressive political attitudes with her niece and Calliope. Mis' Eleanor and Robin quarrel with
Alex about the fate of Chris, a young orphan boy whom Robin wants to
adopt and whom Alex wants to send away. Robin believes that they can
give Chris a better life, but Alex thinks otherwise: "To do the best we can
with ourselves and to help up an under dog or two—if he deserves it—
that's the most Nature lets us in for. . . . Our spurts of civic righteousness
and national reform never get us anywhere in the long run. In the long
run, things go along and go along. You can't stop them. If you're wise, you
won't rush them" (76). Any of Gale's progressivist or suffragist readers
would recognize in Alex's comments the arguments made by those who
disagreed with their efforts; the novel satirizes Alex's traditionalist platitudes and reveals the flaws in his thinking.

Like all the children in Gale's fiction, Chris is a dewy-eyed innocent,
sweet and helpless—a sentimental goad to civic and moral improvement.
Chris's plight gives Gale an opportunity to air another of her favorite
causes: temperance. After his mother's death, Chris has been deserted by
his father, a drunkard who returns to Friendship Village just in time for a
tearful farewell to his son before dying of a wound inflicted in a barroom
brawl. Although the doctor says that the man died of "alcoholism," Mis'
Hubblethwait says, "it was liquor killed him. No use dressin' up words"
(273). Gale's stance on temperance was shared by many suffragists; suffrage was one of the goals of Frances Willard, founder of the Women's

Christian Temperance Union (WCTU), who argued that the "woman's vote . . . would express her higher, selfless nature" (qtd. in Baker 638).[13]

The debate over Chris's fate helps Gale make the case against the Proudfits of the world, as does Robin's disgust for Proudfit's callousness, which leads her to break their engagement. When she tells Calliope about her decision, Calliope realizes how tempting it could be to just "go along" and marry the rich man. Proudfit's path is the "the sheer, clear, mere self-indulgence of the last-notch conservative . . . the quiet, the order, the plain *safety* of the unchanging, of going along and going along" (269). But Robin resists the seductive role of cosseted wife and chooses instead to marry Mr. Insley, a visiting college professor who shares her progressive outlook. Insley is a better man than Proudfit, according to the logic of the novel, not only because he is more compassionate, but also because he values women as workers while Proudfit wants Robin only to be "dainty." Robin and Insley will work "together, yoke to yoke," in a marriage characterized by equality, friendship, and shared visions for a better future. Tellingly, Insley loves Chris and is delighted to adopt him. The simple fact that Robin and Insley want to combine love and work is an important step on the path toward civic improvement: if all men and women could work together the way Robin and Insley will, the future would be a better place.

Gale's suffragist attitudes come to the fore in the final section of *Mothers to Men*, when Mis' Sykes brings a "well-dressed, soft-spoken" suffragist to talk to Sodality. The suffragist, Mis' Lacy, offers a counterpoint to the usual portrayal of suffragists in the media—the "Priscilla Jawbones" that Irwin describes in her memoirs. Throughout this final section Gale subtly attacks a number of antisuffragist arguments, aware of the fact that some of her readers might be hostile to suffrage, no matter how domestically it is presented. The novel's conclusion thus negotiates a balance between Gale's awareness of the need to tread softly and her conviction that suffrage is essential for the country's well-being. Thus Calliope initially says that she has no interest in the vote and is only going to hear Mis' Lacy's talk out of politeness and curiosity, not conviction. None of the Sodality members will say outright that she supports suffrage, but they all agree (out of earshot of their husbands) that they could do their husbands' jobs just as well, or better. Mis' Sturgis goes so far as to say that "it seems as if, if we got the chance, us women might not vote brilliant at first, but we would vote with our sense. The sense that can pick out a pattern, and split a receipt, an' dress the children out o' the house money. I bet there's a lot o' that kind o' sense among women that don't get used up, by a long shot" (295). With her pragmatic assessment of women's common sense, Mis' Sturgis rebuts the antisuffrage argument that women are too delicate and too ignorant to vote. Antisuffrage arguments, observes Sara Graham in *Woman Suffrage and the New Democracy* (1996), characterized women as "undependable, impulsive, and easily corruptible," which were also popular fears about democracy itself. Thus, Graham argues, antisuffragism "meant more than a simple constellation of conservative, misogynist attitudes. It encompassed a tangled calculus of overt sexist sentiment, entrenched adherence to the Burkean concept of virtual representation, racial and class prejudice, and, at its core, a deeply rooted fear of democracy" (21).[14] Although racial tensions are not present in *Mothers to Men*, members of the Ladies Sodality battle these other issues very successfully.

Gale attempts to untangle this complex knot of antisuffrage sentiment by demonstrating how shortsighted the town council is when it comes time to handle any problems having to do with the poor. The town council would prefer simply to ignore these problems in order to think about how to improve their own businesses; they feel no sense of responsibility for anyone other than themselves. Their attitudes change only when one of the youngest—and prettiest—members of Sodality speaks out angrily about the need for women to be involved in community decisions. Letty Ames, the Sodality member who makes this argument, is in love with one of the town's leading bachelors (and he with her); she is also "sweet and shy and unexpected and brave," which does not prevent her from challenging conventional attitudes about femininity. Letty's outburst occurs when a council meeting is interrupted with the news that a young boy is dying of typhoid caused by germs from Black Hollow, a long-stagnant pond, "piled full of diseases," which the council has refused to have filled despite Sodality's continued requests to do so. As Sodality rushes to offer support to the boy's mother by bringing food and caring for her other children, Letty suddenly questions the larger problem underneath the immediate crisis: "All us women can do is carry him broth and bread and nurse him. It's only the men that can bring about the things to make him well. And they haven't done it. It's been the women who have been urging it—and not getting it done. Wasn't it our work too?" (309) Her fiancé protests that Sodality's efforts are "womanly" and provide support "like your mother did and my mother did," but Letty dismisses his comment altogether: "Womanly, *Womanly!* . . . What is there womanly about my bathing and feeding a child inside four clean walls, if dirt and bad food and neglect are outside for him? Will you tell me if there is anything more womanly than my right to help make the world as decent for my children as I would make my own home?" (309). This is political action dressed up as a mother, radical social reform in an apron and carrying a mop—the rhetoric of early-twentieth-century suffrage—and it makes Calliope "thrill" to hear it.

Listening to Letty, Calliope realizes that Sodality's achievements have been "patching up" what others have broken, or accomplished by "scheming"; their hands were full with "ways of serving that they'd schemed for and stole" (311). By contrast, suffrage suddenly becomes the means for directly and consistently doing what women's organizations had been able to do only indirectly and not always successfully. Calliope and the other Sodality women realize that in order to effect permanent change, they need to have a direct say in who governs and what will become policy. Letty's speech sparks a conversion in Calliope about the need for women's rights, which is also, Gale hastens to remind her readers, a need for human rights. Calliope repeatedly insists on the fact of human equality, and admits that "there ain't no more thrilling fact in the universe" than the attraction between men and women, thus illustrating that equality will not eradicate male–female relationships (although she herself remains steadfastly, happily, single and childless). She does, however, chastise those who think that women should not vote because Eve was subordinate to Adam by commenting that "creation itself . . . ailed us . . . Creation is a thing that it takes most folks a long while to recover from" (200). If people could move away from that line of thinking, Calliope muses, then everyone would treat everyone else as equals. After Letty tells the council what it means to be "womanly," Calliope takes her ideas one step further: "Let's pretend," she says to the council and the assembled townswomen, "that we was all citizens and equal. And let's figure things out . . . just like we had the right!" (312). The women at this point do not legally have "the right," but Calliope and Letty demonstrate that political equality is the only way that positive social change can be permanently established.

The novel ends with Calliope's vision of a global sisterhood, a feminist vision of a utopian future. Walking along Daphne Street, Friendship Village's main thoroughfare, Calliope sees her female neighbors all busy at their chores and pictures a "Daphne Street . . . round and round the world, and acrost and acrost it, full of women doing the same" (326). She imagines

away off to the places that Daphne Street led past, where women had all these things . . . where the factories is setting them free, like us here in the village ain't free just yet, and I felt a wicked envy for them that can set their hands to the New Work, that us here in Friendship Village is trying so hard to get in between whiles. And I could see away ahead to times . . . when women, Away Off Then, will be mothers and workers and general human beings such as yet we only know how to think about being, scrappy and wishful. . . . And something in me kind of climbed out of me and run along ahead and looked back at me over its shoulder and says: "Keep up, keep up, Calliope." And before I knew it, right out loud, I says: "I will. I will." (326)

As a subtle reiteration of her politics, Gale names the main thoroughfare of Friendship Village after the nymph Daphne, who resisted Apollo's sexual advances and was changed into a laurel tree to protect her from his amorous advances. This further reflects the distinction between maternalism and motherhood: despite their maternalist rhetoric, Gale's women live on a street named for a powerful—and virginal—goddess. And it is on this street that Calliope's conversion is completed. With her promise to "keep up," Calliope will no longer be satisfied with the indirect, hit-or-miss efforts of women's club organizations.

Calliope's belief in a global sisterhood and the town council's grudging agreement to do something about conditions in the poor neighborhood near Black Hollow conclude the novel on an optimistic note; Friendship Village is transformed into an idealized community created on a foundation of progressive, feminist thought. While not set in an exotic location, Gale's novel is as utopian in its way as the more fantastical feminist utopias created in Irwin's *Angel Island* (1914) and Gilman's *Herland* (1915). Like the worlds imagined in these other novels, the new world imagined at the end of *Mothers to Men*—cleaner, healthier, unified, women-centered—serves to highlight the failures of the society from which it springs.[15] In order to present her utopian message without alienating those readers who might be hostile to her radical ideas, and without lapsing back into the romantic fantasy of her first novel, however, Gale uses the familiar voice of Calliope and the Sodality ladies. The message may be radical, but it wears calico and knows how to bake bread: how could anything threatening to the social order come from a place named Friendship Village, after all?

Mothers to Men represents Gale's strongest expression of political fiction thus far in her career; it is her first clear attempt to unify her politics with her art. Prior to this novel, Gale had established a national audience for her earlier Friendship Village stories, which are less directly political but are nevertheless deeply engaged with women's lives and women's work. The novel uses the same regionalist conventions as those earlier stories—simple plot, idiomatic expressions, country humor—to bring its readers into a comfortable and familiar world that Gale then politicizes, in hopes of creating in her readers the same conversion that Calliope experiences. The novel did not create a big stir when it was published; it was called "charming" and "delightful," and *The Bookman* said that "Miss Zona Gale is one of the unobtrusive authors whose every volume is an assured delight" (December 11, 1911, 445). These reviews unwittingly support Gale's point: enfranchising women and embarking on a path of progressive social reform need not be terrifying. Calliope's folksiness and the familiarity of Friendship Village help to contain the threat of Gale's radical social politics.

Mothers to Men also illustrates how Gale's work both continues and revises nineteenth-century models of female authorship. Its clearly polemical subtexts about suffrage and social reform echo the nineteenth-century idea that women writers should be moral arbiters but with a significant difference: Gale's women seem uninterested in inculcating Christian virtues in the town council; they want direct access to power. Calliope and the Ladies Sodality are less concerned with the state of people's souls than they are with the state of the state; their interests are public and civic rather than private and individual. Although Gale structures her novel along the lines of a conversion narrative, the conversion that Calliope experiences is not the moment of Christian enlightenment so movingly chronicled in novels such as Harriet Beecher Stowe's *Uncle Tom's Cabin* (1852) or Augusta Evans's *St. Elmo* (1866). It is instead a conversion that moves her into the public realm of civic government and into a sense of sisterhood with women all over the world. Calliope and Letty arguing with the town council about its reluctance to implement progressive reform revises the famous scene in Rachel Halliday's kitchen in *Uncle Tom's Cabin*, which Jane Tompkins reads as that novel's most "politically subversive dimension" (142). In Rachel's kitchen, which exemplifies Stowe's conception of female authority and the society this vision could create, people are "motivated by self-sacrificing love . . . and will perform their duties willingly: moral suasion will take the place of force" (142). Female authority thus rests in being a moralizing influence, which as Lora Romero argues in *Home Fronts* (1997), is "conducted . . . through informal, irregular, and unofficial avenues—including cultural expression" (71). When Letty rejects her fiancé's suggestion that she be "womanly . . . like your mother did and my mother did," she is also rejecting the Rachel Halliday model of womanly power in favor of a direct, official, and nonreligious approach.

Gale's attitude toward her own work is also significantly different from the attitude that Susan Coultrap-McQuin attributes to nineteenth-century women writers, who were committed to their work as professionals but who remained essentially private figures, working within the sheltered space of home and family. Of Helen Hunt Jackson, for instance, Coultrap-McQuin remarks that while on the one hand Jackson negotiated her own publication fees and handled all the professional responsibilities of being a successful writer, she "protect[ed] her private family life and conform[ed] to the traditional notion of feminine decorum" (160). The most celebrated exception to this nineteenth-century model is Stowe, who was thrust into the international spotlight with the publication of *Uncle Tom's Cabin*. Even with the immense publicity granted to this novel, however, Stowe remained what Coultrap-McQuinn calls a "domestic feminist," professing to be more interested in helping people to become better Christians than in asserting her own authorial power.

While Stowe saw herself as a professional writer, she did not claim the status of "artist" for herself, which Gale did, an important shift that suggests very different attitudes toward authorial power. Gale saw herself as an artist who was also a "social being"; it is her status as an artist that gives her the authority to comment on her society. Thinking of herself as an artist also bespeaks her deep personal ambitions, which were clear even from her earliest days: during her days as a journalist, Gale gained a reputation for being "about the most ambitious girl in New York at that time—too ambitious, some said" (*The Bookman* 169). Stowe, in contrast, is reported as saying that when she wrote *Uncle Tom's Cabin* she had "no more thought of style or literary excellence than the mother who rushes into the street and cries for help to save her children from the burning house, thinks of the teachings of the rhetorician or the elocutionist" (Bell 104). In her public disclaimers about having any pretensions to artistic style (which may themselves be simply Stowe's savvy manipulations of her audience: how better to prevent critical attacks about literary style than to insist that style was not at all a concern?), Michael Bell argues that Stowe is "conforming rather precisely to the standard rationale adopted by most American women writers of the 1850s" and notes that "ambition here is transmuted into a manifestation of maternal duty" (104).[16] Stowe's representations of domesticity and her willingness to downplay her own literary and cultural authority illustrate why Gale—and Cather and Wharton—found the model of nineteenth-century female authorship limiting: it prevented not only artistic ambition but also the very identity of "artist," which all three writers wanted to claim for themselves.

II

Despite the success of *Mothers to Men* and her other Friendship Village stories, Gale could not find an audience for "The Reception Surprise," a short story that demonstrates her continued interest in commenting on "social disabilities" through its portrayal of an interracial marriage. When she sent this story to Ellery Sedgwick, editor of *The Atlantic Monthly,* he wrote to Gale that, ever since reading "The Reception Surprise," the challenging theme of your story has been more or less vividly present in my mind. I am a New Englander with a good many generations of New Englanders behind me, but I cannot accept the implications of your thesis. Of course, if social equality between whites and blacks is to be established, it must carry with it the right and the propriety of intermarriage between the races. This I find impossible to face, and while I have no silly notions of not sitting down at a table with any *exceptional* member of the race, it would not be in my power to compel myself to live on terms of intimacy with a Negro family. Feeling as I do, I should not like to print your story— (it isn't a story; it is a very adroit and subtle argument.) To discuss it would prolong this letter beyond all reasonable limits; but though you hold my judgement in disfavor, I hope you will believe that I recognize the skill with which you have put forward your thesis. Stories with a purpose, I studiously avoid; but yours I read with attention and great interest. (September 7, 1915, SHSW, emphasis added)

Sedgwick's rejection was echoed by the editor of *Everybody's Magazine,* who belied the title of his journal when he told Gale that "as a nation we aren't quite ready" for the subject of her story.[17] These rejections illustrate the pervasive racism that Gale encountered even within the suffrage movement and among her most radical Heterodite companions.[18] Unlike the politics of many of her white women friends and allies, Gale's conception of sisterhood bridged racial and class divides; she insisted—too idealistically, thought some of her political friends—that equal rights should be applied equally.

Sedgwick's letter makes a distinction between "story" and "argument" that is useful in thinking about how Gale constructed her literary and political career. The boundary that Sedgwick delineates so easily and clearly is not one that Gale recognizes, as illustrated by "The United States and the Artist." The artist is always a social being; argument and art belong together. She thus used her literary celebrity to generate support for her political causes which then, as in *Mothers to Men,* provide plot lines for her fiction. Unlike Sedgwick, who is interested only in the "exceptional" member of the race, Gale affiliates herself with ordinary people, the people whose lives are not usually subject to fiction. Although both *The Atlantic Monthly* and *Everybody's Magazine* declined "The Reception Surprise," Gale had the last laugh: she published the story, under the title "Dream," in her 1919 collection, *Peace in Friendship Village.*[19] By the time she published this collection of stories—her final Friendship Village collection—Gale had become an important literary figure, although she was still a year away from *Miss Lulu Bett,* the novel that would elevate her standing among writers and critics even further.

Gale sets "Dream" in the context of Friendship Village, but this time Gale looks at her villagers through the lens of racial, rather than gender, politics. Although Friendship Village proved hospitable to the feminist progressivism of the Ladies Sodality, its racial politics are much more resistant to change, much to the chagrin of Calliope March. The "dream" of the title refers to Calliope's vision of a community wherein whites and blacks can live "neighborly," but she finds little support for her views among her white neighbors. Unlike the other residents of Friendship Village, Calliope refuses to judge or categorize people, a habit that Mis' Sykes calls "queer" because Calliope thus "miss[es] all the satisfaction of being exclusive. And you can't *afford* not to be" (207). In response to a woman who complains that Calliope does not draw boundaries anywhere, Calliope replies that it's only "them on Mars won't speak to me—yet. But short of Mars—no. I have no lines up" (208). Calliope's willingness to live without boundary markers of any sort belies the pervasive tendency, in the United States after World War I, to emphasize increasingly rigid demarcations of race, ethnicity, and nationhood—markers that members of Sodality are all too eager to enforce.

When an African American family moves into Friendship Village, Calliope is the only person who welcomes them, although before she knows that they are "dark-skinned," Mis' Sykes had been eager to count them as her friends. Mis' Sykes had planned a "reception surprise" to welcome the new family into the neighborhood because she was impressed by the fact that they have servants and a piano: "Folk's individualities is expressed in folks' furniture," she tells Calliope confidently. "You can't tell me that, with those belongings, we can go wrong in our judgment" (207). Her certainty about possessions as a mark of quality is considerably shaken when Calliope tells her that Mrs. Burton Fernandez is "dark-skinned," which Mis' Sykes initially takes to mean "brunette." When she realizes what Calliope actually means, she is outraged; she can't believe that a family "like that" could have misled her. Calliope attempts to demonstrate to her friend that in fact the Fernandez family is all that Mis' Sykes thought they were, but Mis' Sykes cannot see past their color. "Mis' Fernandez has got a better education than either you or I," Calliope argues, "and . . . her two children have been to colleges that you and I have never seen the inside of and never will. And her husband is a college professor, up here to study for a degree that I don't even know what the letters stand for." She concludes by asking Mis' Sykes, "In what way . . . consists your and my superiority to that woman?" (215).

Calliope's ability to accept the Fernandez family as culturally superior neighbors infuriates Mis' Sykes, who can see only that Mis' Fernandez is "black" and that Calliope has "no sense of fitness." Mis' Sykes's logic bases itself first on race, then on "nature," and then on divine will, shifting with the same ease that marked the protean nature of antisuffragist rhetoric. When Calliope attempts to refute Mis' Sykes's arguments, reminding her that Mis' Fernandez in fact is "all you thought you had in that house, and education besides," Mis' Sykes changes her tactics: "It ain't the skin," she says, "don't keep harping on that. It's them. They're different by nature. . . . You can't change human nature!" Calliope has an answer to this, however: "'Can't you?' says I. '*Can't* you? I'm interested. If that was true, you and I would be swinging by our tails, this minute, sociable, from your clothes-line." Mis' Sykes is not convinced by Calliope's mastery of Darwinian logic and shifts her tactics again, this time invoking divine fiat: "If the Lord had intended dark-skinned folks to be different from what they are, he'd have seen to it by now. . . . How do you know that the Lord intended them to be educated? Tell me that!" To this Calliope has no answer other than to appeal to Mis' Sykes sense of pride: she reminds her that all the arrangements for the reception surprise have been made, due entirely to Mis' Sykes's certainty that the Burton Fernandezes were "quality folks," and that to change plans now would be a huge loss of face. Calliope's final comment is that "as fast as those that try to grow, stick up their heads, it's the business of us that tootle for democracy, and for evolution, to help them on. . . . For if some of them stick up their heads, it proves that more of them could—if we didn't stomp 'em down" (218). Curiously, no one in the story remarks on the family's Hispanic last name, which suggests that in Friendship Village at least, race is a more difficult marker to ignore than ethnicity.

Gale demonstrates her commitment to racial equality by adding a detail that gestures to the painful treatment suffered by African American soldiers returning from the war. The Fernandezes' son, who is en route to Friendship Village from France, is a war hero who saved his (white) commanding officer from death. Calliope uses this information to press Mis' Sykes to carry through with the reception, arguing with her that if all else fails she could tell the other Sodality members that the reception was for the soldier, not the family. Calliope asks, "Are you going to let him offer up his life, and go over to Europe and have his bravery recognized there, and then come back here and get the cold shoulder from you—are you?" Adding the African American war hero is another revision to the earlier story and reflects the treatment of African American soldiers in general upon their return from World War I. The 369th Regiment's victory parade up Fifth Avenue to Harlem was a celebration attended by both whites and blacks (although New York's mayor declined to attend), but the heroism of the soldiers in no way altered the treatment of African Americans in the postwar

United States. In fact, according to David Levering Lewis, "by the end of 1919, there had been race riots in two dozen cities, towns, or counties, rampant lynchings and resurrection of the Ku Klux Klan, and a dismal falling off of jobs in the North for Afro-Americans" (23). Calliope's plea to "neighbor" the Fernandez son rather than "honor" him illustrates Gale's awareness of postwar racism in the U.S.

After this conversation, thinking that she has convinced Mis' Sykes, Calliope takes a nap; she wakes up just in time to attend the reception, which "goes off" beautifully, much to her delight and to the delight of the Fernandez family. Unfortunately, at the end of the reception, Calliope *really* wakes up and she realizes that the entire thing only happened in her nap-time dream. In actuality, Mis' Sykes has told Sodality that they "mustn't forget what is fitting and what isn't," which means that none of them will enter the Fernandez house. In a concession to wartime sentiment and with great magnanimity, however, the Ladies have decided that there will be a "public meeting to honor the soldiers—the colored soldier with all the rest. But that's as far as it will go." Reflecting Gale's belief that communities should form through affiliation rather than enforced and external markers, Calliope pleads with Sodality: "He don't [sic] want to be honored! . . . He wants to be neighbored—the way anybody does when they're worth it" (231). Being neighborly, in Calliope's mind, means allowing difference to strengthen rather than threaten the community; in her mind, having the Fernandez family as neighbors "is like seeing the future come true right in my face" (212). The story ends with her melancholy comment that "what hadn't happened was more real for me than the things that were true" (231).

While the story ends with a defeat of Calliope's liberal principles, it is still a clear statement of Gale's nascent cosmopolitanism and her desire to effect social and political changes through her writing. Although some critics bemoaned the fact that Gale had returned to Friendship Village after the harsh realism of her 1918 novel *Birth, Peace in Friendship Village* sold very well, which meant that Gale's vision of an integrated society was carried to a large audience. Like Calliope, Gale refuses to acknowledge race-based distinctions, an attitude that led her to challenge her less accepting friends. In a letter to Lula Vollmer, a playwright and fellow Wisconsin resident, Gale observed that despite Vollmer's good intentions, she sees African American women only as "the lower class . . . devot[ed] to the mistress." If Gale were to invite her to lunch in New York "with Jessie Fauset, that brilliant young author of *There Is Confusion*, [Vollmer] wouldn't come. Yet Jessie Fauset is a powerful creative artist, a student and a scholar, a graduate of Cornell, a Phi Beta Kappa, and a lady. More she is a spirit filled with humanity and with love for it." Sounding even more like Calliope, Gale concludes her letter by saying that the "new Negro" has begun to "flower forth," and "on another planet it would be a dramatic and vital occurrence" (April 7, 1926, SHSW). But on Earth, this dramatic flowering is ignored, and the United States, like Friendship Village, falls far short of Gale's optimistic visions.

From her earliest days in New York, Gale had been involved with African American writers and artists, well before "the Negro was in vogue."[20] Her interest in and commitment to racial equality was matched by Ridgely Torrence, her one-time fiancé and the playwright who wrote a series of three one-act plays that were staged with an all-black cast in 1917—the first all-black cast ever seen in a Broadway theater. The production received rave reviews, but the show closed after a week's run, due to poor timing: it opened on the day that the United States declared war on Germany. Although Gale ended their romance in 1911, she and Torrence remained close friends and often commented on one another's work; she was probably in the audience on opening night, along with other literary and social celebrities.[21] In *Theater Arts Magazine,* Gale wrote that "these plays are no imitation of the drama of the white race. Neither are they the pseudo-delineation which the American dramatist has too often offered as interpreting a type-negro. . . . Here is a race, infinitely potential, moving before one in individuals highly differentiated and as terribly intent—you see now at last—on their own living as any Anglo-Saxon is intent on his own. The Colored Players strike at a provincialism which has been in one's way, it appears, not only socially, but artistically" (158). Through her relationship with Torrence and her own interest in striking at racist "provincialism," Gale met and became friendly with a number of important figures in the New Negro Renaissance, including James Weldon Johnson, Charles S. Johnson, and Jessie Fauset. Gale shared with these writers and intellectuals the view that the artist must be a "social being."

Gale's friendship with Fauset led her to write the introduction to Fauset's novel, *The Chinaberry Tree* (1931), although their friendship receives little comment in studies about either writer. The two women shared a network of relationships and a similar attitude about how to use their literary influence. Fauset came to New York in 1919 from Washington, D.C., where she had been teaching school for a number of years; well-educated and sophisticated, she started working with W. E. B. Du Bois at *The Crisis,* the magazine that Du Bois had started in conjunction with the NAACP. Like Gale, Fauset was a believer in affiliation and collaboration, which she put into practice as the literary editor of *The Crisis,* a role that caused Langston Hughes to call her a "midwife" of the Harlem Renaissance.[22] While working on the magazine, according to Deborah

McDowell, Fauset "built bridges with young, aspiring writers whose talents and potentials she recognized"; McDowell also credits Fauset with moving the magazine "into the forefront of literary and racial modernism" (xiii). Both Fauset and Gale used their literary authority to further others' careers—Fauset through her work at the magazine, Gale through the scholarships she endowed at the University of Wisconsin; both willingly introduced younger writers to influential editors, agents, and publishers. They shared friendships with such people as Fannie Hurst, Jean Toomer, Charles S. Johnson, James Weldon Johnson (whose wife, Grace Nail, was a Heterodite), and Georgia Douglas Johnson, among others.[23] Both Fauset and Gale maintained webs of relationships that extended far beyond their home territories; both were committed to writing in and about the United States, although Fauset's extensive travels abroad give her novels a more cosmopolitan flavor. Each writer is concerned with and writes about the need for social change, particularly the inequalities surrounding gender and race; their friendship moves beyond the conventional portrait of white–black relationships during this period.

When Fauset departed *The Crisis* in 1926, its literary influence waned, held hostage in part by Du Bois's adherence to rigid editorial ideas about what African American fiction should and should not do. Replacing Du Bois's magazine as an influential literary voice was *Opportunity*, the magazine started by Charles S. Johnson for the Urban League. Johnson, also trained as a sociologist, initially wanted the magazine to function as a scholarly journal, but he realized the magazine would be more useful if it became a chronicle of black America's cultural life. Johnson "understood the social function of literature, but . . . avoided the expression art-as-propaganda, and . . . suggested repeatedly that writers and artists had a responsibility to themselves as well as to the community," observe Abby Johnson and Ronald Johnson in their study of literary politics in African American magazines (51). Like Gale, Johnson understood that while artists might create within their own four walls, they also have a social responsibility. His magazine facilitated important connections between the community and its artists without insisting that portrayals of the African American community be unfailingly positive.

In part because she shared Johnson's understanding about the role of the artist in the community, Gale agreed to serve as fiction judge for the literary contests sponsored annually by *Opportunity* from 1924 to 1927. George Hutchinson, in *The Harlem Renaissance in Black and White* (1995), argues that Gale's participation in the *Opportunity* contests and her attention to issues of race and class exemplify the "extensive connections between the interest in regional realism, American cultural nationalism, and New Negro writing" (215). In the first year of the contest,

Zora Neale Hurston's story "Spunk" won second prize, and Gale wrote to Johnson requesting an additional copy of it, so that she could "send it to Mrs. Wharton in France" (April 12, 1925, SHSW).[24] In the *Opportunity* column announcing the winners, Gale is quoted as saying that the stories "revealed great treasure" (May 1925, 130); the same editorial mentions Fauset's first novel, *There Is Confusion* (1924), and Jean Toomer's *Cane* (1923) as examples of work that reveal "with some measure of faithfulness something of the life of a people; something of those subtle forces which sustain their hopes and joys, stiffens them in sorrow" (May 1925, 131).

The publication of *There Is Confusion* became the occasion for the dinner at the Manhattan Civic Club that is now better known as the launching for the so-called "New Negro writers." Hosted by Charles Johnson and Alain Locke, the dinner introduced a number of new African American writers—most of whom, not uncoincidentally, were men—to the African American "establishment" and to white intellectuals, editors, and writers, including Gale. In a letter to Alain Locke, Johnson listed as invitees Carl Van Doren, H. L. Mencken, Robert Morss Lovett, Ridgely Torrence, Zona Gale, Oswald Garrison Villard, Mary Johnston, and "about twenty more of this type. Practically all of these are known to some of us, and we can get them" (qtd. in Hutchinson 391). At this dinner—ostensibly in honor of Fauset—Fauset was herself overshadowed, even neglected, in a display of misogyny that Gale surely would have noticed and that may in fact have led to the two women becoming friends. According to Hutchinson, Locke wanted to make sure that "the event was not to feature Jessie Fauset," and Charles Johnson hastened to reassure him, writing to him that the evening was "not exclusively for Miss Fauset or anybody else. The real motive for getting this group together is to present this newer school of writers" (390). Neither man, however, seemed to relay this information to Fauset. In a letter written well after the event, Fauset accused Locke of "distorting" the idea for the evening, which "originated with Regina Anderson and Gwendolyn Bennett" (Hutchinson 390). Fauset wrote to Locke that she "still remembered the consummate cleverness with which you that night as toastmaster strove to keep speech and comment away from the person for whom the occasion was meant" (qtd. in Wall 70). Fauset's anger, expressed many years after the fact, comes as a result of realizing that, as would happen decades later in the Black Arts movement of the late 1960s, women and women's experiences did not fit smoothly into the "new movement" of the 1920s, just as women and gender issues would not mesh with the radicalism of the leftist 1930s, or with the New Criticism of the 1950s.

Increasingly marginalized by the male cultural elite who were shaping the Renaissance in their own image, Fauset began to have difficulty getting her work published. Despite her early and steadfast commitment to African American politics and literature, her work was not considered "exotic" enough to interest white publishers and she was similarly doubted by her African American contemporaries. Claude McKay described her as "prim and dainty as a primrose," and added that her novels were equally precious (qtd. in McDowell xxx). Challenging opinions like McKay's, Thadious Davis argues that Fauset's work is in fact "catholic and global in its reach . . . [and] complicates simplistic orthodoxies. For [Fauset], 'blackness' was not synonymous with Afro-American, but included black people worldwide" (xiii). Davis's comment seems equally applicable to Gale, who also wanted her work to address global concerns. Both Fauset and Gale wrote about and lived within their local communities and used this local focus to challenge social and political realities. This strategy eventually resulted in both writers being dismissed as naïve, and their work being misread as unsophisticated and nonexperimental. Such misreadings, however, stem from an inability or a refusal to examine what motivated their work and from an unwillingness to reimagine what counts as innovative or radical art.[25]

Like the Burton Fernandez family, Fauset's characters are middle-class African Americans whose search for personal happiness and security is often thwarted by the distortions of a racist society. But the sheer fact of their middle-class existence made Fauset's characters seem unexciting to publishers, who wanted something "hot," like Claude McKay's *Home to Harlem* (1928). Seeking help for *The Chinaberry Tree* (1931), Fauset asked Gale to write an introduction to the book, turning to her not as a patron but as a friend. She knew Gale, was familiar with her work, and shared Gale's political and social viewpoints. In a letter to Gale, Fauset tells her that the characters in *The Chinaberry Tree* "don't begin to measure up to the capable and efficient colored women you've been meeting at conventions" (October 22, 1931, SHSW).[26] And because of this, she goes on to say, she cannot get the book published: "The joke of it is that the people in my story . . . are just decent ambitious folks with sensibilities. Yes—their like is unknown" (October 22, 1931, SHSW). Her "decent ambitious folks" are, in their own quiet way, as revolutionary as Hurston's Janie Crawford; Fauset's characters defy what had become by then stock conventions in the sensationalist novels made popular by McKay's novel and by Carl Van Vechten's *Nigger Heaven* (1925). Fauset rejects sex and sensationalism, cabarets and clubs, and instead focuses on the ways in which women struggle for autonomy and individualism.

In writing her introduction to the novel, Gale seizes on this apparent paradox—that Fauset's characters were too conventional to be believable—as a way of arguing that Fauset's work remedies a serious flaw in the American literary tradition. Gale notes that "only the uneducated Negro" gets portrayed in literature, despite the fact that "group after group has entered fiction—the New Englander, educated and uneducated, the Southerner, the Middle Westerner, the far-Westerner, the Canadian, developed or primitive" (1931, vii). Why then, Gale asks, do publishers insist on supplying readers only with a steady diet of "travesty and comedy [about] the uneducated Negro with his dialect and his idiom, his limited outlook"? Fauset's work presents a challenge to readers because it refuses to participate in these stereotypes; her characters are "living lives of quiet interests and pursuits . . . interests social, domestic, and philanthropic," and are not at all flamboyant or spectacular. Expanding her regionalist litany into an assertion of shared national identity, Gale notes that the people about whom Fauset writes "are to be met, not only in New York and Chicago, but in the smaller towns of the East, the Middle West and the South" (viii). In other words, the essay suggests, middle-class African Americans live happily outside of New York; they are not only the products of Harlem.

The introduction concludes with Gale's own rejection of conventional attitudes about race relations in the United States. She notes that the characters in Fauset's novel are uninvolved and relatively uninterested in white culture: they are "quite unconnected with white folk" and make decisions "without . . . consideration of those [whites] about them." Her comments suggest that perhaps white culture is not the powerful and pervasive force that it believes itself to be; it is possible, Gale asserts, for African Americans to live without wanting to emulate or to be involved with white America. Fauset's novel articulates the damage caused by the national obsession with race, but the worlds in which her characters move are peopled almost exclusively with nonwhites. Gale's introduction not only highlights Fauset's focus, but goes one step further by pointing out that Fauset's characters "carry on their lives . . . as if there were no white people in America save those who serve them in shops and traffic." Here Gale describes the cultural autonomy of African Americans, a world in which whites are not at the center of American culture and may in fact "serve" rather than be served. As Gale sees it, Fauset's novel thus breaks down distinctions and dismantles social hierarchies: we are all, Gale concludes, "fellow countrymen," and thus none is superior to any other.

Fauset liked Gale's introduction a great deal and wrote her to say that she was "immensely pleased with the idea of seeing my name coupled with yours" (October 22, 1931, SHSW). In another letter she noted that

Stokes (the publisher) is as "proud of [the book] as I am, which is saying much" (November 25, 1931, SHSW). In the 1995 reprint of Fauset's novel, however, Gale's introduction is not included, and there is in fact no mention of Gale's efforts on Fauset's behalf; the relationship between the two women has been erased. Despite this erasure, the editor of the reprinted edition describes Fauset's work in ways that are also appropriate for Gale's: "By writing novels that many readers and/or critics perceive to be sentimental," argues Marcy Jo Knopf, "Fauset masks her revolutionary and modernist consideration of miscegenation and black female independence" (*The Chinaberry Tree* [1995], xiii). Gale too deployed sentimental forms in order to consider nonsentimental subjects; Gale, like Fauset, "understood the importance of the power of sentimental fiction to propel citizens to political action, or at least to sympathize with causes such as feminism and racial uplift" (xii). Given that Fauset sought Gale's help with this novel and that the two women were friends who corresponded as equals, as peers within a literary world, what might explain Gale's erasure?

Blaming the shifting fortunes of literary history seems one possibility: despite her 1921 Pulitzer prize for the stage adaptation of *Miss Lulu Bett*, by 1995, Gale was an obscure literary figure, and Fauset had become more important. It is easy to imagine that an editor might think an introduction by an apparently unknown writer is inconsequential. Another, more complicated, possibility also presents itself in the dual tendency to downplay black–white interactions in the 1920s and 1930s and to overlook collaborative models of literary sisterhood. The model of the solitary artist, of the individual and singular achievement, still prevails, as illustrated by this new edition of Fauset's novel. Tellingly, although Fauset's work has been the subject of increased critical attention of late, study of her work has lagged behind interest in Zora Neale Hurston and Nella Larsen, her less affiliative contemporaries. Ann duCille, in *The Coupling Convention* (1993), points out that Hurston has become "the essential black literary foremother," who is often presented "as if without precursor, model, example, or inspiriting influence" (80, 82). What duCille calls "Hurstonism" is simply another manifestation of literary history's contradictory tendency to celebrate the unaffiliated individual, the solitary artist, and then to make that figure into a representative touchstone for all those who follow. The structures of literary history cannot or will not accommodate collaborative models of literary authority.[27] Both Gale and Fauset wrote from within marginalized communities, in an attempt to bring those communities into the center, but literary history seems not to have followed their examples. Instead it seems that only by rejecting the identity of the marginalized community can one hope to move to the center, to authority.

By the time she wrote the introduction to Fauset's novel, Gale's optimistic belief that the federal government would solve the nation's pressing social problems had given way to a belief in the transformative powers of spirituality and mysticism. In 1924, her political hero Robert La Follette had been defeated in his campaign for the presidency; the National Origins Act had passed in Congress; and women had failed to make significant inroads in American political life, despite having been awarded the vote four years earlier.[28] During this disappointing time, Gale began work on *Preface to a Life*, a novel that clearly details her shift away from institutionalized political processes. While the goal of her utopian aesthetics did not change, the process by which that ideal society would be achieved did change: instead of beginning with communal changes that would lead to individual autonomy, Gale began to suggest that individual enlightenment would lead to civic improvement.

III

Mysticism and spirituality had always been a part of Gale's rhetoric, even in her most political moments, as illustrated by her essay supporting the Equal Rights Amendment, "What Women Won in Wisconsin" (1922). In this essay she claims that "women have a spiritual genius which has never been given social expression. It is precisely this which they could liberate into the world, for the general welfare, if all these meshes of little circumstances hampering them could be swept away and they could be given the moral backing of a general consciousness of equality of opportunity" (185). This essay, published in the *Nation*, argues that Wisconsin—and the other states in the union—should pass the Equal Rights Amendment in order to unleash women's collective "spiritual genius" and thus improve both individual lives and the world. Gale's essay must have been convincing, because she was chosen to help draft the amendment that became state law in 1923. When national ratification of the amendment failed, further political transformations began to seem impossible, and inner transformations became a necessity. Gale's later fiction returns again and again to the idea that "life is something more than what we think it to be" (Simonson 96). Within this realization, however, rest the seeds of sweeping political and social changes.

Reading Gale's mystically inflected novels is difficult because there are very few critical paradigms that help to situate or contextualize them. Mysticism and spiritualism have not traditionally been included in accounts of "serious" American literature, which may partially explain why Gale's work has disappeared from literary history.[29] But in the early years of the twentieth century—as in its last years—spiritualism and mysticism were taken quite seriously by a great number of people and Gale's mystical novels sold very well. Gale does not proselytize about a particular creed or religious outlook—in fact, most Western organized religions come off quite poorly in her novels. She draws instead on a number of different schools of mystical thought and combines them with her studies in sociology and science—merging, for example, Charlotte Perkins Gilman, Thorstein Veblen, and Albert Einstein with Georges Gurdjieff, Krishnamurti, A. R. Orage, and Theosophy. The various sources of her mystical beliefs share some common themes: transcendental unity with the cosmos; universal, spiritual love; and a gradual progression towards a higher state of being that may include some sort of reincarnation or out-of-body experiences. From Theosophy, the spiritualist movement started by Madame Blavatsky in the late 1800s, Gale took the ideas that everyone has tremendous untapped possibilities for spiritual growth and that each individual soul is thought to be evolving and working its way through numerous incarnations on the cycle of return to God (Gilchrist 11). Gale, however, avoided use of the word "God" in her mystical writing, preferring instead to use terms like spirit, goddess, octave—terms that she got from Gurdjieff and Orage.

Gale's optimism about the perfectibility of human consciousness extended to an optimism about technological developments as well, which she saw as bringing people closer to an exalted, almost divine state. In essays and short stories, she refers glowingly to the inventions of Marconi and to airplanes as evidence of humanity's infinite progress: scientific achievement brings with it a concomitant spiritualization. In "Children's Children," an unpublished short story, Gale imagines that in the futuristic world of 1979, everyone has his or her own airplane, used as easily as automobiles. With the "habit of swift motion" comes a "new perception . . . brimming with life" (4). Anticipating this image is a moment in *Preface to a Life* (1926), when Bernard sees an airplane overhead, its "great wings drenched in pure brilliance, bright surfaces and phosphorescent edges, binding immensity to immensity, moving in cloudy and fiery light like a god, the whole limpid, prismatic" (307).

Gale wanted her mystical fiction to show her readers how to achieve a higher plane of existence, which in her thinking would help them to spiritualize their experiences and fill them with universal love. Experiencing life in this fashion would, in turn, lead to the abolition of war and racial hatreds, the creation of a more compassionate state, and an increased environmental awareness.[30] In this later work, Gale's primary emphasis shifts from the community to the individual; she hoped that transformed and enlightened individuals would use their spiritualized visions to improve the world around them, as happens in the bestselling *Preface to a Life*. Gale's spiritual experimentations do not obviate her feminist sensibility; she simply links her feminism to mystical rather than political transformation. In a letter to Dorothy Canfield Fisher, she calls the spirit that moves through us all the "Mother principle" (February 2, 1927, SHSW); it is this principle that will transform the life of Bernard Mead, the hero of *Preface to a Life*.

Prior to his spiritual awakening, Bernard is trapped in a middle-class existence that he had never wanted for himself but that he hadn't had the courage to reject. He marries a woman he doesn't love because he can't bring himself to leave her for the woman he does love, and he takes over his father's lumber business after his father's sudden death although he has no interest in either business or lumber. In many respects Gale's novel is of a piece with other novels of the mid-1920s that create portraits of affluent middle-class lives undergirded by despair: at the end of Cather's *The Professor's House* (1925), Professor St. Peter recovers from his nearly fatal asphyxiation and realizes that the rest of his life will be lived without joy; Kate Clephane is once again in self-imposed exile on the Riviera, having lost her daughter to her ex-lover, at the end of *The Mother's Recompense* (1925); Jay Gatsby floats dead in a swimming pool at the conclusion of *The Great Gatsby* (1925); Clyde Griffiths languishes in jail waiting to die at the end of *An American Tragedy* (1925). Gale's novel, in contrast, offers Bernard's spiritual awakening as the solution to his existential crisis.

Spiritual awakening, in *Preface to a Life*, has nothing to do with organized religion, which Gale portrays as a source of the hypocrisy and complacency against which Bernard must fight. All the residents of Pauquette, Wisconsin, where Bernard has lived his entire life, claim to be Christian because they go to church on Sundays, but their regular attendance hides very un-Christian behaviors. As Bernard strolls through town, he realizes that each house harbors a secret: in one house lives a man whose father had helped arrest a rich man who was jailed but then set free on a technicality, although "the town knew that he had both disgraced and robbed a woman who trusted him." In another house lives Elf, who "had got from his wife's mother her eighteen hundred dollars and had invested and lost it, and then sent her to the poor farm"; and down the street is "Alex Golithar, who had sailed from the old country with his wife and three children but they were stricken with the plague in the steerage and he left them one by one in the sea; and he stepped foot in Boston alone, and now lived on the bluff with a new wife" (166). Through these vignettes, Gale highlights the difference between professing Christian virtues and actually practicing them. Western religion, whether

Protestant or otherwise, seems to bring no one any peace and in some cases even leads to suicide: one man in town, after "setting out an avenue of two hundred maples . . . had gone to confession, though previous to that time he had not entered a church in fifty years; and the next morning they found him hanging from a hook in the barn" (166). Although Bernard himself had "set his foot down early" against going to church with his family, he is nevertheless surrounded by religious hypocrites who refuse to acknowledge or to share his spiritual vision.

Another cause of Bernard's sense of entrapment is his inability to see himself outside traditional gender roles. He has married a woman he does not love, but he refuses to allow the woman he does love to help him to escape his marriage because he cannot allow himself to be anything other than "the boss." Alla Locksley, his would-be lover, proposes that they move to Italy together and that he could use some of her money to start a business of his own, which outrages Bernard: "what a ghastly idea—that you'll set me up in business." In response Alla accuses him of having the "vanity of the middle-class American . . . sheer egoism it is, and the need of the American man that everything shall be of *his* providing" (94). Rejecting Alla's offer of partnership, Bernard remains with his small-town wife, Laura; their marriage embodies the middle-class enervation that Gale wanted her spiritual teachings to dispel. After years of marriage, Bernard and Laura have nothing to say to one another other than to talk about Laura's latest redecorating scheme. They have both become fat; their physical corpulence mirrors their inner flabbiness.[31] The Mead family spends an inordinate amount of time at the table discussing what they have eaten, are eating, will eat, an example of the mindless insistence on corporeal reality that Gale saw as gnawing away at the spiritual well-being of the country. Furthering this idea is the fact that Bernard sometimes feels like he lives in the "soft esophagus of a giant animal"; something, quite literally, is eating at him, swallowing him up (96).

Deep in the maw of his marriage and a capitalist, patriarchal economy, Bernard flourishes financially, but he knows that something is missing. Not until he sneaks away from his family to seek out Alla Locksley again, years after he rejected her offer of escape, does he experience his first epiphany. This moment will set in motion his gradual emergence into a more spiritualized state of being. He goes in search of Alla after an old friend accuses him of "dying and drying up—you're like a man in a husk" (158), but like Newland Archer at the conclusion of *The Age of Innocence* (1920), when Bernard reaches Alla's house, he can't bring himself to go inside. Instead he sits outside, watches her house, and looks at the stars. Sitting under the trees, he begins to examine his life and finds it wanting: "What did he want? . . . Something more than anything that he knew."

Although at this moment he has no answers for his questions, giving a voice to his doubts opens him to a transcendent vision:

> For an instant it seemed as if his look might pierce the horizon, might sweep the earth with that deep scrutiny. . . . What he was looking upon was not mere background . . . not just earth and growth. . . . It was as if familiar areas had risen to rejoin space. It was as if the sky were filled with aisles of brightness. . . . innumerable trails had been blazed and cut through the colorless air, so that brilliance flowed down from some unsuspected core of color and light . . . as if at any moment music might begin. . . . Here was some secret of the design of octave and spectrum, of flame and crystal. . . . And he was in it, it was in him. All this he felt not as idea, but as emotion. . . . So this was the way it was!—even though he could not, for his life, have defined what he felt to be true about it. . . . For one instant of time he was penetrated by the actual substance of his terrific certainty. (199)

His vision vanishes almost as soon as it occurs, leaving him physically exhausted but spiritually exhilarated. When he returns home and sees his family gathered around their dinner table, oblivious to his absence, he murmurs to himself, "It's not enough," to which his wife replies, "Not enough? What *of*? We thought we had such a nice dinner." Laura's misunderstanding—and her automatic assumption that Bernard is talking about food—highlights Bernard's growing inability to make himself understood to his family, who cannot conceive of an experience such as he has just had.

While this first epiphany does not immediately cause Bernard to change the patterns of his life, he slowly becomes aware that his position in the universe is very different from what he had always imagined. His inarticulate attempts to explain his changing perceptions to his family merely estrange them further; they begin to think that Bernard has lost his mind, because in middle-class Pauquette, mystical experiences are unheard of and somehow inappropriate.[32] The family is so worried that they call an "alienist" in to consult with Bernard, but the alienist does not understand Bernard either. Bernard tries to explain that far from giving in to his "cruder self," which is what the alienist suggests, his visions reveal emotions and insights that "belong to a self I've never reached yet . . . not to the one I've left behind!" (275, ellipsis in original). Although Gale's mysticism often found expression in the language of science and technology, in this novel, science—in the guise of psychology—is found wanting: it draws people down into the body while Gale's mysticism wants to lift people out of their bodies onto a spiritual plane.

Bernard, the Mead family, and Alla Locksley represent different points along the spectrum of consciousness described by Gurdjieff as "Sleeping State, Waking State, Self-Consciousness, and Cosmic Consciousness" (Kerman and Eldridge 139). The Meads, with the exception of Bernard's mother, are all still sleeping, and Alla, with her insistence on independence and on living without regard to convention, has achieved a level of self-consciousness that attracts Bernard to her: "I've loved being alone," she tells him, "I shouldn't mind being buried in Asia." She tells Bernard that she "handled her own business; she had . . . adopted a child, a grown girl, who was at school in the East," and Bernard realizes that she was "completely self-reliant." And yet her self-reliance and self-sufficiency do not extend to an understanding of Bernard's cosmic consciousness. Bernard had refused to escape with Alla, a decision that forces him to search for meaning in ways that he would not have done had he left his airless marriage. When Bernard, during his first epiphany outside Alla's house, encounters the "secret of the design of octave and spectrum," he is experiencing a Gurdjieffian moment. Gurdjieff believed that the highest calling of humankind was to "develop himself as an essential unit in the hierarchical organization of the universe, fitting into his place in the grand pattern of successive 'octaves.' Each of these, akin to the octave in the musical scale, in turn becomes a segment of the more inclusive octave at the next higher level." Bernard, like the followers of Gurdjieff, has embarked on the process of becoming "one note in the next larger octave" (Kerman and Eldridge 139). Through his experiences, Bernard moves beyond Alla's self-consciousness towards cosmic consciousness; he finds a "new way of experiencing all. It was not a point but a process . . ." (Gale, *Preface* 345, ellipsis in original).[33]

One step in Bernard's process is to unlearn his reliance on conventional masculine roles and to stop blaming his wife's parochialism for his own misery. *Preface to a Life* illustrates the flawed structure of American marriages, which reduces wives like Laura Mead to the status of a dependent, as if she were one of Bernard's children. Bernard's loveless marriage embodies Gale's postsuffrage critique of a culture that still prevents women from attaining their full potential. Gale's feminism emerges both in the portrait of a marriage that stifles both partners and in her depictions of the cosmic principles that "penetrate" Bernard and make him a more compassionate man. When he goes to one of his lumber camps to settle a labor dispute, for example, he arrives with the desire "strong within him . . . to break the men." After a long walk in the woods during which he experiences another epiphanic moment, however, he "found his compromise with the men" and no longer sees himself as a "good king" (243). Through his mystical experiences with the "Mother principle," Bernard becomes less invested in hierarchical structures: he allows a union to form among his workers, sets aside land as a park preserve, and realizes that Laura has her own feelings of dissatisfaction and disillusionment—some of which are due to his own shortcomings, not hers.

The cosmic certainty that so deeply penetrates Bernard he names "The Mother. One being. One of the Godhead . . . *The Mother* . . . The Mother, moving, shining, flowing into light, light of the Godhead" (297). Later, Gale makes the point even more explicit: Bernard looks into the sky and imagines the "goddess in whom no one any longer believed . . . it breathed deeply and waited, it was carrying its children to some birth." The cosmos is both female and neuter, an "it" that will eventually give birth to a more enlightened race. These "goddess" moments enable Bernard to overcome his anger at his family's unwillingness to believe his experiences, so that by the conclusion of the novel he feels "the emotion of the multitude of them all . . . and [none of them] were alien. They, the multitude, were but one . . . one web, one spirit" (340). This feeling of unity with the world—expressed in terms of an almost Whitman-like *copias*—is the culmination of Bernard's awakening, similar to Calliope Marsh imagining a global sisterhood at the conclusion of *Mothers to Men*. Calliope has imagined a world "Away Off Then," where men and women work together in complete equality; Bernard envisions a world where humanity's baser selves will be left behind and everyone can "move and shine like light and act like gods and see like gods" (335). Gale's political feminism has become a goddess-centered mysticism that most of society cannot or will not experience, but it gives Bernard the strength to return to his family, to sit with them around the dinner table while they debate the merits of different flavors of jelly.

Bernard's awakening enables him to become a better individual and a better member of his family and his community; his enlightenment is an affiliative and unifying experience, not a solipsistic one. While Gale's mystical novels continue her progressive feminist project of attempting to create a more egalitarian and compassionate society, they do so by giving primacy to the individual experience over the communal. Gale's emphasis on individual spiritual transformations places her in a long line of American women who used spirituality as a means of self-actualization. In "Women and Individualism in American History" (1989), Linda Kerber argues that for many eighteenth- and early-nineteenth-century women, "Heightened religiosity and a new community of believers could provide paths for self-fulfillment and the expression of personal independence possible in virtually no other sector of society" (594). Kerber claims that for these women, "the rhetoric of religion provided justification for behavior which a secular society would otherwise not countenance" (596). While

Gale herself would not seem to be a woman in need of self-actualization, the mystical rhetoric of her novel provided her with a way to talk about Progressive-era reforms that, by the mid 1920s, were no longer at the forefront of social consciousness.

Gale's mysticism also establishes a place for her within the tradition of American transcendentalism, combining the optimism of early Emerson with a Thoreauvian sense of public conscience. Bernard's epiphanic moments—all of which happen outside, away from inhabited spaces—echo Emerson's famous moment of apprehension in "Nature" (1836), in which he describes "a perfect exhilaration . . . standing on the bare ground,—my head bathed by the blithe air and uplifted into infinite space,—all mean egotism vanishes. I become a transparent eye-ball; I am nothing; I see all; the currents of the Universal Being circulate through me; I am part or particle of God" (10). Barbara Packer argues that "Nature" emerged out of Emerson's dissatisfaction with Christianity as "a historical religion" and his longing to find its "ethical truths inscribed elsewhere" (378); similar impulses fuel Gale's writing.[34] Her skepticism about governmental reform leads her to mysticism, but not as a retreat from public life. Like the Thoreau of "Civil Disobedience," Gale maintains that even one individual can have tremendous influence on the world and that it is the obligation of each honest man (or woman) to speak against injustice. Gale, like Emerson and the other transcendentalists—particularly Thoreau—had read extensively in Eastern religion and philosophy, but her mystical writings are seldom acknowledged as operating within this tradition.[35] She blends transcendentalism with other strains of Eastern philosophy and spiritualism to create a hybrid fiction that blurs conventional categories of discussion: *Preface to a Life*, for instance, is a humorous and satiric realist novel except for those moments when Bernard is lost in a spiritual reverie; it is a portrait of a marriage and a portrait of small-town society; it pokes fun at organized religion but wants us all to become "like gods"—it is, in short, as one reviewer called it, "a curious novel." And yet despite its curiosities, the novel is utterly clear about its intention: to awaken readers from their lives inside the "soft esophagus of a giant animal."

Gale's mystical novels move toward a clear resolution of social ills, even if her ultimate goal—a more compassionate world—is not always realized within the frame of the novel itself. In her efforts to articulate this vision, however, some reviewers thought she lost the specificity that had made *Miss Lulu Bett* such a success: "Miss Gale is more concerned with spiritual experience as a separate experience than with the spiritual experience of a particular person," wrote the reviewer in the *New Republic*. "It is a case of the cart before the horse" (November 24, 1926, 23). Another reviewer caught the similarity between Gale's novel and other novels of the 1920s, calling it "the other side of Babbitt . . . a little terrifying to behold." This same review calls the novel a comedy of manners, a mischaracterization that arises from the reviewer's gendered expectations: "Women novelists excel in the comedy of manners, for a woman's life is a chain of human relationships and she rarely exists vividly outside of them" (*New York Herald Tribune,* November 7, 1926). *The Saturday Review of Literature,* on the other hand, wrote that "the intent and sweep of [Gale's] novel encompass the meaning of life itself and the metaphysical questionings of her protagonist, whatever may be thought of their clarity, probe even beyond the limits of human experience" (December 4, 1926, 364). The reading public seemed to agree with the *Saturday Review* critic, because the novel became Gale's biggest seller, outstripping even *Miss Lulu Bett.* None of the reviews, however, mentioned the social ramifications of Bernard's enlightenment—his support of unions, growing distaste for capitalism, criticism of organized religion, the feminist portrayal of spiritual awakening. Even H. L. Mencken, a notorious cynic, admired the novel enough to consider breaking his rule against publishing serials in *American Mercury:* the novel had "tempted [him] sorely," he wrote; "it is certainly an excellent piece of work." Despite his admiration for the story, however, he "decided reluctantly that it would be unwise to break the rule against serials. . . . For my irresolution I needn't apologize, I hope. My very strong desire to get you into the magazine was to blame for it" (July 14, n.y., SHSW).

In a profile piece about Gale that ran three years before the publication of *Preface to a Life, The Bookman* detailed the arc of her career from her early days in New York to the success of *Miss Lulu Bett.* The writer concludes his essay by saying that Gale "seems to be overcoming her early sentimentality, her gravest danger as an artist. For a long period I stopped reading her altogether; for no one can thrive on a diet of chocolate drops. In her last two novels [*Birth* and *Miss Lulu Bett*] she redeemed herself with me. Is she of the caliber that will press forward now or will she drop back into an easy and comfortable popular vein? It will be interesting to watch her development from this crossroad" (172). Tellingly, the writer of the piece suggests that the real test of Gale's caliber will be whether or not she resists mere popularity; worthy fiction cannot be popular fiction, according to this formulation. But with *Preface to a Life,* Gale managed, again, to defy conventional wisdom: the novel garnered popular success and critical acclaim. Her success emerged as a result of her stubborn refusal to hide her political attitudes or her spiritual beliefs; her commitment to being an artist who was also a "social being" remained unshaken.

CHAPTER THREE

SISTERHOOD AND LITERARY AUTHORITY IN *THE HOUSE OF MIRTH*, *MY ÁNTONIA*, AND *MISS LULU BETT*

Writing to Dorothy Canfield Fisher in 1923 to praise her latest novel, the influential newspaper editor William Allen White tells her that "we poor men are having a really hard time. . . . First you took our ballot from us; then you deprive us of our booze, and it looks as though you are going to rob us of even the alphabet" (236). White's letter clearly links women's literary authority to a concomitant loss of male authority: women cannot gain power, it seems, unless men lose power. In his construction, power cannot be shared, because as women gain writerly authority, men become, quite literally, speechless. White's comment depicts a steadily encroaching female presence that moves from political power to social reform to the power of speech itself, with each step further disenfranchising men. His mixed emotions are particularly interesting, given that White in fact supported suffrage; his letter indicates the widespread ambivalence that greeted white women's enfranchisement. Suffrage was an unavoidable issue in the first part of the twentieth century; arguments both pro and con suffused public discourse. Fanny Butcher, a friend of White's and the longtime literary editor for the Chicago *Tribune*, wrote in her memoir that

> woman suffrage was a burning question in my twenties. . . . It wasn't something you could be indifferent about. If you weren't for women's rights to the same life, liberty, and pursuit of happiness as men's, you were against your sex. Or if you believed a woman's place was in the home, watching over her babies and the biggest baby of them all, her husband, you were sure that women who wanted to have a voice in the elections, who wanted

the right to run their own financial affairs, to own their own inheritances, to be doctors and lawyers and stockbrokers were termites gnawing at the very foundations of the already infested national structure. . . . The controversy over votes for women got mixed up with every phase of American life—politics, morals, industry. The antivote faction tied it up with free love. Employers blamed it for upping their wage budgets. (178–79)[1]

Suffrage, in short, was everywhere, and anyone who was a public figure was expected to have an opinion about the issue.

When suffrage leaders realized that they had to alter their campaign tactics if they hoped to sway public opinion, they learned how to use the news media to foster their public relations efforts and promoted prosuffrage fiction and drama as ways to reach out directly to women across the country. Although these forms were often denied critical legitimacy, they were tremendously popular at the grassroots level, proving that there was an audience eager to hear the suffrage message. In her article about suffrage fiction, Sowon Park argues that "the suffrage movement was an unprecedented stimulus to women writers . . . [and] suffrage literature in *quantitative* terms, marked a new epoch in the socio-cultural context of writing for women" (451). Suffrage also provided a stimulus to female actresses and dramatists, who staged suffrage dramas and the immensely popular suffrage pageants that were often the highlight of marches and rallies. Gale's close friend, Fola La Follette, made a career for herself acting in suffrage dramas, which became extremely popular, particularly when performed by someone like La Follette or Ethel Barrymore.[2] Despite the popular success of these forms, however, they were seldom taken seriously by the critical establishment. La Follette's husband, George Middleton, discovered this when he attempted to bring his feminist play *Nowadays* to the Broadway stage. He and La Follette "gave it a . . . convincing test," he explains, by "reading it throughout the country . . . [proving] that the play had audience appeal, had any one in the professional theatre been willing to give *Nowadays* a chance" (136). Even with their wide network of connections in the theater world, however, Middleton and La Follette could not find someone willing to produce the play on Broadway.

As the suffrage campaign intensified, suffrage rhetoric, both pro and con, permeated public discourse and shaped the contents of magazines. The question of how women should be portrayed in the magazines became a "nub of contestation" for magazine editors, argues Richard Ohmann in *Selling Culture* (1996). Ohmann observes that "a woman was unsettlingly 'new' if she disrupted old understandings of the feminine. Then the rhetoric of limit-setting [in the magazines] grew stern . . . all the [women's] magazines labored uneasily with the received idea of the feminine. All felt free to constitute it or allude to it as a puzzle, a difficulty, a subject. . . . The woman's essence [had been] thrown into doubt, and . . . had to be arduously reshaped and patrolled" (272).[3] The public debate about women's roles affected attitudes toward women within the publishing world, which began to reject the qualities that had enabled nineteenth-century women writers to merge their professional lives with the cultural roles assigned to women: "Masculine values were being propounded in order to bring control of the literary marketplace to men," explains Susan Coultrap-McQuin, and as a result women in both the United States and Britain were being "edged out" of the literary professional world. But those women writers who chose to adopt the "masculine" values of anti-sentimentality and anti-domesticity ran the risk of being characterized as suffragists—and thus being seen by antisuffragists as "gnawing at the very foundations of the already infested national structure" (198). For writers like Gale and Canfield Fisher, who were in fact supporters of suffrage, being described as a sort of feminist termite was, while unflattering, not entirely inaccurate. But for writers like Wharton and Cather, who were publicly more ambivalent about suffrage and feminism, being allied with this political movement presented more of a problem.

As writers who were deeply invested in shaking off nineteenth-century traditions of female authorship, Cather and Wharton did not want to ally themselves with "old-fashioned" views of women, but they did not want to be labeled as New Women, either. Neither the nineteenth-century model of "lady authorship" nor the twentieth-century model of activist-writer seemed to fit. How then, to rob men of the alphabet, to use White's phrase, and wrest literary authority for themselves without being automatically seen as writing for a *cause*—suffrage, social reform, temperance, or, even worse, feminism? Further, given the immense popularity of writers like Stowe, Southworth, Fern, and Evans, becoming a best-selling author in the early twentieth century—if one were female—carried with it an additional risk: popularity itself became an indication of being nonauthoritative, nonintellectual.[4] Given the implicit threat in becoming too popular, another question faced Cather and Wharton: once they had established themselves as significant literary voices, could they also establish control over their public images so as to retain their literary authority? Gale faced her own version of these same questions, although for her the issue was how to break away from the stifling popularity of her Friendship Village stories and find an audience for her politically radical fiction that did not utilize regionalist folksiness.

The novels that for each writer marked her "breakthrough" into the rank of serious literary artist—*The House of Mirth* (1905), *My Ántonia*

(1918), and *Miss Lulu Bett* (1920), respectively—provide answers to the question of how Wharton, Cather, and Gale managed to negotiate this complicated literary and political terrain. These three novels, which span the tumultuous fifteen-year period in which the United States fought a world war and granted women the right to vote, represent a significant shift in the way that each woman thought about herself as a writer. Wharton's comment about writing *The House of Mirth*—that she had found the "kingdom of mastery over [her] tools" in the process of its composition (*Backward* 941)—applies equally to Cather and Gale. While all three writers had published prior to these novels, it is to these books that each writer pointed as a turning point in her career. Reviewers agreed with their assessments, universally hailing these novels as significant achievements. *Miss Lulu Bett* was heralded as a "signal accomplishment" by Constance Rourke in the *New Republic* (316); Randolph Bourne claimed that with *My Ántonia*, Cather had moved "out of the rank of provincial writers and given us something we can fairly class with the modern literary art the world over that is earnestly and richly interpreting the spirit of youth" (qtd. in Woodress 301). Reviews of *The House of Mirth*, observes R. W. B. Lewis, were permeated with the sense that "Edith Wharton was one of the two or three most serious and accomplished writers of fiction on the American scene and that [*The House of Mirth*] was undeniably her most important work to date" (*Wharton* 154). Each of these novels marks the moment when its author robbed men of the alphabet and found the strongest expression of her own voice. They also mark each writer's engagement with the struggle over women's rights that suffrage activism had made unavoidable.

These novels significantly revise the possibilities available to women by illustrating the ways that domesticity and the domestic arts can lead women to economic self-sufficiency, a linchpin of early-twentieth-century feminism. There is, however, a significant difference between the structures of Wharton's and Cather's novels, on the one hand, and Gale's, on the other, a difference that can be explained by Wharton's and Cather's ambivalence about affiliating themselves with suffrage politics in particular and "women's causes" in general. While the central plot of Gale's breakthrough novel charts the movement of its heroine from economic subservience to independence, Wharton and Cather position their economically self-sufficient characters on the periphery of their novels. Like Poe's purloined letter, Wharton's and Cather's challenges to patriarchal structures are hidden in plain sight, in novels that seem to represent the futility of such resistance. The women in these novels—Carry Fisher, Tiny Soderball, and Lena Lingard—use traditionally feminine talents to create successful business opportunities for themselves that allow them to

escape traditional domestic arrangements. Carry, Tiny, and Lena are outspoken and independent, and maintain emotional relationships with
women rather than with men. They represent viable alternatives to con-
finement within socially prescribed gender roles even as the central plots
of both novels seem to illustrate the difficulty of escaping those roles. A
description of Carry Fisher helps to illustrate this point: Carry does not
"talk of herself without cause," but when she does, her conversation
"served . . . the purpose of the juggler's chatter while he shifts the contents of his sleeves" (262). Carry's talk is a smoke screen, hiding her ulterior purpose. And so it is with these novels: Lily Bart and Ántonia
Shimerda so fill the center stage of each novel that the other characters
can go about their alternative careers with impunity. In *Miss Lulu Bett*, on
the other hand, Lulu's transformation from drudge to employed worker *is*
the plot of the novel.

In both *The House of Mirth* and *My Ántonia*, the central narratives dis-
tract readers from the fact that existing on the margins of both novels are
female characters whose successful lives suggest alternatives to Lily Bart's
chloral-induced death and to Ántonia Shimerda's stunning fecundity. By
marginalizing these viable alternative narratives for women's lives, Wharton and Cather avoided accusations of being directly involved with "the
woman question." But the peripheral plotlines involving Carry Fisher,
Tiny, and Lena nevertheless illustrate that sisterhood and female affiliation are not only possible but necessary for women to create successful
lives for themselves. As in their letters to Gale, in their novels Cather and
Wharton create hidden communities of spirit that flourish because of
their secrecy. In *Miss Lulu Bett*, on the other hand, sisterhood is central to
Lulu's escape from stifling domesticity: only by affiliating herself with
other women does Lulu gain self-awareness and autonomy.

Despite the different positions that they occupy within the novels
themselves, these characters—Carry, Tiny, Lena, and Lulu—share the
ability to sell their domestic skills in the open market. They all have what
Harriet Beecher Stowe, in *The Minister's Wooing* (1859), calls "faculty":
"To her who has faculty nothing shall be impossible. She shall scrub
floors, wash, wring, bake, brew, and yet her hands shall be small and
white; she shall have no perceptible income, yet always be handsomely
dressed" (528). The housekeeper with faculty effortlessly manages an
amazing array of tasks: "She shall not have a servant in her house—with
a dairy to manage, hired men to feed, a boarder or two to care for, un-
heard-of pickling and preserving to do—and yet you commonly see her
every afternoon cool and easy, hemming muslin cap-strings, or reading
the latest book. She who hath faculty is never in a hurry, never behind-
hand." This paragon of domestic virtues is also a wonderful neighbor, al-

ways willing to help "Mrs. Smith, whose jelly won't come . . . to show Mrs. Jones how she makes her pickles so green . . . to watch with poor old Mrs. Simpkins, who is down with the rheumatism" (528). In her discussion of this passage, Ann Romines points out that Stowe both "valorizes faculty and gently mocks the idea of domestic competence it embodies" (5). Stowe's description of faculty articulates what Romines describes as the association between "women's work and . . . female power" (5). Because culture "consumes the products of the housekeeper's labor, the fact and the process of that labor are suppressed" (6). Female work and female power, therefore, are in constant struggle against invisibility and erasure. Carry, Tiny, Lena, and Lulu all learn how to transform their "invisible" labor into visible capital and, thus, into financial security and self-sufficiency.

Wharton, Cather, and Gale significantly revise Stowe's idea of "faculty" so that it ceases to be purely domestic labor and instead enables women to achieve permanent economic and social independence. Just as suffragists were expanding ideas about motherhood into the political arena, so do Wharton, Cather, and Gale expand traditionally feminine, domestic skills into modes of female autonomy and self-sufficiency. This "applied domesticity" allows their heroines to achieve economic independence and to escape mandatory marriage and motherhood. These female characters flourish by learning how to manipulate "the system"—or elude it altogether—and, at the same time, their authors learn how to represent themselves in the literary marketplace in order to control and manipulate the literary and gender politics that would otherwise control them.

I

Late in *The House of Mirth,* in fact, shortly before her death, Lily Bart seeks refuge in a little restaurant on Fifty-ninth Street that is crowded with "sallow preoccupied women [who carry] . . . bags and note-books and rolls of music . . . all engrossed in their own affairs . . . busy running over proof-sheets or devouring magazines" (318). None of the women notices Lily, although she searches the crowd "craving a responsive glance, some sign of intuition of her trouble" (318). Often read as Wharton's indictment of the New Woman, the women in this café are so wrapped up in their own lives that they cannot even offer Lily a friendly smile to ease her solitude. Ironically, although Lily has spent her entire adult life under the scrutiny of society's eyes, at this moment, out in public and surrounded by women, she seems invisible.

While this short scene may seem unimportant to the structure of the novel as a whole, it illustrates a number of concerns that are central to my discussion of Wharton and the literary marketplace. The women who surround and ignore Lily carry with them the accoutrements of the publishing world—proof-sheets and magazines—a world that was becoming very familiar to Wharton as she became a more established literary figure. At the same time though, in the midst of this café filled with women, Lily is invisible, which is not usually what happens when she appears in public. Lawrence Selden, for instance, has no problem at all picking Lily out from the crowds at Grand Central: she stands out, in his eyes, like an expensive jewel. But in the café, Lily is lost, "stranded in a great waste of disoccupation" (318). She vanishes in the crowded room of women, all of whom are busy at something, all of whom appear to have professional lives. Lily's invisibility points to Wharton's own anxiety about how—or if—her work will vanish in the crowd of other women writers in the literary marketplace. Lily's search for a "responsive glance" also suggests the search for sympathetic readers that made Wharton so appreciative of Gale's intuitive interpretations, which are "balm" to her.

At the same time, however, Wharton is *becoming* one of these women in the café, busy with proof-sheets and magazines; *The House of Mirth* marks the moment when, in her own words, Wharton changed from a "drifting amateur into a professional" (*Backward* 941). Wharton's professionalism carries with it an additional set of difficulties, namely how to manage the public aspects of being a professional writer and how to establish the public image that was increasingly part of what an author had to do to sell books. In *The Labor of Words* (1985), Christopher Wilson notes that at the turn of the century writers found themselves "part of a system which depended on [their] professional practice—and image" (66). Wilson also contends that "publishers recognized the advertising value and relative thrift, not only of existing news channels—say, newspaper tabloids, which might carry a literary event—but of the author's celebrity itself" (82). Wilson does not address how the question of public image changes if the writer in question is a woman, but as *The House of Mirth* illustrates, creating the wrong public image can destroy a woman more easily than it can a man: Lily is alone and desperate in the café precisely because her image had been—incorrectly—tarnished in the public eye. Thus even as Wharton learned to think of herself as a writer during the composition of *The House of Mirth*, she needed to learn how to present *herself* as a writer to her reading public.

Lily Bart is often seen as the central text in *The House of Mirth*, a kind of blank page on which anyone can write what she pleases.[5] But what is often overlooked is the novel's other text: Carry Fisher, whom Wharton describes as having "the air of embodying a spicy paragraph" (57). Unlike any of the other guests at Bellomont, the sumptuous Trenor estate, Carry moves freely between New York's old money and its new; she seems at home in any context. Carry supports herself by introducing the nouveau riche to the established upper class; she offers her social grace, polished manners, knowledge of society arcana, and conversational skill to those women who otherwise would be unable to penetrate the most exclusive drawing rooms in New York. Aware of the power of scandal to titillate and attract, Carry blends her knowledge of social convention with her "spicy paragraph," creating a text that people will pay to read: she markets this script to her audience of "dull people," as Judy Trenor calls them. Carry is an impresario whose productions effectively revamp the shape of Old New York; like Wharton herself, Carry establishes a symbiotic relationship with this world, seeing its faults and foibles quite clearly but being unwilling to leave that world entirely because nowhere else seems any better. Carry's ability to chart her own path through this world and to write her own script for herself and her daughter becomes Wharton's representation of possibilities beyond Lily's beautiful death or Gerty Farish's charitable dinginess.

Given Wharton's lifelong interest in houses and the construction of domestic space, the fact that Carry is the only character in *The House of Mirth* who has her own house underscores Carry's importance as a viable alternative to Lily's fate.[6] Lily herself ends her days in a boarding house, and Gerty's small rented apartment is squalid, dirty, uncomfortable; it is only attractive for the brief moment that Lawrence Selden comes to visit, and then only because Gerty believes he might love her. Through Gerty, Wharton parodies New Women and their involvement in civic reform: Gerty is a hanger-on who "typifies the mediocre and the ineffectual . . . [with an] assumption that existence yielded no higher pleasures" (93). Carry is also involved in reform movements, although apparently without Gerty's earnestness. At Bellomont, Lily observes Carry talking to Percy about "municipal reform . . . [which] had been preceded by an equal zeal for socialism, which had in turn replaced an energetic advocacy of Christian Science. Mrs. Fisher was small, fiery, and dramatic; and her hands and eyes were dramatic instruments in the service of whatever cause she happened to espouse" (48–49). Carry's interest in the world outside the golden bubble of Bellomont contributes to her status as an alternative to Lily Bart: Carry knows that there is more to life than hats and husbands. Her house at Tuxedo, in contrast to Gerty's apartment, offers a "firelit quiet" and a "congenial atmosphere" (260). Carry herself is a woman much like Lily in her beauty and upbringing, but very unlike Lily in her ability to chart a safe course through the dangerous waters of New York society. Although Judy Trenor says Carry is "a perfect vulture . . . and hasn't the least moral sense" (90), Carry is not the hypocrite that Judy is, nor is she a predator like Bertha Dorset, whose latest lover is described as looking "like a galley slave" (249).

The Old New York society of *The House of Mirth* values stability, conformity, and decorum but does not want to inquire too closely about how these ideals are achieved or maintained. In a world that privileges stability above all, domesticity—or the appearance of domesticity—becomes a cardinal virtue, which is something that Carry understands and Lily does not. Lily cannot create the illusion of domesticity long enough to land herself a husband: her tea-pouring for Percy Gryce on the train to the Trenor's house party attracts him initially, but the stories spread by Bertha Dorset drive him away, fearful of Lily's "wild" nature. Carry, on the other hand, manages to manipulate this society and its conventions to her own ends. She is a businesswoman who integrates the worlds she lives in, seducing Old New York into accepting the nouveau riche. She manipulates society itself into patterns it hadn't known existed and transforms it in the process. When Carry helps the arriviste Louisa Bry plan a party, "society . . . succumbed to the temptation . . . the protesting minority were forgotten in the throng . . . and the audience was almost as brilliant as the show" (138). Carry's juxtaposition of old-world money and values with crass social climbers mirrors what Wharton herself does in novels like *The House of Mirth* and *The Custom of the Country* (1913). The society portraits that Wharton creates so vividly are more penetrating versions of the *tableaux vivants*—Carry's idea—that are in part responsible for the success of Louisa's party.

Carry creates successful illusions because she knows what people want; she is a good reader and a good writer, whose skills enable her to fulfill people's desires. As Lily falls ever further from social grace, Carry is the only one who reads her situation clearly and is brave enough to say so, even though "the light projected" by her commentary has "the cheerless distinction of a winter dawn" (265). Like any good writer, Carry names what she sees, even if it means reporting on her own weakness. After she snubs Lily in public, Carry apologizes by saying: "The truth is I was *horrid*, Lily, and I've wanted to tell you ever since. . . . Look here Lily, don't let's beat about the bush: half the trouble in life is caused by pretending there isn't any. That's not my way" (242). As a reader of people's hidden desires and of complex social situations, Carry is well-suited to offer advice to Lily; unlike Lily, Carry "carries" her own burdens and finances her own position.

Like the dramatist that Wharton herself always wanted to be, Carry writes scripts and stages performances that allow the actors—her "dull

people"—to present themselves as they would like to be seen. The handsome check paid to Carry by Louisa Bry is the result of Carry's ability to
create a believable fiction about Louisa's popularity. Carry makes it seem
as if Louisa had been sought out by those who would otherwise (without
Carry's introductions) have shunned her: "Louisa . . . is a stern task-
master . . . she was always laying traps to find out what I thought. Of
course I had to disown my oldest friends, rather than let her suspect she
owed me the chance of making a single acquaintance—when, all the
while, that was what she had me there for" (262). Carry's ability to combine the new rich with the old so smoothly speaks to her successful manipulation of traditionally feminine talents: social graces, good manners,
pleasing conversation, easing strained moments, and fulfilling the needs
of others. (Or at least appearing to put others' needs before her own—satisfying Louisa enables Carry to achieve her own goal of time alone with
her child.) In order to succeed financially, however, Carry must make herself disappear; her efforts on Louisa's behalf must become invisible, just
as the housekeeper with "faculty" must appear never to labor openly. And,
as in the literary marketplace, only if her fiction is successful does Carry
get royalties, or in this case, Louisa's handsome check.

Carry's public successes enable her to take a house at Tuxedo, a domestic private space that is hers alone. Unlike Judy Trenor, Carry does not
have to filter her likes and dislikes through her husband, and unlike
Gerty, Carry can afford to rent an entire house and staff, instead of only
a woman who comes in to do the washing up. Despite being rented,
Carry's house has "an air of repose and stability" (260), and when Lily
goes walking outside, the landscape is covered with an idyllic "golden
haze" (265), similar to the grounds of Bellomont, which further links
Carry to established New York society. At home, Carry drops the persona
she maintains to pay the bills, which allows Lily to realize that "Mrs.
Fisher's unconventionality was, after all, a merely superficial divergence
from an inherited social creed" (260). Presenting herself publicly as a
"spicy paragraph" is Carry's cover story; allowing herself to be misread, as
it were, pays the bills for her cozy private life. In private she becomes a
"solicitous hostess" and "expansively maternal"; she tells Lily that "it's
such a blessing to have a few quiet weeks with the baby" (262). Lily wonders whether, if Carry had "time and money enough, she would not end
by devoting them both to her daughter" (262). Thus, while at the center
of Wharton's novel is the established social class whose creed helps to destroy Lily, the novel also offers its readers the image of Carry, whose position on the margin affords her not only the luxury of privacy but also
the luxury of offering refuge to others. Unlike the other women whom
Lily knows, Carry's "sympathies were . . . with the unlucky, the unpopu-

lar" (261), which is why both Lily and Simon Rosedale are welcome in her house. Because Carry writes her own script, she can give solace to Lily when no one else will. Carry has what Lily wants—independence, security, and a child—and presents Lily, at least fleetingly, with an opportunity to experience the community of spirit that Wharton imagines in letters between herself and Gale.

In writing *The House of Mirth,* Wharton says, she gained "what I most lacked—self-confidence" (*Backward* 941). Her letters to her publishers about the novel display her newly found authority in their sharp instructions about illustrations, proof-reading, and other details. She writes to William Crary Brownell that although she "sank to the depth of letting the illustrations be put in the book," she could not let Scribner's add to the frontispiece the verse from Ecclesiastes that gave the novel its title. Such a pointed reference "inculcates a moral," she says, and so she has "taken the liberty of drawing an inexorable blue line through the text" (*Letters* 94). She mentions in a letter to Charles Scribner that she has sent him an author photograph, "with my eyes down, *trying to look modest?!"*(95).[7] Being photographed for her books had become a regular—although distasteful—event, something that she did even for her first novel, *The Valley of Decision* (1902). Writing to Brownell about that book, Wharton comments that she "quakes . . . at the thought of being 'done' fundamentally by [the newspaper that was going to run her photograph] for its superficial investigations have not been exactly caressing" (58). This letter also demonstrates her burgeoning awareness of what it takes to sell books: she tells him that he will have to provide "the Wanamaker Touch that seems essential to the booming of fiction nowadays," because she "could sooner write another 2 vol. novel!" (58). Nevertheless, following this disclaimer is a compressed description of the novel and another selling point: "No novelist . . . has ever dealt with this particular period of Italian life" (58). Her desire to sell books ultimately overcomes her initial distaste for "booming." By the time *The House of Mirth* is published she no longer protests that she does not have the "Wanamaker touch." She feels powerful enough to tell Scribner's how they should—and should not—publicize the book and complains angrily when she sees that the first copies of the book carry the sensationalist tag that "for the first time the veil has been lifted from New York society" (qtd. in Lewis, *Wharton* 151). She demanded that Scribner remove "that pestilent paragraph" from the book and told the publishers that she thought "in the House of Scribner, the House of Mirth was safe from all such Harperesque methods of *réclame*"—again displaying both her knowledge of and distaste for the methods of advertising and marketing that help fiction to "boom."

Wharton was at best ambivalent about commercial considerations: she wanted her books to sell but she was reluctant to participate in marketing and advertising campaigns. Her anxieties about the marketplace can be linked to the literary world's tendency to see popular fiction and serious literature as mutually exclusive categories, a distinction that would plague her—and Cather and Gale—for the length of her career.[8] Yet, although Wharton professed distaste for "booming" fiction, she also needed, as Amy Kaplan has observed, "to see her name circulate in the marketplace" (67) in order to consider herself a professional writer. Wharton describes the power of this desire in *A Backward Glance,* when she details her response to the publication of her first volume of short stories: "*I* had written short stories that were thought worthy of preservation! Was it the same insignificant *I* that I had always known? Any one walking along the streets might go into any bookshop, and say: 'Please give me Edith Wharton's book,' and the clerk, without bursting into incredulous laughter, would produce it, and be paid for it, and the purchaser would walk home with it and read it, and talk of it, and pass it on to other people to read!" (869). Wharton's books, like Carry Fisher's spicy paragraph, will mingle among classes, be recommended to others, and be talked about. Being published—being public—imbues Wharton herself with significance; the public text gives authority to the private self. The act of publishing seems to call the "I" into being and transforms it into something other than it was before. Although this comment refers to Wharton's earliest professional life, it nevertheless illustrates why Wharton participates in "booming" her fiction even as she claims that she does not know what to say: she needs the transformative power of the public text.

Wharton's ambivalence about publicity mingles with her ambivalence about her popularity. She wants her work to be bought and sold in the marketplace, and for people to "talk of it," but she wishes she could control how they talk and what they say. She writes to Brownell that she felt "hopeless" at the "continued cry that I am an echo of Mr. James . . . & the assumption that the people I write about are not 'real' because they are not navvies and char-women" (91). Wharton's success with *The House of Mirth* established her as a "serious" author and ensconced her in the public imagination as the chronicler of New York society, but her focus on the urban upper class linked her in the public imagination with Henry James. Her choice of subject matter is not entirely her fault, she explains to Brownell. All she can write about is "what I happen to be nearest to, which is surely better than doing cowboys de chic" (91). Once her work, her name, and her image begin to circulate in the marketplace, however, she can no longer control how they will be read; the people who pay the bookshop clerk may decide to link her with James, or to decry her subject matter, or to assume that she can only write about one subject.

Her desire to be free of James's long shadow and her sharp awareness of literary trends may perhaps explain the dramatic difference between *The House of Mirth* and her next full-length novel, *The Fruit of the Tree* (1907), which, while not quite dealing with "navvies and char-women" comes quite close, focusing as it does on factory workers, corporate reform movements, and the debate over euthanasia. The novel is a departure from much of Wharton's early fiction because it deals with such contemporary issues and because her heroine, Justine Brent, is a self-sufficient career woman, a New Woman whose abilities as a nurse are matched by her compassion for the working class. Brent comes to work for an old school friend, Bessy Westmore, a wealthy young widow with a young daughter. Bessy's second husband, John Amherst, manages the factory that Bessy owns, but the two of them disagree violently about the scope of the progressive reforms that Amherst wants to bring to the factory and to the factory town. In addition to such anomalous subjects, the novel offers a pointed example of Wharton's ambivalence about sisterhood. When Bessy falls off a horse, she badly injures her spine and pleads with Justine to put an end to her misery. Justine knows that "the poor powerless body before her was not yet a mere bundle of senseless reflexes, but her friend Bessy Amherst, dying and feeling herself die . . ." (432, ellipsis in original). Her affection for her old friend and her desire to alleviate her suffering leads Justine to administer a lethal dose of morphine, an act of friendship that kills. The novel never offers a final decision about whether or not Justine did the right thing, but the fact remains that the clearest act of sororal sentiment in the novel has deadly consequences. Sisterhood is fatal.

The novel's final scenes point to Wharton's concerns about what happens to a text when it leaves its author's hands: it becomes a public document over which she has very little control. Several years after Bessy's death, Amherst and Justine marry, drawn together by their mutual interest in progressive reform. Justine is thus in the audience when Amherst presents the blueprints for the factory workers' recreation center, which he says was Bessy's idea. Justine knows the truth, however, which is that Bessy had the plans drawn up for her *own* use; she had no intention of sharing them with the workers and was in fact trying to spite her husband, whose attention to the factory she resented. Amherst, Justine realizes, "knew nothing of the original purpose of the plans. . . . It was grotesque and pitiable . . . to have [Bessy's] petty impulses of vindictiveness disguised as the motions of a lofty spirit" (628). In his misreading of the blueprints and Bessy's intentions, Amherst has "create[d] out of his regrets a being who had never existed" (628). Justine does not correct

Amherst's perceptions; no one can control his interpretations, and his (false) idealization of Bessy's ideas becomes the truth. Once a text is made public, anything can happen to it, just as the author herself can be completely reimagined by a willful reader.[9] Any author can be re-read by a reader, but the stakes are higher for women than for men because women have been traditionally more subject to the controlling, and punitive, gaze of the public eye. A woman can be misread for being in the wrong place at the wrong time, as happens to Lily Bart; judged to be a fortune-hunting murderess, as happens to Justine Brent; or dismissed as merely an imitative Jamesian, as happened to Wharton herself.

Wharton's attempt to distance herself from James, however, seems to have succeeded: a number of reviewers mentioned that in this novel she has "developed her own style" (qtd. in Tuttleton 154). But her dip into contemporary social situations also caused the reviewers some consternation, particularly her choice of heroine: Justine, trumpeted the reviewer of the *Independent*, "becomes terrible and dangerous" because of her mercy killing. Such a woman "might kill her own baby if it had epilepsy, or her husband if he was hopelessly paralyzed" (qtd. in Tuttleton 152). The reviewer in *The Bookman* thought the novel was a "better book" than *The House of Mirth*, but at the same time, cautioned that "the persons of the drama are indeed somewhat conventionalized into the guise of 'types' . . . it is possible to feel that [the book] is a wonderfully clever invention, not an organic growth" (qtd. in Tuttleton 150). This review sounds a bit like one of Wharton's letters to Gale: it pays Wharton a compliment and then undercuts the praise with several damning details. The book is good, but the characters are poorly drawn; it is wonderful, but somehow unnatural.

The Fruit of the Tree demonstrates Wharton's efforts to break free of James's shadow, but it also reveals her anxiety about becoming a public figure: readers might create "a being who has never existed" when they buy and read her books. Her refusal to affiliate herself publicly with any group or community emerges from this anxiety; if she remains publicly aloof, then there is less context for misinterpretation or mislabeling.

II

Like Carry Fisher, Tiny Soderball and Lena Lingard are peripheral characters whose individual stories are overshadowed by a central narrative. All three are economically self-sufficient women who market traditionally feminine skills as a way to survive on their own terms: Carry "markets" social graces, good manners, and conversation; Tiny makes a fortune from running boardinghouses in Alaska; Lena becomes a successful dressmaker. And just as in *The House of Mirth*, Carry's narrative suggests an alternative to the fates of all the other women in the novel, so do Tiny and Lena suggest, in *My Ántonia*, possibilities for women beyond the backbreaking labors of prairie farming or passionless urban marriages.

Cather introduced strong heroines who led unconventional lives in two earlier novels—*O Pioneers!* (1913) and *Song of the Lark* (1915)—but Tiny and Lena are of particular interest because Cather claimed that *My Ántonia* was her own favorite novel. While Alexandra Bergson and Thea Kronborg do manage to escape conventional expectations for women's lives, the endings of both novels circumscribe their heroines in the most conventional means possible: marriage. The marriages are not depicted as any sort of passionate fulfillment (Thea's is mentioned so quickly that readers could be forgiven for not realizing that it had happened at all), but each narrative nevertheless ends with its unusual heroine safely contained within the boundaries of heteronormative behaviors. These two early novels are complex explorations of women's lives, but the Tiny-Lena-Ántonia triangle exemplifies Cather's ambivalent involvement with the questions of feminism and the power available to communities of women.

Unlike these earlier heroines, Tiny and Lena never marry and are quite clear about their intention never to do so; they are alternatives to the "rich mine of life"(926) that is Ántonia Shimerda, an image that reduces her to a kind of ambulatory womb. Although Cather titles a section of the novel "Lena Lingard," once Jim leaves Lincoln (and renounces his crush on Lena), Lena more or less drops out of the novel, surfacing again only in the Widow Stevens's tale about her adventures after Lincoln. Like Carry Fisher, Tiny and Lena market typically feminine talents in order to break out of the conventional narratives available to women; they use domesticity to escape the limits of traditional domestic arrangements. Both Tiny and Lena are able to create private spaces for themselves that allow them to escape the narrow and judgmental public gaze. Their path to freedom moves from Black Hawk to Lincoln and finally to San Francisco. Only in a city at the very edge of the country are they able to create lives that are completely their own.

Lena Lingard's resistance to marriage and motherhood causes raised eyebrows in Black Hawk and in Lincoln, but in San Francisco she becomes just another successful businesswoman. When she tells Jim that she will never marry, Jim assumes that it is just a question of time before she meets the right man, an assumption that reveals his limited and limiting imagination. He ignores Lena's typically succinct reasoning: "Men are all right for friends, but as soon as you marry them they turn into cranky old fathers, even the wild ones. They begin to tell you what's sensible and what's foolish, and want you to stick at home all the time. I prefer . . . to be accountable to nobody. . . . It's all being under somebody's thumb" (891–92). Earlier in the novel, Lena counsels Christopher, her younger brother (whom, interestingly, she calls "Chrissy") to buy a handkerchief for their mother monogrammed with "B" for Berthe rather than "M" for mother: "I'd get the B, Chrissy . . . it will please her for you to think about her name. Nobody ever calls her by it now" (822). Lena's steadfast refusal to marry is hidden in this advice to her brother, as is a warning to those who would marry: marriage and motherhood erase a woman's singular identity. In order to maintain her independence, Lena refuses to take responsibility for any man's emotional well-being: "I can't help it if he hangs around," she says of one overly ardent suitor, adding "I can't order him off. It ain't my prairie" (820). Instead of ordering him off the prairie, she herself leaves, moving to Lincoln and starting a dressmaking business. With her first financial success, she builds and furnishes a house for her mother, who has been living on the prairie in an earthen dugout house, like many other immigrant families (including the Shimerda family). Lena's "feminine" talent at needlework becomes a powerful tool that enables her not only to free herself from traditional expectations but also to improve the material conditions for the rest of her family.

Similar to Alexandra Bergson in *O Pioneers!*, who uses the fields of Nebraska for her canvas, Lena is an artist who is never referred to as such. Jim sometimes finds her "alone in her workroom, draping folds of satin on a wire figure, with a quite blissful expression of countenance" (885). Lost in blissful thought, Lena spends hours in her private workroom imagining new designs, which she then sells to her growing list of customers. Like any artist, Lena has the ability to transform things: the cast-off clothing she inherits from others she "makes over for herself very becomingly" (108). She helps Ántonia to infuriate the fashionable women of Black Hawk by precisely copying their outfits for her, thus transforming Ántonia from immigrant to fashion plate for a fraction of the cost. Lena's pleasure in working alone with her needle echoes a comment that Cather made in a letter to Elizabeth Sergeant about how working ideas off her pen was on the whole a peaceful chore, now that she had found a flat of her own where she could isolate herself (December 7, 1912, Morgan Library Collection). Working ideas off the pen makes writing sound like needlework, stitching ideas to paper within a private, uninterrupted space. In Lena's transformation of cast-off clothing into beautiful, new-looking ensembles, we can see a trope for Cather's writerly self. Cather took the stories of immigrant women she knew in Nebraska and transformed them into novels for public consumption. Things that no one thought were important or "fit" subjects for novels, Cather "made over for herself very becomingly," just as Lena does with others' discards.[10]

Lena combines commerce and art and makes a successful living doing the thing she loves best in the world. Her business acumen is denigrated by Jim, whose parochial imagination cannot reconcile Lena's sexuality with her financial success; in his mind, the two are incompatible. Like the housekeeper with "faculty," Lena manages to make her labors look effortless. Even the ease with which she works causes Jim to doubt her: in his eyes she is too "easy-going [and] had none of the push and self-assertiveness that get people ahead in business" (885). He can envision only one way of getting ahead, but Lena has found a way to use her traditionally feminine skills to carve out an alternative path to success.

Tiny Soderball's path to success is perhaps the least typical of all the characters that I discuss in this chapter and is certainly the clearest challenge to conventional narratives of femininity in My Ántonia—perhaps in all of Cather's novels. Readers and critics tend to overlook Tiny, however, who is rarely mentioned in discussions of the novel.[11] Cather encourages this oversight by limiting the tale of Tiny's adventures to three quick pages of the novel. When Tiny leaves Black Hawk, she goes to Seattle and runs a rooming house, then joins the Alaskan/Canadian gold rush in a sort of Jack London-esque adventure story: to get to the gold fields, she "went in dog-sledges over Chilkoot Pass, and shot the Yukon in flatboats . . . [then] started for the Klondike fields on the last steamer that went up the Yukon before it froze" (895). Girls like Tiny were a "menace to the social order" (840) in Black Hawk, but on the Alaskan frontier Tiny makes her fortune by creating the illusion of safe domesticity. She sets up a hotel for the miners and feeds them homemade bread for which they pay in gold. Her domestic illusions are rewarded by a dying Swede who deeds his claim to her because he thinks it "great good fortune to be cared for by a woman, and a woman who spoke his own tongue" (896). Tiny sells her hotel, invests the money, and goes off to the gold fields, where she turns the Swede's claim into a "considerable fortune" (896).[12] This fortune is a result of her "daring" (895) and her ability to market her domestic arts. Tiny moves effortlessly from bread making to hotel keeping to gold mining, just as the housekeeper with "faculty" can do everything from keep house to manage a dairy. Tiny manufactures domesticity for the marketplace and, like Carry, is well paid for the success of her illusions. Also like Carry, Tiny uses the success of her manufactured domesticity to fund her own alternative housekeeping arrangements off the beaten track—San Francisco, in Tiny's case.

Tiny enacts the quintessential American dream: a loner from humble beginnings, she carves a fortune for herself out of the wilderness and leads her life in defiance of social conventions. Although in Lincoln Tiny seems capable only of flirtation, she is in fact quite ambitious. Jim Burden remembers her "arching her shoulders at [men] like a kitten," but he also suspects that the men who frequent her boardinghouse "might be afraid of [her]" (895). Tiny revises the male adventure story, a kitten who beats the wolves at their own game. She pays a price, however, for her flight to freedom: she loses three toes to frostbite and seems emotionally frostbitten as well. Her independence and self-sufficiency, which allow her "a house of her own" (912) and "solid worldly success" (895) preclude or prevent an ability to love: "nothing interested her much now but making money. The only two human beings of whom she spoke with any feeling were the Swede, Johanson, . . . and Lena Lingard" (896).

Tiny and Lena reject heterosexual marriage and are the central figures in one another's emotional lives. The intimate friendship between them flourishes on the edges of established society and on the edges of the novel itself. Their relationship cannot happen at the novel's center; they need more freedom than can be found in Black Hawk or even Lincoln. In Nebraska, Tiny and Lena are threats, the sort of women who men dance with but never marry, who had seemed fated to become the wives of immigrant farmers, like their mothers before them, and like Ántonia herself. But as Tiny says, "Frisco [is] the right field" for both of them (896). When Jim goes to visit them, he notices that "Tiny lives in a house of her own, and Lena's shop is in an apartment house just around the corner" (912), and that they take care of one another in concrete and tangible ways: Lena makes Tiny's clothes, and Tiny looks after Lena's accounts. Each has found ways to be a caregiver and a housekeeper, but in ways quite different from Ántonia's relentless domesticity. Their arrangement suggests a West Coast variation on a "Boston marriage" and implies that outside the conventions of mainstream society, women can create a domestic space that fulfills rather than suffocates their needs.

Lena and Tiny remain unwed and childless; they re-create themselves away from, and out of, Black Hawk. Their housekeeping arrangements in San Francisco echo the women's lives created by Cather's mentor Sarah Orne Jewett in *The Country of the Pointed Firs* (1896). In both cases, alternatives to social conventions exist on the periphery—the periphery in Jewett's case being sheerly geographic (although she did not think of Maine as peripheral, her readers would have), while in Cather's novel, the alternatives are peripheral both geographically and narratively. Tiny and Lena illustrate that sisterhood is possible, useful, and fulfilling, but that it may be attained only outside or away from public scrutiny—just as sisterhood exists in Cather's letters but not in her public comments about the world around her.

In her biography of Cather, Sharon O'Brien argues that by the time Cather wrote *The Song of the Lark,* she had experienced a "creative breakthrough" that emerged out of the "vital, imaginative continuity she had established with the women in her own past . . . [and her construction of] a receptive female audience" (448). Cather took great joy, says O'Brien, in writing Thea's story, and went so far as to tell Horace Greenslet that he should advertise the book "in women's colleges. Students at Smith, Barnard, and Radcliffe would like Thea, [Cather] knew: they also wanted that defiant, unsentimental kind of success" (448). The shift from the defiant success of Thea, at the center of that novel, to the marginalized successes of Lena and Tiny indicates a significant change. Thea is Cather's last unequivocally positive heroine: a strong central character who leads a productive, creative life. Cather's subsequent central female characters, Ántonia Shimerda included, are thwarted or diminished in some fundamental fashion: Ántonia by the end of the novel is grizzled, toothless, asexual; Myra Henshawe is manipulative, destructive, and terrified, as is Sapphira Colbert; Marian Forester is punished for her seeming promiscuity and debased by Ivy Peters; Lucy Gayheart suffers an unhappy love affair and drowns. Paradoxically, even as Cather gained confidence as a writer, she became overtly less defiant in her fiction; thus what is publicly unconventional in *The Song of the Lark* becomes a much quieter challenge in *My Ántonia.* Communities of women become a private source of strength rather than a defiant declaration.

In writing *My Ántonia,* Cather solidified her reputation not only as a serious literary figure but also as a Midwestern writer whose sympathies and energies were with the wide-open spaces and simple people who lived there. Cather actively cultivated this image, knowing that it would be more marketable to her readership than that of an epicurean, sophisticated, Greenwich Village–dwelling lover of women. From her years working as a journalist and as managing editor of *McClure's,* Cather had a deep understanding of what would and would not sell; she was profoundly aware of how an author's image could help to sell books. In the years between writing *O Pioneers!* and *My Ántonia,* Cather served as the ghostwriter for S. S. McClure's autobiography, an experience that she claims helped her to create the voice of Jim Burden.[13] This ghostwriting experience also provides a trope with which to discuss Cather's shrewd management of her own image. She ghostwrites a marketable "Cather": an image that highlights regional affiliations and masks gender issues, sexuality, and urbanism. As part of this image, Cather downplays her own literary authority, representing herself as a writer whose work flows to the surface without effort; she is merely a conduit for the stories of others. She says that her prairie novels (unlike *Alexander's Bridge* [1911] and *Song of the Lark*) emerged without "arranging or 'inventing' . . . [were] sponta-neous and took [their] own place" (*On Writing* 92). The spontaneous writer and prairie persona act as cover stories for a different Cather—the opera-loving lesbian whose elegant tastes are matched only by her so-phisticated attention to the craft of writing. Her public identity—the middy-blouse-wearing, plain-speaking country writer symbolized by her famous Steichen portrait—disguised power as simplicity and cloaked Cather's modernist experiments as "just stories."

Cather's adept presentation of self and her skilled manipulation of im-ages for public consumption created the iconically simple figure that is a far cry from the woman Stephen Tennant encountered when he met Cather at her Park Avenue apartment for the first time. Tennant, a flam-boyant gay Englishman who wrote the introduction to *Willa Cather on Writing*, described Cather's far-from-Midwestern outfit when she invited him to afternoon tea: "black satin pyjamas, a brilliant flamingo-pink tunic, and a cream shirt" (Hoare 212). Cather, in private, is a dandy, a far cry from the gently smiling, prairie woman in the Steichen photo. But readers remain resistant to images of an urbane Cather, as Betty Jean Steinhouser's attempts to stage a one-woman show based on Cather's life demonstrate. Steinhouser says that she "tried to duplicate Cather's evening dress. . . . I knew she liked to dress up and wear hats and all that." Audiences did not like this representation of Cather, however. They wanted the "middy blouse and the tie," so Steinhouser changed her en-semble in order to "give the people what they wanted and what makes them feel comfortable" (qtd. in Carlin 3). Readers (and indeed many crit-ics of Cather's work) are "comfortable" when Cather presents herself—or is presented—as a "typically American," the phrase used to laud both Mc-Clure's ghostwritten autobiography and *My Ántonia*.[14]

The critical success that greeted *My Ántonia* firmly established Cather in the ranks of serious American writers. It also gave her the confidence to break with Houghton Mifflin, which had published her previous nov-els. Her reasons for leaving Houghton Mifflin had to do with her con-viction that Houghton did not aggressively market her work. Cather claimed that she had to supply her own review copies of the novel to the *New York Globe*, and she was furious at a review that claimed "nobody had been afraid to say the book was unique in American fiction except her publisher" (Woodress 307). While Horace Greenslet, Cather's editor at Houghton Mifflin, eventually refuted these charges, the damage was done, and in 1921 Cather left Houghton Mifflin for Alfred Knopf.[15] In leaving Houghton for Knopf, Cather firmly allied herself with the pro-gressive forces of the publishing world; Alfred Knopf was a purely twen-tieth-century phenomenon, who merged aesthetics with advertising in

Photo 5   This image of Cather from 1926 solidified her public image as the plain-speaking prairie writer. Reprinted with permission of Joanna T. Steichen.

ways that resulted in profits for all concerned.[16] Affiliating herself with Knopf meant allying herself with a publishing house that distributed some of the most important work of both the New Negro Renaissance and modernist movements, yet despite this, Cather's image remained that of the Nebraska prairie writer, which is what critics and reviewers celebrated when they praised *My Ántonia*.

Cather's public image as the "president of the Girl Scouts," to use Katherine Anne Porter's phrase, seems at odds with her private life and her life with Edith Lewis in the very heart of Greenwich Village, which

Photo 6   Cather looking more like the urbane writer described by Stephen Tennant.
Reprinted with permission of the Nebraska State Historical Society

as early as 1910 was recognized as home to an emerging neighborhood of
gays and lesbians (Chauncey 235).[17] Like Tiny and Lena in San Francisco, Cather and Lewis lived outside the mainstream; their housekeeping arrangements in the heart of New York's Greenwich Village offered
both women the opportunity to live as they pleased without detection or
comment. The Village was a neighborhood where—unlike other neigh-

borhoods in New York in the early teens and twenties—two women seen together ran a greater risk of being thought lovers than if they were seen together elsewhere in the city. Although her Village address would seem to reveal the nature of her relationship with Lewis, the relationship stayed hidden, a ghost in plain sight, cloaked both by Cather's public silence and by cultural attitudes that presumed and assumed heterosexuality. Cather's secrets, in other words, allow her to have it both ways: she creates an authorial persona that seems somehow "above it all" while her novels continually engage the ideas and innovations that also involve her more self-evidently "modernist" literary contemporaries.[18] Reinforcing this public image were reviewers' comments about *My Ántonia* that praised her "artistic simplicity" (Woodress 301) and avoidance of the "usual methods of fiction" (Thacker 30). The public image that Cather created was marketable and powerful—and *safe*. To become more publicly queer, less of what Terry Castle has called an "apparitional lesbian" (4), would be to risk not only open expressions of homophobia but also to be affiliated, for good or ill, with a specific group and set of definitions.[19] It is telling, for instance, that *My Ántonia* omits any mention of World War I or women's suffrage, two of the most significant struggles of the early twentieth century. Bringing these events into her "simple" story would belie Cather's apolitical intent; instead we have to look to the periphery and the stories of Tiny and Lena in order to see how Cather indirectly allied herself with the struggle to bring women into the political arena.

III

Gale's novel, *Miss Lulu Bett,* is different from *My Ántonia* and *The House of Mirth* because Lulu's challenge to social norms is central, rather than peripheral, to the novel. Lulu's story is similar, in many ways, to the story of Sinclair Lewis's Carol Kennicott, although Lulu escapes completely from Warbleton, Wisconsin, and Carol returns to Gopher Prairie, Minnesota. Published in the same year, both *Main Street* and *Miss Lulu Bett* were heralded as compelling and important portraits of contemporary U.S. culture, and critics debated about which was the more significant novel. While Lewis's novel has remained in the critical canon, however, Gale's novel has not, despite its popular success and critical acclaim and the fact that Lulu's gradual emergence from grim sexless drudge to autonomous sexual woman is a classic feminist awakening: Lulu is a kind of self-actualized Cinderella.

Gale's efforts to publish *Miss Lulu Bett* built on the critical success of the prophetically named *Birth*, the 1918 novel that marked a dramatic departure from the Friendship Village stories. Like *Miss Lulu Bett*, *Birth* also describes small-town life as stifling and parochial; the characters are either unaware of anything outside their own lives or are aware that there is something more to life but are unable to articulate their ideas. Although *Birth* was a critical success (despite one reviewer's comment that the title made it sound like a "treatise from Mrs. Sanger"), it sold very poorly because it was such a departure from what Gale's readers were used to. But Gale claimed to be finished with Friendship Village, as a query letter she wrote to the editor of *Harper's* indicates: she describes a "novelette" that she is readying for publication (*Miss Lulu Bett*) and then mentions that she has a collection of short stories ready for publication "under the title *The Two Souls* . . . there is no connecting thread, and they are *not* Friendship Village stories; but they are the ones of the last few years which I would care to preserve" (n.d., SHSW). Negotiating serial rights for *Miss Lulu Bett* was difficult, because the novel was too long to run in a single magazine issue and too short to serialize for any length of time. Nevertheless, sure that *Miss Lulu Bett* was a significant piece of writing, Gale wrote to Rutger Jewett at Appleton telling him that she would be delighted to show him the manuscript under the following conditions: "a special understanding for good advertising both here and in England, and a thousand advance royalty would be the terms on which I would care to submit it. On those terms, would you care to read it?" (July 1919, n.d., SHSW). Despite her disdain for Friendship Village, the stories had made her financially secure and thus able to declare the terms on which she would let her material be read; the letter demonstrates both her financial security and her literary power. Jewett accepted her terms, and the novel became Gale's first to be published by Appleton.

    Miss Lulu Bett is set in Warbleton, Wisconsin, a small Midwestern town populated by what H. L. Mencken called the "booboosie." Lulu lives with her sister and brother-in-law as the family beast of burden: she cooks, cleans, and tends to her aged mother and to Dwight and Ina's two children. Middle-aged and unlovely, Lulu has all but given up on any hope of happiness when Dwight's brother, Ninian, arrives for a brief visit and sweeps Lulu off her feet. In a rather bizarre sequence of events, Dwight performs a wedding ceremony for Ninian and Lulu that begins as a joke but results in a legal union because Dwight is a justice of the peace. Ninian and Lulu agree to abide by the "joke" and leave town, but Lulu returns alone a month later. She announces that Ninian might still be married to his first wife, who had left him many years before, and who he assumes is dead, although he has no proof of the fact. Dwight and Ina are horrified that they might be related to a bigamist and insist that Lulu not tell anyone what has happened, that she should instead allow people to think she has been deserted. After several months of agonized waiting, Lulu gets a letter from Ninian saying that his first wife is in fact alive, living in Brazil, and that, as a result, Lulu and Ninian's marriage will be annulled. Lulu decides to leave town again, this time on her own, but before she leaves she prevents Diana Deacon, the teenaged daughter, from eloping with someone she doesn't love. In the novel's final twist, a piano salesman in Warbleton professes his love for Lulu, proposes to her, and the two leave town together. The Deacon family is amazed at Lulu's boldness—as is Lulu herself—and the novel ends with Lulu's flight to freedom.

The novel was both highly praised and an immediate best-seller; its success freed Gale from her role as the chronicler of rosy-colored Friendship Village stories. Published two years after the end of World War I and a year after the passage of the Nineteenth Amendment, *Miss Lulu Bett* emerged out of a combination of disillusionment and hope. Gale was bitterly disappointed that her hometown blithely supported the war effort and condemned her pacifist views as possibly traitorous. At the same time, she was elated by the potential for social change created by the enfranchisement of women. The Deacon family represents all the small-minded social attitudes that Gale wanted to change, and the Deacons' marriage illustrates the gender inequities that Gale hoped would be eradicated with suffrage.

While Carry Fisher, Tiny Soderball, and Lena Lingard all seek private spaces wherein they can escape the limiting and judgmental eyes of society, Lulu Bett needs to become a public figure, to exist outside the kitchen, as it were, before she can achieve self-reliance and self-sufficiency. Gale's novel suggests that forced domesticity suffocates a woman's free will but that domestic skills can also become the tools with which to create economic freedom, ideas that are peripheral to the narratives of Wharton's and Cather's novels. Unlike Carry, Tiny, and Lena, Lulu has never thought of herself as pretty or powerful, but by the conclusion of the novel, she establishes herself as an attractive, self-sufficient woman. She begins to free herself from domestic enslavement after she has entered—and left—a heterosexual relationship and after she has forged an alliance with another woman who also suffers at the hands of the household patriarch, Dwight Deacon.

It is the arrival of Ninian Deacon, Dwight's ne'er-do-well brother, that sets Lulu on her unexpected journey toward self-discovery. In her first conversation with Ninian, she tells him she is "Miss . . . from choice" and asks "what kind of a Mr. are you," a question that Ninian says he has never thought about before (47). Lulu finds herself telling Ninian that she wants to do something with her life before she dies—an ambition that she did not know she had until she had an interested audience. In subsequent conversations, Lulu finds herself suddenly capable of repartee, a talent she finds "terrifying," an "alien tongue" (78). This new language is spoken by some "other Lulu, whom she had never known anything about" (78). Even the worldly Ninian is surprised by her verbal skills: "I don't see how you do it," he says, "come back, quick like that, with what you say" (78). Only after Lulu masters this "alien tongue" does she free herself from enslavement with the Deacon family, as if she literally needs a new language in order to redefine herself.

When Lulu returns alone after her month-long honeymoon with Ninian, the Deacons are astonished, but their astonishment deepens at Lulu's unrepentant attitude and what they consider her flamboyant behavior. Their first shock occurs when Lulu tells them that she wished Ninian had kept his secret even longer: "I kind of wish he hadn't told me till we got to Oregon" (125). Her statement indicates the first stirring of a rebellion that she does not yet recognize; she has not realized how badly she wants to escape the Deacons' household. She imagines that marriage is her only avenue of escape, which is why she cedes all responsibility to Ninian. If Ninian had taken her farther away, she could have used that as an excuse for not returning to Dwight and Ina. But having been away from Warbleton and treated as more than just the kitchen drudge has begun to alter her perceptions. She continues to wear the new clothes that Ninian bought her, for instance, including a daring red dress and a fashionable hat that she uses both to provoke the town gossips and to shield herself against their whispers. Walking down the streets of Warbleton after her return, Lulu hears people talking about her and feels ashamed. But when she sees herself in a shop window and notices her fashionable reflection, she feels "surprise and pleasure. 'Well!' she thought . . . [and] abruptly her confidence rose" (142). Instead of allowing herself to be misread, she creates for herself a countertext that provides comfort and courage.

Her pleasure in her own appearance literalizes her awakening process: she begins to see herself differently, which causes problems with the Deacons, who don't want her to change. Dwight attempts to bully her into admitting that Ninian's excuse is a "cock-and-bull-story" and that he had in fact "tired of her and sent her home" (139), but the new Lulu refuses to cave in, which Dwight and Ina find "incredible." Dwight wants to protect himself from the potential scandal of having a brother who is a bigamist, and he doesn't care if his self-protection is purchased at Lulu's expense. He wants Lulu to remain in the kitchen; his power rests on his ability to dominate her.

Lulu's brief marriage not only exposes her to the world beyond the Deacons' kitchen but also awakens her sexuality. She and Ninian are away for a month, traveling as husband and wife, which implies a sexual relationship, as does the intimate act of Ninian choosing her clothes—first undressing and then dressing her. With Ninian, Lulu sheds the identity that the Deacons forced her to inhabit. Unlike other heroines of realist fictions who are undone by their sexuality and sexual experiences—like Carrie Meeber, Carol Kennicott, Edna Pontellier, Ellen Olenska—Lulu's sexual experiences give her power and strength. And because Lulu escapes Warbleton—and chooses another, more worthy, man as a partner—her sexual experiences serve ultimately to reward rather than to punish her.[20]

None of the other women in *Miss Lulu Bett* achieves Lulu's level of self-sufficiency and articulateness, and none of them fully understands her misery or her desire to be free of Warbleton. The possibility of sororal support seems almost impossible—even Lulu's own sister, Ina, refuses to help when Lulu asks her to make Dwight stop teasing her. Although Dwight is "like a bad boy with a frog . . . [and] he found a dozen ways to torture [Lulu]," Ina refuses to join her sister against her husband. Ina has utterly given herself over to Dwight and is not "the woman to cry for justice for its own sake, nor even to stand by another woman." She assumes that "no matter what Dwight's way was, wouldn't [it] be better?" (145) The other two women in the household, Ina and Lulu's mother and the Deacons' eldest daughter, Diana, have their own reasons for ignoring Lulu's plight: Mrs. Bett, despite her dislike for Dwight, depends on Dwight's charity; and Diana is too busy flirting with the next door neighbor to pay any attention to her Aunt Lulu. It is with Diana, however, that Lulu forges an unlikely alliance, one that allows Lulu to realize the full extent of her power. Only by helping another woman, an act of sisterhood that flies in the face of Dwight's authority, does Lulu find the strength to leave Warbleton and seek paid employment elsewhere. Sisterhood, for Lulu, enables individual self-fulfillment rather than limits it.

When Lulu catches Diana trying to elope with Bobby Larkin, she realizes that Diana wants to escape the Deacon household as badly as Lulu does, and is willing to marry a man she does not love to do so. Lulu reminds Di that both of them know what it is like "to be hushed up, and laughed at and paid no attention to, everything you say [sic]" (206). Despite the difference in their ages, Lulu realizes that they "actually shared some unsuspected sisterhood. It was not only that they were both badgered by Dwight. It was more than that. They were two women. And she must make Di know that she understood her" (208). When Diana admits that she does not love Bobby, Lulu convinces the couple to return home and promises Diana that she will not reveal a word about what has happened. She keeps her promise, even when Dwight commands her to tell him where Diana had gone with Bobby. By remaining steadfastly silent in the face of Dwight's demands, Lulu asserts her newly found power; her silence highlights her refusal to be bullied. Her silent challenge startles the family, who realize that they had not "ever seen Lulu look like this"; they are even more shocked when she speaks out directly against Dwight's wishes: "She threw up her head . . . and said 'If you cannot settle this with Di . . . you cannot settle it with me'" (230). Lulu refuses to answer Dwight's questions but does not lie to avoid the issue; she is able to manipulate the "alien tongue" to her own advantage. Lulu's defense of Diana—her act of sisterhood—signifies Lulu's readiness to strike out on her own; sisterhood gives her power and the courage to rebel. In *The House of Mirth* and *My Ántonia*, these acts of sisterhood occur only peripherally: Carry helps Lily Bart, and Tiny and Lena aid one another, but these acts are made to seem incidental rather than central.

Defying Dwight on Diana's behalf marks the final stage of Lulu's emergence from the kitchen. Having firmly established herself as an autonomous individual, Lulu decides to leave Warbleton for good, on her own terms. She accepts a job as a housekeeper at a hotel in the next town—the same work she has been doing for the Deacons without pay—and packs her bags, sure that she can earn a living with her domestic skills. On her way to the train, she stops to say good-bye to Neil Cornish, an aspiring lawyer who the Deacons had hoped would fall in love with Diana, and Lulu's only friend. She explains to him that Ninian's letter has finally arrived with the news that his first wife is still alive and that he is still, in fact, married. Lulu is delighted with this news because it proves that Ninian did not toss her aside out of boredom, as Dwight had continually implied. Cornish listens to all this quite calmly, but when she tells him that she is leaving, the intensity of his good-bye startles her: he tells Lulu that she has been "a jewel in [the Deacon] home" and that she "made the whole place. . . . I felt at home when you came out" (250–51). When Lulu protests that it is just her cooking he likes, Cornish replies that it goes beyond "just the cooking" (251). As their conversation continues, Lulu has the sense that Neil, unlike anyone else she knows, "gave her something, instead of drawing on her . . . she could talk to him" (186). Cornish is atypical in Lulu's experience because he listens to what she says; like Ninian, he sees her as more than just the family drudge, but unlike Ninian and his brother, Cornish does not want to control her.

Cornish is not shocked at Lulu's decision to leave town but is instead impressed by her decisiveness. When he suddenly proposes, Lulu is astonished and pleased; Cornish's proposal reverses the dynamic of the relationship she had with Ninian. Now it is Lulu who has swept someone off his feet; Lulu who is the worldly one, the one who has explored beyond the boundaries of Warbleton. Rather than needing someone to take her away, Lulu has already decided to leave, and it is her choice whether or not to leave alone. Cornish asks whether she could "risk it" with him and mentions a house they could rent together in which to make a home; he thinks in terms of things they can do together, as a "we." It is a reiteration of the Cinderella story—Lulu gets the closest thing that Warbleton has to a prince. But this prince is a suffragist's hero, who will work in tandem with his wife and respect her individuality.

In creating a novel that she characterized as "an honest portrayal of the . . . domestically enslaved woman," Gale also created a very unconventional heroine and illustrated the degree to which she was influenced by Gilman's ideas. In her introduction to Gilman's autobiography, Gale writes that Gilman "had a thousand suggestions. . . . Women must be released from drudgery . . . and they must be released from the individual kitchen. . . . [Gilman] longed for the release of the married through professional house service" (xxiii). Gilman discussed the idea of "professional house service" in "Domestic Economy" (1904), arguing in favor of communally run households that assigned various housekeeping tasks to paid professionals, rather than expecting the wife and mother to be "cook, laundress, chambermaid, charwoman, seamstress, nurse and governess" (159). Lulu is enslaved because she is neither appreciated nor paid; real freedom, argue both Gilman and Gale, comes only with economic independence, which is what Lulu leaves Warbleton to find. Gilman's and Gale's shared awareness that women need to be economically self-sufficient can be seen in Wharton's and Cather's novels, although their financially independent women are carefully relegated to the margins.

Gale's novel articulates feminist ideas that challenge traditional possibilities for women's lives. Although initially Lulu seems to be an odd choice for a heroine—a middle-aged spinster who is not clever, pretty, or humorous—her movement from domestic entrapment to self-sufficiency rewrites the established plots available to women characters. Unlike other women in novels written between 1900 and 1920, who are trapped by their "sex appeal," or who get what they want materially only to realize that they have sacrificed personal happiness, Lulu gets it all. Carrie Meeber sits alone in the dark at the end of *Sister Carrie;* Ellen Olenska is exiled from New York and isolated from the man she loves; Carol Kennicott returns to Gopher Prairie; Edna Pontellier swims out to sea. Experiencing sexual pleasure or exploring beyond the boundaries of conventional heterosexual marriage results in misery, unhappiness, and death, but Lulu's happy flight from Warbleton arm-in-arm with a man who adores and admires her breaks this pattern.

Lulu's escape struck a nerve with readers; the novel garnered glowing reviews and sold so well that Gale was asked to dramatize it for the stage. After a one-performance preview at New York's Sing Sing prison, the play debuted on Broadway on December 27, 1921, at the Belmont Theater.[21] When Gale adapted the novel, she radically altered the novel's ending, making it an even stronger feminist statement. The play's ending has Lulu refuse to marry Neil Cornish, telling him "not yet—not yet!" Marriage will have to wait, she tells everyone, because she is going away, alone. To the horrified Deacons and the stricken Cornish she announces: "[I'm going] away. I thought I wanted somebody of my own. Well, maybe it was just myself . . . I want to see out of my own eyes. For the first time in my life. . . . Good-by, all of you. I'm going I don't know where—to work at I don't know what. But I'm going from choice!" (Barlow 160–61). Like Huck Finn "lighting out for the territories," Lulu leaves familiar domesticity for something new and unknown; she chooses work rather than marriage as her destiny. Not only is she leaving alone, but she also assumes that she will work: the question is only *at what* she will work, not *if* she will work. Leaving and working are both Lulu's choice, and it is hard to say which would be more disconcerting to her audience: her refusal of marriage or her acceptance of employment.

Gale changed this radical ending, however, after about ten performances. The rewritten ending obligingly finds Ninian's first wife long-dead, so that Ninian can return to rescue Lulu from the Deacons; the character of Neil Cornish is written out entirely. While a number of critics approved the feminist ending, seeing in *Miss Lulu* a Midwestern version of Ibsen's *Doll's House,* audiences were less appreciative; Gale seemed to have overestimated her audience's capacity to sympathize with such a radical figure. In 1921, despite the flapper and the suffragist—or maybe because of them—America was not ready for a Broadway heroine who so completely and happily jettisoned the trappings of middle-class femininity. Judith Barlow suggests that in the aftermath of suffrage, the theater had become "if possible, even more conservative" (xii). Proving that audiences weren't ready for such radicalism is the fact that the new "happy ending" increased ticket sales, resulting in a run of almost two hundred performances and a road show of about six hundred performances that "received almost unanimous raves [on tour]" (Barlow xxiv). The play's tremendous profits and the popularity of the touring company led Paramount Studios to buy the rights to the play, which it made into a successful movie.[22] New York *Variety* noted that as of May 20, 1921, in the thirty-first week of its run, the play was making between five and six thousand dollars weekly; Miss Lulu's misery and subsequent escape made Gale a very wealthy and very well-known writer.

Gale's acquiescence to commercial taste reveals the extent to which she was willing to compromise in order to have her message heard. To some degree, however, she was caught in a no-win situation: her radical ending had led some critics to label the play as nothing more than feminist propaganda, while the revised ending led other critics to accuse her of pandering. The revised ending caused a firestorm among reviewers, who debated the relative merits of the two endings, with most choosing the more radical version. The popular success of Gale's play with the revised ending proves what William Dean Howells once said to Wharton: that what "the American public always wants is a tragedy with a happy ending" (Wharton, *Backward* 894). When Wharton adapted *The House of Mirth* for the stage, working with Clyde Fitch, she refused to change the ending of the novel, despite reviews that called the play "doleful" (Benstock, *Gifts* 155). If Lily were to live, then by Wharton's own definition, the society in which Lily lived lost all significance. Lily's death anchors one of the novel's central ideas: that "a frivolous society can acquire dramatic significance only through what its frivolity destroys" (Wharton, *Backward* 940). In Gale's novel, however, what matters most is Lulu's realization that she is a self-sufficient, independent woman. Once Lulu has come to this understanding, whether or not she leaves with Neil Cornish becomes unimportant.

The debate over the play's two endings led Gale to write a letter to the editors of several New York papers, in which she asked:

> Why at this moment is the unmarried ending the artistic ending? . . . Why in *Miss Lulu Bett* is Lulu less artistic in marriage at the final curtain than in going off to work for herself? . . . Why is marriage inartistic?
>
> Thirty years ago the woman's declaration of independence would have been propaganda, fifty years from now it will be a common-place, to thousands of us it is a common-place now. Art is longer than this.
> . . . .
> I am in this same attitude—I think that the open ending is the artistic ending. When *Miss Lulu Bett* is published as a play, it will have the open ending. But when I analyze the impression, I find only one reason for its validity; that is, if any least violence is done to character or construction in order to achieve the so called closed ending. Perhaps the new drama is going to face the truth that there is no "ending" happy or unhappy, anywhere in living. Perhaps it will be free to use its episodes, so long as they convince, without labeling them. (Gale Archives, Performing Arts Library, n.d.)

While changing her politically outspoken message suggests that Gale is a crass opportunist, the revision enabled her tale of middle-aged flight and domestic escape to be seen on stages across the country, thus getting her message to more people. Although audiences might not see the full extent of Lulu's rebellion against patriarchal and economic oppression if she leaves Warbleton with a man, they would at least see her kick over the traces of her miserable life and realize that even plain, middle-aged spinsters can experience passion.[23]

Judging from reviewers' comments, the central feminist message of the play did not get lost, "happy ending" notwithstanding. The *New Republic* claimed that Gale's writing is part of the

> wonderful Discovery of America . . . being done by Willa Cather, Sherwood Anderson, Sinclair Lewis, Floyd Dell, Edith Wharton. But . . . Miss Gale has done [in *Miss Lulu Bett*] authentically what perhaps only a *feminist,* and certainly only what an *artist* can do. She has shown, in perfect American terms, the serious comedy of emancipation . . . that famous conflict between the tribe and the growing feminine individuality . . . in which defeat may mean an immense gain of respectability but must mean a complete loss, in spite of our pet institutions of that liberal adjustment of personalities called civilization. (January 12, 1921, emphasis added)

The review not only assumes that *feminist* and *artist* are compatible terms but also asserts that the union of the two has produced a quintessentially "American" drama, corroborating Gale's belief that the artist must also be a "social being." The *Detroit News* echoed the sentiments of the *New Republic* review, praising Gale's play in feminist terms: Miss Lulu climbs "to the emancipated womanhood of the last act as a symbol of woman's slow toil for freedom through the centuries. She is the silhouette of some marching future for women everywhere" (Derleth papers, SHSW). Notwithstanding the critical outcry about her changes, five months later, in 1921, Gale's play won the Pulitzer prize for drama, beating out, among others, Eugene O'Neill's *Emperor Jones*.

Curiously, despite Gale's outspoken support of suffrage and reviewers' comments about the play's feminist politics, Gale's public persona was seldom connected to radical politics. Publicity interviews describe her soulful good looks, and her political views are downplayed in favor of her homespun Portage homilies. In "The Everlasting Persistence of This American Girl" (1921), a long interview published in *American Magazine,* Gale is celebrated for her small-town roots, her love for her parents, and "her sincerity about life" (Sumner 136). There is no mention whatsoever of Gale's involvement in suffrage politics, her feminism, or her support for La Follette's pacifist stance in World War I. She becomes instead the "American girl," who is "slender, almost fragile, with soft brown hair, clear

Photo 7   Zona Gale, circa 1915–1920. Reproduced with permission from the State Historical Society of Wisconsin.

grayish eyes, and almost incredibly small hands" (138). Even calling her a girl somewhat blurs the issue—Gale was forty-six when the interview was conducted. In this same interview, Gale defines her professional ambitions with goals similar to those mentioned by Wharton and Cather: in

Photo 8 Gale at about the time *Miss Lulu Bett* was published. Reproduced with
permission from the State Historical Society of Wisconsin.

order to think of herself as a success, she needs to conquer the marketplace. At the University of Madison, she says, she won "some prizes for
writing . . . but that wasn't the same thing as having people *buy* what I
wrote" (137). All three share an interest in achieving both commercial
and aesthetic success, but Gale's method for achieving these things is
markedly different from that of her friends.

It is difficult to say who dictated the tone of Gale's literary publicity
articles, because Gale certainly did not hide her opinions about politi-

cal and social issues from her reading public. Like Wharton and Cather, Gale is subject to being molded into a conventional and recognizable image—in her case, an "American girl," and in their cases, a society lady and a prairie pioneer, respectively. Gale's public image may have been influenced by her good looks; she was, by all accounts, considered something of a beauty—sometimes to her detriment. An early newspaper editor of hers told an interviewer that when Gale first applied to him for a job, for instance, he thought that her "personal charm was so marked that—well, genius doesn't always have personal charm. . . . But the miracle happened—she had insight and sympathy and she could put both to paper" (December 1922, *Century*, n.p.). Her newspaper stories were often accompanied by her photograph, in fact, and she became known as that "good-looking reporter" (qtd. in Simonson 24). Gale's ethereal beauty masked a steely determination to succeed, however, which occasionally meant—as in the case of the revised ending of *Miss Lulu Bett*— that she compromised the fullness of her radical vision in order to convey even some small portion of it. Thus she allowed herself to be presented as the "American girl," on the one hand, while at the same time she publicly asserted herself as a feminist, pacifist, and socialist.[24] There are two Gales available to the reading public, depending on how it wanted to imagine her: the doe-eyed, aphoristic author and the radical, political writer.

As the excerpt from the *New Republic* indicates, reviewers and audiences of *Miss Lulu Bett* seemed more willing to accept the conjunction of feminism and art than those who conducted Gale's publicity interviews: a play with a feminist message could (and did) play in Peoria—and in New York. Although the country might be slightly anxious about the status of its newly enfranchised women, it was ready to celebrate Lulu's liberation and to see her story as its own. *Miss Lulu Bett* cannot be called "suffrage literature" per se, but it reflects the new ambitions of U.S. women eager to bring their domestic "faculty" to the marketplace and to the ballot box. The novel and the play also reflect Gale's own confidence about moving out of the confines of Friendship Village. While she was working on *Miss Lulu Bett,* she was also traveling the country giving readings and speeches about La Follette progressivism, racial equality, world peace, Unitarianism, antimilitarism, and the Equal Rights Amendment. Her public work to reform society helps her to imagine, it seems, a society in which women like Miss Lulu might be able to escape their stifling situations. In contrast, consider Wharton's *The Age of Innocence* (1920), in which the threateningly unconventional Ellen Olenska is effectively exiled from family and country; there is no room for Ellen in May Welland's hermetically sealed universe.

Despite the lesson offered by Gale's success, neither Wharton nor Cather ever publicly affiliated themselves with feminism. Cather publicly professed disdain for women with causes—among whose company she included suffragists—but chose for her life partner a woman whose New Woman characteristics cannot have escaped her: Edith Lewis was a graduate of Smith and a self-sufficient, self-supporting career woman when she met Cather. Although she became Cather's devoted companion, Lewis continued to work, first at *McClure's* and then at the J. Walter Thompson advertising agency. The powerful emotional bond she shared with Lewis notwithstanding, however, Cather does not allow a sororal community of spirit to flourish in her novels, other than on the margins, as is the case with Tiny and Lena.[25] Wharton, on the other hand, privately came to support feminism through the influence of Jean du Breuil de Saint-Germain, for whom Wharton wrote a eulogy in 1915. Wharton wrote that he

> opened her eyes to a question of which—I admit to my shame—I had not until then understood the immense social implications. . . . He made me see that the only thing that matters, in the feminist movement, is the fate of . . . those poor hard-working women who accept their long misery with an animal fatalism because they do not know they have a right to a more humane existence. In short, one would be tempted to say that women who argue for the right to vote could very well do without it, but it is necessary for those women, so much more numerous, who do not even know what it is, or why others are demanding it in their name! (*Uncollected* 200–201)[26]

Wharton—sounding surprisingly like Gale here—supports suffrage because of what it can do to alleviate class-based suffering, but she never makes these views public.

Because the novels with "New Women" heroines like Justine Brent and Thea Kronborg were not as critically successful as the novels in which unconventional women were less directly presented, Wharton and Cather became convinced that obliqueness was the best approach. In turn, because they were so successful, their strategy of indirectness has become part of feminist literary history, a "sacred tradition," which is what Justine Brent realizes will become of Amherst's interpretation of Bessy's blueprints (630). Wharton's and Cather's apparent hostility to sisterhood and to feminism now appears inevitable, rather than being seen as a deliberate choice made out of both artistic and commercial considerations. Their decisions about how to "rob men of the alphabet" look very different, however, when compared with Gale's straightforward descriptions of female emancipation. Gale's successes demonstrate that literary authority and literary sisterhood do not necessarily have to be at odds with one another. When each writer decides to take World War I as her subject, however, her literary authority is sorely tested; no form of "alphabet robbery" seems capable of describing war.

CHAPTER FOUR

WOMEN AT WAR: CROSSING THE GENDER–GENRE BOUNDARY

At the end of Wharton's "Writing a War Story," the famous writer Harold Harbard says to Ivy Spang—the author of the war story in question—that he finds her work "puzzling . . . queer . . . you've gotten a hold of an awfully good subject . . . but you've rather mauled it, haven't you?" He goes on to tell her how much he admires the story's accompanying photograph, a picture of Ivy dressed in her nurse's uniform (she is a nursing volunteer at a hospital), in which she looks like a cross between "Mélisande lowering her braid over the balcony and Florence Nightingale advancing with the lamp" (364). When Harbard notices Ivy's unhappiness at having her writing so quickly dismissed, he says, "You were angry just now because I did not admire your story; and now you're angrier still because I do admire your photograph. Do you wonder that we novelists find such an inexhaustible field in Woman?" (*Collected Short Stories* 370). Harbard's comment suggests that Ivy should be consoled by his admiration of her picture, as if the success of her image mitigates her authorial failure. His remark anchors her within a limited frame of representation; she can be only the beautiful object, never a member of "we novelists," who are, it seems, always only men.[1]

Ivy's story appears in *The-Men-at-Arms*, a new magazine that was "to bring joy to the wounded and disabled in British hospitals," but only her photo provides comfort, not her prose. The soldiers love the picture, telling her that they have never seen "such a jollier photo" and asking for copies to keep as a "jolly reminder," although one wonders what it is, exactly, that they want to be reminded of. Her image has more value than her words; it is the photo that will be copied and circulated, not her story. The picture becomes the Betty Grable pinup of the hospital ward, and Ivy becomes an unwilling celebrity, or rather, she is celebrated for something other than what she intended. Her fate illustrates how quickly women can lose control over their public image and how severe were the consequences for a woman who attempted to write about the war: Ivy is ridiculed, humiliated, and patronized. Despite the fact that World War I saw a loosening of gender roles for both men and women, there was an equal movement in the opposite direction—an increasing emphasis on deeply traditional images of women that could be deployed as pro-war symbols. Popular war-support posters included images of Lady Liberty striding across battlefields, sword uplifted, urging the purchase of war bonds; a pietà-like Red Cross nurse, captioned as the "greatest mother in the world," cradling a tiny soldier in her arms; scenes of mothers, wives, and children gazing out the window, urging their men to "Go!"[2] The beautiful nurse is another such image, and it is clear that the men in Ivy's hospital ward find her most useful in that guise—even though all Ivy does is serve tea-trays.

Harbard equates soldiering with war writing, and because Ivy has never done the former, she will never succeed at the latter. She fails as a war writer, in short, because she is a woman. But Wharton also calls into question what constitutes authorial knowledge, which complicates any easy reading of this story. Wharton directs her derisive irony in two directions: at the male literati who, like Harbard, want to preserve women as decorative objects and at those members of the younger generation (male and female) who think that manifestos and platitudes will grant them admission into the club of "we novelists." Ivy fails on two fronts: she knows nothing about the war and she knows nothing about writing. Ivy's ideas about literature and writing are cribbed from faddish literary magazines: she "knows," for instance, that mornings are sacred to great writers, that one should abandon the "superannuated habit" of starting each line of poetry with a capital letter, that "no one" bothers with plot or subject these days, and that she should avoid reading anyone else's work lest her own ideas be contaminated. Ivy's certainty that "mornings were sacred" would be an in-joke to Wharton's friends, who knew of Wharton's habit of spending the mornings writing, even to the extent of having a special lap-table made for her so that she could write in bed while traveling. This moment of self-mocking aside, the litany of things that Ivy believes to be true about writing contradicts Wharton's own beliefs. In a letter to Victor Solberg, Wharton wrote that "you seem to think that the risk of being subject to the influence of great poets is one that young writers fear. There cannot be a greater mistake than this, or one more de-

structive to any real poetic culture. . . . The great object of the young
writer should be, not to fear these influences, but to seek only the greatest, and to assimilate them so that they become part of his stock-in-trade"
(*Letters* 411). Ivy's fear of being "contaminated" thus demonstrates the
failure of her aspirations before she has even begun.

Given Ivy's inadequacy as a writer, Harbard's criticism seems suddenly
warranted, and his views sound startlingly similar to Wharton's own. In a
letter to Gale, Wharton wrote that "the expressionists and impressionists
and all the rest of them can't wholly befog the fact that the novel has *got*
to have a subject, as much as a picture or a vase or any chosen object of
representation has to, by the mere fact that selection operates" (April 14,
1923, SHSW). The conclusion of Wharton's story thus cordons off the category of "we novelists" against the young upstarts who would claim membership in her group without having her knowledge and experience. The
only two people who know anything about literature in this story are the
wounded novelist and the old French governess, whose suggestions that
Ivy "find a plot" and start "by thinking about a subject" (362, 363) echo
Wharton's comments to Gale. Mademoiselle eventually gives Ivy a subject, a wounded soldier's story that Mademoiselle had written down while
tending to him in the hospital; the soldier's story becomes the "good subject" that Ivy ruins. The French woman and the English man have authentic knowledge about writing, nursing, and soldiering that Ivy can
only imitate and echo. Harbard's comment about women as an inexhaustible field, which concludes the story, raises questions about gender,
age, and knowledge that would become central for Wharton and Cather
as they wrote their own war stories. Wharton's story presciently illustrates
what critics would say about her war writing, and that of Cather and
Gale: that their war fiction was inauthentic; that they had "rather mauled"
their subject; that as women they shouldn't have attempted to write about
the war in the first place.

When Wharton, Cather, and Gale decided to write about the war—
a subject that each saw as a demanding and unavoidable topic—they
challenged the deeply held belief that war concerns only men and that
the war novel is a male genre. As "Writing a War Story" demonstrates,
readers come to war fiction with certain expectations—primarily that
war stories are written by men with military experience of some sort or
another. The literature that emerged out of World War I, in particular,
emphasized the link between soldiering and writing, giving rise to an entire school of soldier-poets, like Wilfrid Owen, Sigfried Sassoon, and
Robert Graves, as well as Hemingway, Dos Passos, and Ford. Lynne
Hanley has pointed out that until relatively recently, it has been assumed
that women "have no story to tell" about war because they "are presumed

to be absent from war. . . . The only woman who can claim authority to speak about war is the rare woman who has been at least near the combat zone" (7). The war novel thus becomes a man's purview; the only "war story" available to women is that of tending the home fires and waiting for the returning hero. The editors of *Arms and the Woman* (1989) describe this apportioning of subject matter as the "dualities of front and home front, militarist male and pacifist female [that] have traditionally structured—and so perpetuated—the war story" (Cooper and Munich 16). Wharton, Cather, and Gale ignore this gender–genre boundary, however, and create war stories that critique not only traditional militaristic rhetoric but also the very idea that as women they are to remain silent about the brutal conflict raging around them.

In each writer's war fiction, traditions and conventions are inverted and in fact become the tools that each uses to comment on gender roles, nationalism, and her own position as a middle-aged artist in wartime. Wharton's *A Son at the Front* (1923), Cather's *One of Ours* (1922), Gale's *Heart's Kindred* (1915), and stories from her 1919 collection, *Peace in Friendship Village*, interrogate the idea that there is only one "authentic" war experience and only one way to represent that experience. Their writing challenges the equation between soldiering and writing and demystifies the deceptively beautiful language used to mobilize and glorify soldiers. Both Wharton's *A Son at the Front* and Cather's *One of Ours* present the war as something necessary but not necessarily glorious; Gale's work, on the other hand, supports an unequivocal pacifism and questions the very concept of war itself: how can a civilized world justify such violence? Gale's war stories present pacifism as the only sane response to a militarized world. In her war stories, there are no frontline battles, no blood, no wounded, and no dead bodies, but she is nevertheless waging the same battle that Wharton and Cather are: the right to represent the war and responses to war as she sees fit.

Wharton's and Cather's war novels are studied less frequently than their other novels, but when they are discussed, it is generally in the context provided by the male soldier-writers who made their name during this period. Gale's pacifism, which is inextricably linked to her feminism, provides an alternative and equally important context for Wharton's and Cather's novels, and highlights the strength of the international peace movement in the years just prior to World War I. The World Peace Organization was founded in 1910, the same year that Andrew Carnegie gave ten million dollars to the Carnegie Endowment for International Peace; five years later, the International Congress of Women (ICW) met at The Hague to discuss world peace. Regardless of whether they are reading Gale's dovish fictions or Wharton's and Cather's soldier stories, however, reviewers uphold the gender-genre boundary, relegating all three writers to the status of "lady author." When the reviews are positive, the genre fades as an issue and the novels succeed *despite* being about the war, but when the novels fail, it is because no woman can have "authentic" knowledge about war or war-related issues. For Cather and Wharton this categorization was particularly galling, as it attempted to eradicate what they had worked so hard to create: a public authorial self that had nothing to do with other women writers. Nevertheless, by confronting reader expectations about war writing, each writer moved from writing about the war into new and successful phases of her career; her war fiction and the responses to it shape the direction of future work.

In *A Son at the Front* and *One of Ours*, Wharton and Cather find that men at war are an "inexhaustible field" and focus their attentions on the deaths of beautiful young men. While the novels are different from one another in many ways, the handsome dying soldier provides common inspiration. Cather's romantic Claude and Wharton's enigmatic George are brothers-in-arms, subject to similar scrutiny by their middle-aged creators. Each writer inverts the traditional artist–muse relationship described by Harold Harbard and makes a beautiful boy into her muse, an inversion that Wharton makes explicit by creating as her protagonist a middle-aged male painter whose favorite subject is his soldier-son. Both novels address one of the terrible paradoxes of war: the young die but the old and middle-aged survive, left behind to try to make sense of a world "broken in two," as Cather famously described it. At the same time, however, in the literary world that these writers inhabited, young men were making their literary fortunes with writing about the war, creating what would come to be considered the "authentic" books about the war and the postwar era. On the battlefield, young men were dying by the thousands, but in the literary marketplace, youthful voices were coming more and more to the fore—voices that were often downright dismissive of their older, female peers. By asserting themselves as war writers, Cather and Wharton stake a claim for themselves as important contemporary voices and refuse to be relegated to the prewar era. Their war novels thus should be read not just as novels that are about a world at war but also as reflections of each writer's anxieties about and ambitions for her position in the postwar world. In their portrayals of a world at war and the dissolution of prewar absolutes, as well as the implicit gender confrontation created by taking on the genre of "war novel," Cather and Wharton oppose masculine modernism, taking for themselves a part of the postwar literary playing field that had been previously marked "men only."[3]

Gale's war writing is less involved with questioning literary or generational politics and more engaged with questioning the very concept of war itself. Her pacifist novel and short stories interrogate the feelings of nationalism and xenophobia that ran high in the United States before and after the war; she continually outlines a worldview in which differences are embraced and idealism triumphs. Her pacifism, however, does not diminish her commitment to feminism. Instead, her work reminds us that World War I occurred as the conflict over women's rights was coming to a boil and that in the United States, at the very least, the right to suffrage was inextricably linked to wartime rhetoric and relief efforts. Gale appropriates the sentimental images being used to foster pro-war feeling in order to argue against the war: instead of gazing in mute adoration and approval at their departing soldier-sons, Gale's mothers speak out strongly against soldiering and insist that it is their right as mothers to keep their children safe. In *Women's Fiction and the Great War* (1997), Suzanne Raitt and Trudi Tate have pointed out that in order for countries to wage war, they "must invest in an image of peace worth fighting for, a peace which is imagined through images of an idealized and nostalgic pre-war Golden Age" (5). Instead of looking backward toward some peaceful past, however, Gale argues that this peaceful golden age could be *now* if countries could only shift away from nationalist and militarist paradigms.

Gale does not use a soldier's body for her muse; instead, she self-consciously inverts rhetorical structures rather than gender roles, although as always in her work, it is the women who occupy center stage and who are the centers of both radicalism and morality. While Gale's war writing looks very different from Wharton's or Cather's, she too experienced a significant shift in focus after the war. Doubly disappointed during the war years, first by the U.S. decision to enter the war and then by NAWSA's support of the war effort, Gale's postwar work reflects her disillusionment. Although idealism triumphs in *Heart's Kindred,* the defeat of the peace movement led her ultimately to the more critical attitudes expressed in *Peace in Friendship Village,* published four years later.

I

Gale was a charter member of the Women's Peace Party (WPP), founded in January 1915 by a group of women that included Jane Addams, Carrie Chapman Catt (leader of NAWSA), and Rosika Schwimmer. At the first organizational meeting of the WPP in Washington, D.C., Gale was elected chair of the propaganda committee, a position that may have spurred her to write *Heart's Kindred.* The climax of the novel takes place at a feminist pacifist convention and uses excerpts from actual speeches made by prominent members of the WPP, including Schwimmer and Addams. The WPP pledged to support suffrage, arguing that one reason wars were fought was that women were not allowed to participate in the decision making because they could not vote. The peace movement in both the United States and abroad became a divisive factor, however, because while most pacifists were suffragists, not all suffragists were pacifists, and they were not sure they wanted pacifist support. The WPP suffered a setback when Catt decided that NAWSA would support Wilson's "preparedness" campaign, setting aside her pacifist principles in favor of pragmatic politicking. Catt wanted Wilson, in exchange for suffragist support, to endorse a suffrage amendment when the war was over. Catt's decision meant that mainstream suffrage swung towards militarism, a decision that many suffragists saw as a betrayal of the movement's primary goal.

It was in partial response to NAWSA's acceptance of militarism that Alice Paul founded the National Woman's Party (NWP, formerly the Congressional Union), ironically a more militant organization than NAWSA. Because of the conflict between NAWSA and the NWP, the suffrage debate heated up during the war years and suffragists were increasingly subject to violent reprisals. Women who went on hunger strikes after they were arrested were force-fed; those who were not demonstrably in favor of the war effort were loudly decried as traitors; picketers in front of the White House were subject to physical and verbal abuse. Irwin remembers

> the intensive militant fight which Alice Paul instituted and which lasted from 1917 to 1920. Our pickets were mobbed, man-handled by mobs, knocked down, injured. They were arrested and sent to jail where they were badly treated and where they hunger-struck. Alice Paul was taken to a hospital and her sanity investigated. But all the time, more and more women came forward to march on the picket line. All the time, streams of gold flowed into the coffers of the National Woman's Party. All the time our speakers, young, fresh, incredibly brave, articulate, able—were streaming through the United States, telling the rest of the country exactly what was happening to the American women in Washington. Presently the arrests stopped. But women were not enfranchised. In a campaign which had features of incredible beauty, Alice Paul went on from militant tactic to more militant tactic, actually, in public, burning President Wilson's words wherever he spoke of liberty. One by one, Congressmen and Senators were brought over to our cause. (461)

Paul declared that her tactics, which on more than one occasion caused riots, were the fault of the government and not the NWP: "The responsibility is with the government and not with the women of America, if the lack of democracy at home weakens the government in its fight for democracy 3,000 miles away" (qtd. in Graham 107). Paul's vocal, "unladylike" picketers disrupted NAWSA's carefully constructed images of suffragists as women who were inherently peaceful and compassionate and who wanted the vote only so that they could "mother" the society at large. Because of the NWP's singular focus on suffrage, pacifists could continue to work for suffrage without fearing that they would be asked to support the war, which caused many pacifist suffragists to switch their allegiances from NAWSA in support of Paul, as Gale did. Although NAWSA dismissed their efforts, Paul and the WPP felt justified in taking credit when the Nineteenth Amendment finally passed, arguing that their dramatic tactics made the issue impossible to ignore.

Despite the fact that pacifism was thought to be a quintessentially womanly trait, until the formation of the WPP, all pacifist organizations were headed by men. It was in part to combat the sexism of pacifist organizations that the WPP was founded in the first place. In a letter to Jane Addams asking her to chair the new organization, Catt wrote that the four current national peace societies were "all well endowed . . . very masculine in their point of view. It would seem that they have as little use for women and their points of view as have the militarists" (qtd. in Alonso 61). The misogynist attitudes of pacifist men notwithstanding, being a pacifist was considered both feminine and vaguely traitorous by the U.S. government and by the press. Even a figure like Addams, who was something of a national hero for her settlement work, was portrayed in the news "as an unpatriotic subversive out to demasculinize the nation's sons" when she returned to the United States from The Hague after the ICW conference (Alonso 69). Feminist pacifists thus disrupted accepted female behavior in several directions simultaneously: they upheld deeply conventional ideals of womanhood by being nonviolent, but their pacifist beliefs made them traitors; they were bad mothers if they did not stay home to tend to their children and bad mothers if they wanted to keep their children at home rather than send them off to war; their pacifist agitation interfered with the masculine business of nationbuilding and warmongering, but pacifism was a man's business.

Both Gale's pacifism and her feminism made her deeply suspect in the little town of Portage. Anne Firor Scott points out that after 1914 "pacifist" stopped being a "term of distinction" and became instead "equated with [being] a German sympathizer or traitor" (*Visible* 134). Gale's father was so afraid that the people of Portage would think of his daughter as a traitor that he bought war bonds in her name to forestall criticism. Catt was accused of being pro-German, despite her support of Wilson, because she had continued her friendship with Rosika Schwimmer, a Hungarian feminist and pacifist. Schwimmer, in turn, was accused of being a German spy (Graham 101). Even if she were not a pacifist, a woman's membership in the NWP could cause problems, as Inez Irwin notes in her memoir: when she and her second husband, Will Irwin, were planning to travel to Europe as war reporters, "there was a hitch. As I was a member of the National Woman's Party, the State Department refused me a passport. And so, after our wedding, we went immediately to Washington, where, in a brief telephone conversation, Bill's old friend, Franklin Lane, Secretary of the Interior, smoothed out the passport incident" ("Adventures of Yesterday" 558). Affiliating oneself with an unladylike cause, as Irwin's story illustrates, had consequences potentially more severe than simple social opprobrium.

These sentiments did not prevent Gale from clearly delineating the goals of feminist pacifism in *Heart's Kindred*, which combines the structure of a conversion narrative with real-life speeches and events in an effort to make pacifism seem practicable rather than idealistic. During the time that she was writing *Heart's Kindred* and in the years immediately following its publication, Gale was traveling the country, reading and lecturing on behalf of various pacifist causes, including antimilitarism and antipreparedness.[4] The celebrity status she had achieved through her Friendship Village stories served to attract people, if not entirely to her cause, then at least to listen to her arguments. Gale's novel traces the moral development of a violent mountain man, Inger, who evolves from being an unprincipled killer (it is hinted that in an angry rage, Inger once killed a man) to a principled killer (his willingness to kill for patriotism) to a pacifist who believes that "killing is killing," no matter what the context. Along this path, Inger also becomes a feminist, although he does not consciously realize that this has happened. Inger's transformation occurs on both a public and a private level: publicly, he is swayed by speeches made by Jane Addams and other women pacifists; privately, he falls in love with the beautiful pacifist Lory Moor. Public demonstrations and private emotions combine to create a new man, one who feels a sense of "heart's kindred" with all of humanity.

Inger's conversion happens on the journey that he takes with Lory from the tiny mountain town of Flagpole to Chicago and then to Washington, D.C., a journey that begins when Lory seeks him out "comradely . . . as one being of another" (70). Inger has never been treated as a "comrade" by a woman before, nor had it ever occurred to him that such a thing was even possible, that men and women could be "comrades" rather than lovers. He helps Lory escape her drunken father, who wants her to marry a man she hates as payment on a gambling debt. As they travel from Flagpole to Washington, in search of relatives with whom

Lory thinks she can find refuge, Inger realizes "it *is* a job to be a woman," a thought that illustrates his burgeoning awareness of patriarchal double-standards. As he learns that women are more than just saloon girls or mothers through Lory's example, so too does he learn that violence is not necessarily a fact of life.

When Inger and Lory go to a rally about war preparedness, Inger experiences another step in his conversion journey, a movement from killing for no reason to killing for a reason. The arguments of the pro-war speakers, by appealing to Inger's patriotism, teach him that there is more to killing than just "tearing things up." At this rally, several pacifists attempt to speak, but they are shouted down; Inger thinks that they should be run out of the country. He does not yet see what Lory sees—that "killing is killing"—but his partial transformation has prepared him to understand the message of the women's peace convention.[5]

Inger stumbles upon the convention unknowingly, when he is swept up in a crowd of people making their way to the Capitol building. In the rotunda he sees a group of "soberly dressed women" up on a platform, which startles him because until that point the only women he had seen on platforms were dancehall girls. Looking at the women more closely, he thinks that if the dance-hall girls were "dress[ed] . . . like this—dark and plain—they wouldn't look so different" (193). His comment is an expression of Gale's conviction that all women are sisters under the skin—or under their petticoats. As the speeches begin, Inger's first response is to question the women's patriotism, and he wonders why they aren't being arrested. When the first woman, a Dane, says that women should "show . . . how unworthy it is of the citizen of the twentieth century to be used . . . as food for cannon," Inger is stupefied. What she says "sounded to him like treason for which they should fall on her and drive her from the hall." Subsequent speakers do not alleviate his suspicions, particularly a woman from Germany who calls for her audience to "perform your duty as wives and mothers, as protectors of true civilization and humanity!" When Inger hears her words, he thinks he has stumbled upon a plot: "Were these a few traitors who had come here to teach American women to play traitor too?" (199–200). The women's speeches draw on the same ideas about womanhood as were used in preparedness posters—soulful mothers gazing at their soldier sons, or garbed like women warriors, spurring men on to greater victories—but the pacifists use these images to argue against military involvement, an inversion similar to the suffragist strategy of using maternalist rhetoric to lobby for the vote.

In their drive to protect civilization and humanity, the women of the convention (which is never given a specific name) offer a range of arguments in support of pacifism, including the prevention of crimes against women and the fact that pacifism could be good for the economy. Like Gale, the women in the novel see pacifism as a pragmatic rather than an idealistic position; they are convinced that it is the only sane response to an increasingly militarized world. Gale uses actual speeches and footnotes the name of the speakers as a way to forestall criticism that her pacifist vision is merely a sentimental romance; she wants her readers (and critics) to see that pacifism existed in the "real" world, outside the pages of her novel. The novel's speakers include Jane Addams; Johanne Rambusch, from Denmark; Lida Gustava Heymann, from Munich; Rosika Schwimmer, from Buda Pesth [sic]; Louie Bennet, Dublin; Emily Hobhouse, London; Clara Zettkin, Stuttgart. After Addams read an early draft of the novel, she wrote to Gale that it "does seem most important that women should be able to formulate a sense of kindred, which certainly is sadly needed at this time" (July 29, 1915, SHSW). She also sent Gale a copy of the speech she gave at The Hague, which Gale incorporated into the novel.

In their efforts to convince their audience, the women don't pull any punches; they are, for 1915, rather blunt about the effects of war on women. Rosika Schwimmer tells the audience that "they don't want us to find out that there is no glory, no big patriotism, no love for anything noble, nothing but butchery and slaughter and rape." Without flinching, she goes on to explain that

> you know the story of the War-brides. You know how agents of the different churches compete with military rulers in glorifying this kind of prostitution. But do you know of the concentration camps with the compulsory service of women? You may have seen the full reports of the atrocities committed on the Belgian women—but you didn't the get the other reports about the same kind of atrocities committed by *all* armies on female human beings between the ages of five and eighty-nine in all the countries where the game of war is being played. *Women of the world, what are we waiting for?* (206)[6]

From this argument, the talk turns to pragmatics: how best to shift the world from a "psychology of war" to a "psychology of peace." One speaker mentions that "war depends on economic conditions beyond our control," to which someone replies that just as "trade was a thought before it was trade," so too might it be with peace—just a thought at the moment, but on the verge of becoming a reality. Other speakers and audience members make the connections between "unfair trade legislation by one country against another down to the sale of toy weapons and soldiers; and from competing expenditures for national defence down to military drills in schools and colleges" (215). By establishing the links between governmental and individual behaviors, Gale tries to show her readers that pacifism is not merely about stopping the war in Europe but is against militarism in all its manifestations. The novel calls for a drastic paradigm shift, away from "war . . . the out-worn way to settle differences" to a "world programme for permanent peace without armistice and a council of nations looking toward the federation of the world" (216–17).

Gale's vision and the vision shared by other feminist pacifists is global, not particular. Inger's transformation is complete only after he accepts that "the people are heart's kindred, met here for their world-work, which the nations must cease to interrupt" (234). His moment of spiritual unity—of empathy beyond the border of his own experience—is the hallmark of Gale's spiritual belief. It is also one of the touchstones for her feminism, as well: that women should be able to imagine themselves with their sisters all over the world. One of the reasons why the pacifist movement, in its most radical feminist pacifist guise, posed such a threat to national governments is that it called for the dissolution of nationalist boundaries in favor of a global community. In *Three Guineas* (1938), Virginia Woolf articulates this idea in her formulation that "as a woman, I have no country. As a woman I want no country. As a woman my country is the whole world" (109). In much the same way that Gale refused to participate in *any* war-related activities, including relief work, Woolf goes on to say that a pacifist woman "will bind herself to take no share in patriotic demonstrations; to assent to no form of national self-praise; to make no part of any claque or audience that encourages war; to absent herself from military displays, tournaments, tattoos, prize-givings, and all such ceremonies as encourage the desire to impose 'our' civilization or 'our' dominion upon other people" (109). Pacifism, insists Gale, will "know nothing of treaties; nor will it know anything of those other ways of secret warfare by which great nations seem to keep clean hands: the ways of 'high' finance through 'peaceful penetration' . . . it will know nothing of nations. The little loyalties will go. National pride, national 'honor,' patriotism—all the little scaffolds will fall away" (218). Nationalism, in Gale's mind, provides both the rhetorical rationale and the practical excuse for militarism of all sorts, and should thus be avoided or eradicated altogether. This is Inger's final lesson and the final lesson of the novel itself: national boundaries are not worth fighting for because ultimately, they are only constructs, imagined lines that could just as easily be redrawn in other directions, binding us together rather than keeping us apart.

As a pacifist feminist, Gale occupied a risky position, as did her like-minded comrades. While *Heart's Kindred* ends on an optimistic note—Inger's transformation, we are to believe, could be our own—the members of the WPP and the women who attempted to travel to the ICW meeting in The Hague experienced governmental harassment and public outrage.[7] Although *Heart's Kindred* is not Gale's best work, writing it—and confronting the U.S. military establishment—helped her begin to break away from Friendship Village, a break that, as we have seen, she would complete with the publication of *Miss Lulu Bett*. In the novels she published after *Heart's Kindred*, Gale's work reveals her disappointment with a world and a town that embraced militarism. Gale's pacifist position did not soften as the war progressed; she remained adamantly against nationalism and refused to be involved with any war-related activities. She wrote to Addams that she wished

> we might keep the Peace Party, as a party, clear of all that save for which it was organized. In all this raising of $100,000 for the Red Cross, in all the enhancement of effort toward organized relief, can not the Party, as a party, stand . . . for its purpose, its reason for being. . . . For it seems to me with deep conviction that in this insistence our duty lies, rather than in such suggestion as that of 'showing loyalty and patriotism by offering our services for work' . . . [or] 'of each state Branch [of the WPP] entering some form of public service and thus letting our opponents perceive our readiness to serve our country.'—Those suggestions were made in April to the state chairmen, but . . . I cannot bear that the Woman's Peace Party, as a party, should do relief work in war time. It seems to me far worse than the suffrage party, as a party, rolling bandages. It is vitally important that a strong anti-war party should persist; and if the woman's branch of that anti-war party slips into woman's ancient work of relief and conservation so now invited by war, surely it will lose some great indefinable strength of spirit. (June 16, 1917, SHSW)

Gale herself was against participating in war-relief work, as this letter clearly demonstrates, but she nevertheless saw that for many women such activities provided an unprecedented opportunity to participate in public life.[8] Her awareness that many women found war work liberating becomes a thread through her last collection of Friendship Village stories, *Peace in Friendship Village*, in which she uses her small town to critique national and political ideologies.

Gale's pacifist feminism runs through the entire collection of stories, which were written between 1913 and 1919. The two stories in the collection that were written at the close of the war reflect Gale's faith in the League of Nations as a beginning point for a more peaceful, unified world, a belief she shared with many of her feminist pacifist colleagues. When the war was over, the WPP changed its name to the Women's International League for Peace and Freedom (WILPF) and opened its membership to women from all nations. The WILPF protested the terms of the Versailles Treaty, which included placing all the blame for the war on Germany. The women approved the terms of the League of Nations but thought that membership should be open to all nations and that the operating principles should be more democratic. They also wanted inclusion of a "Women's Charter," which would stress equal rights and opportunity for all women including suffrage, protection against slavery, property and civil rights after marriage, equal child custody rights, the right to retain citizenship instead of automatically losing it upon marriage, open education and job opportunities, equal pay for equal work, the end of prostitution, legitimizing the rights of children born out of wedlock and the responsibilities of the father to that child; food for children and—perhaps the most radical plank of all—"economic provision for the service of motherhood" (Alonso 82). In the early 1920s, the women who were members of the WILPF were harassed by the government, which caused some women to lose their jobs and others to be put on government lists as "dangerous, destructive, and anarchistic" (Alonso 83). Late in her life, Gale rather proudly told a friend that she had been included on this list.

In its satiric portraits of contemporary U.S. society, *Peace in Friendship Village* indicates the direction of Gale's future work and illuminate several of Gale's ongoing themes: the importance of women's work and women's communities, the necessity of breaking down the barriers created by xenophobia and nationalism, and the recognition of community responsibility and interconnectedness. Although Gale's pacifism is clearly a force in these stories, she takes a less dogmatic approach than in *Heart's Kindred*. The women in Friendship Village speak for many women who experienced a loss of purpose after the war, when their labors on behalf of the war effort were deemed no longer necessary. "We've been some use in the world," sighs one young woman, "and now we've got to go back to being nothing but happy." Her friend observes that "we'll have to play bridge five nights a week to keep from being bored to tears," to which another woman replies: "We can't go back to that. . . . At least, I *won't* go back to that. But what I'm going to do I don't know." Calliope realizes that "it was a shame to close down the Red Cross and send them back to their separate church choirs and such, to operate in, exclusive" (3).[9]

The older members of the Ladies Sodality also feel an encroaching purposelessness, wondering, "What under the sun are we going to do now that our war work's done?" Calliope observes that "of course we were all going to do what we could to help all Europe, but saving food is kind of a negative activity, and besides us ladies had always done it. Whereabouts was the novelty of that?" (21). Mis' Sykes, who wants always to have an answer, although Calliope usually proves her wrong, suggests triumphantly that "there's some talking about more military preparedness right off, I hear. That means for another war. Why not us start in and knit for it *now?*" (22). The solution to the women's sense of loss comes in the form of community work—but for a different community than they are used to. Instead of beautifying parks and implementing hygiene programs, they will work with the newly arrived European immigrants who have settled in Friendship Village. Calliope realizes that the relationship between the immigrants and Friendship Village will be a reciprocal one; that there is a thing or two that "they [the immigrants] can teach us" (19).

Despite Calliope's tolerant views, many Ladies Sodality members—and the town itself—initially display the xenophobic attitudes that swept the United States during and after World War I. The European immigrants all live in the Flats, on the outskirts of the village, which "didn't seem ever to count real regular in real Friendship Village doings. For instance, the town was just getting in sewerage, but it wasn't to go in down on the Flats and no one seemed surprised" (26). Mis' Sykes continues the distinction between "us" and "them" when she warns people to lock their doors because of the "foreigners" in town. Calliope attempts to break down this distinction by asking her, "Where were your mother and father born . . . and *their* folks, where'd *they* come from?" When Mis' Sykes gets to the inevitable "there was three brothers come over together," Calliope pounces:

> Well, where'd they come from? And where'd their folks come from? Were they immigrants to America, too? Or did they just stay foreigners in England or Germany or Scandinavia or Russia, maybe? . . . For all we know, it takes in a dozen nations with their blood flowing, sociable, in with yours. It's awful hard for any of us . . . to find a real race to be foreign to. I wouldn't bet I was foreign to no one . . . nor that no one was foreign, for certain, to me. (54)

Calliope, as one Sodality member complains, "don't draw the line *nowheres*" (208). The Sodality ladies break down their nationalist barriers, however, when they go down to the Flats to try to find the mother of a child who has suddenly appeared on Mis' Sykes's front stoop. Because the child cannot speak English, the women have no choice but to go door to door, hoping to reunite mother and child. When the mother is finally found, Calliope says, "We couldn't make more head nor tail out of what she was saying. . . . But we could understand without understanding . . . it was in her heart" (38). All the women, it seems, speak this heart language—somehow they even figure out that the little boy had strayed away from his older sister, who was supposed to mind him—and as a result, the

women from the village suddenly realize that "it don't look . . . like we'd
have a very hard time knowing what to do with ourselves." They decide
to "teach them women how to feed [their children] better and cost no
more . . . [how to] take care of them when they're sick" (43). Even more
importantly, sewerage, and what Mis' Toplady calls the "skeptic tank" get
laid to the Flats, because "it belong[s] there just exactly as much as in the
residence part." Unlike the story "Dream," in which Calliope's vision of a
unified town proves to be illusory, in this story, the title comes true: there
really is "Peace in Friendship Village."

Calliope, like Gale, refuses to "draw lines" between us and them; she
also sees that Friendship Village will benefit from its new immigrant
neighbors. One of *Peace in Friendship Village*'s central themes is this an-
tixenophobic, antinativist message, most clearly expressed in "The Story
of Jeffro," first published in *Everybody's Magazine* in 1915. When she
reprinted the story in *Peace in Friendship Village*, Gale added a prefatory
note that highlighted the story's message:

> When I have told the story of Jeffro, the alien, someone has always said:
> "Yes, but there's another side to that. They aren't all Jeffros." When stories
> are told of American gentleness, childlike faith, sensitiveness to duty, love
> of freedom, I do not remember to have heard anyone rejoin: "Yes, but
> Americans are not all like that." So I wonder why this comment should be
> made about Jeffro.(45)

Jeffro, a Jewish immigrant to Friendship Village who wants only to earn
enough money to pay for his wife's passage to the United States, embodies
the virtues that Gale lists here as "American." Despite this, Jeffro is called
"that Jew peddler" by inhabitants of Friendship Village, is shot by soldiers
who are trying to break through a picket line that he has joined, and loses
his tiny savings account when the town bank collapses. When he hears
about the bank collapse, he exclaims to Calliope: "And now I understand.
You throw dust in our eyes, free fire-engines, free letter-carriers, free this
and free that, and all the time somebody must be laughing at how it makes
us fools! I hate America. Being free here, it is a lie!" (70) Eventually, however, the town rallies to his aid—helping him plant a garden, finding him
work—and Calliope thinks that perhaps "Friendship Village knows things
America hasn't found out yet—but of course that can't be so" (74). The
story suggests that Calliope's fist thought is correct: Friendship Village *had*
discovered something that America had not, and her words caution Americans against blindly believing in their own superiority.

All of Gale's fiction resists the nativist attitudes pervasive in the
post–World War I United States. In an unpublished story about a Jewish

caddy at a WASP-y country club, Gale continues the argument against anti-Semitism that she began in "The Story of Jeffro." When the elegant Miss Oliphant selects Hugo as her caddy, he tells her, "What little blood I have . . . is Jewish blood." Miss Oliphant doesn't mind, however: "What's your middle name and when's your birthday and what's your favorite flower and, Hugo, I care just as much about one as another and as to blood, you ought to drink more orange juice and milk. Go and get some, before we start" (2). In "The Feast of Nations," Calliope tells Mis' Sykes that she has a "strain of . . . English and a touch of me way back was Scotch-Irish and I've got a little Welsh. And I'd like to find some Indian but I haven't ever done it. And I'm proud of them all" (4). *Peace in Friendship Village* combats domestic rather than international battles, and articulates a vision of a cosmopolitan United States that finds difference exciting and energizing rather than threatening. In *Postethnic America* (1995), David Hollinger defines a cosmopolitan society as being "more oriented to the individual, whom it is likely to understand as a member of a number of different communities simultaneously" (86). Calliope's cosmopolitan vision allows her to see that Jeffro belongs both to Friendship Village and to the "old world" where his wife still lives, while his presence in town improves both his own life and the life of the town itself; it is a reciprocal relationship. Gale's feminist pacifism leads her to reject the racist and nativist attitudes that mark so much of the U.S. fiction produced in the years during and after World War I; Calliope believes that at the end of the war, everyone will become members of the "League of the World" and stop fighting over "which [country] was the best one" (18). Rather than privileging "American-ness" as some sort of ultimate goal, Gale's stories seek what Hollinger describes as the cosmopolitan goal of "voluntary affiliations of wide compass" (86). Thus although Gale's pacifist fiction seems to uphold traditional images of women—compassionate, peaceful, maternal in their outlook if not in physical fact—she deploys these images to radical ends, seeking always to create a world in which the "little scaffolds" of nationalism, chauvinism, and racism cease to matter.

II

Next to Gale's adamant pacifism, Wharton's and Cather's war writing looks almost jingoistic by comparison; their war novels seem, on the surface, to tell the sorts of stories against which Gale was writing. Both *One of Ours* and *A Son at the Front* draw on a number of war-novel conventions: young men eager to do battle; grieving parents and sweethearts;

beautiful nurses; hospital scenes and tearful partings; heroes and cowards. Both novels also demonstrate an awareness of the homoerotics of soldiering, another hallmark of World War I fiction. In addition, they both interrogate the structure of the "war novel" and describe the conflicted awareness of the postwar artist, themes that emerge in both the canonical literature about the war and the writing at the core of so-called high modernism. Cather's experiments with structure and voice and Wharton's depiction of an artist struggling with questions about the place of art in the postwar world would seem to position these two novels squarely within the intersecting canons of modernism and war fiction, but this is far from the case. Instead, these novels are considered minor works that fail to do justice to their subject, a testament to the sturdiness of the gender–genre boundary, which precludes the possibility that a woman could write a "good" war novel.

Most of the reviews of *One of Ours* upheld this gender–genre boundary and lambasted Cather for attempting to write about the war. Paradoxically, however, it was the first of Cather's novels to hit the best-seller lists and was particularly popular with soldiers. Claude Wheeler, the protagonist of *One of Ours*, seems like precisely the type of man Gale wanted to rescue from recruitment manual rhetoric. Claude thinks of the war only in terms of heroism and glory; he believes in all the jingoist language and never changes his mind, even at the moment of his death. He embodies what much of America wanted to believe about itself when it entered the war—that they were larger-than-life heroes who would rescue the world. Elizabeth Sergeant notes that *One of Ours* was popular because "thousands of American parents and many American veterans, too, saw the rewards of their sacrifices here displayed gloriously" (181). From the moment Claude enlists, he burns with patriotic passion: "He believed that he was going abroad with an expeditionary force that would make war without rage, with uncompromising generosity and chivalry" (1194). Claude "loved the men he trained with—wouldn't choose to live in any better company" (1194). He is an unrepentant romantic, and it is his romantic voice that contributed both to the drubbing the novel took at the hands of reviewers and to its immense popularity. It is easy to read the novel's tricky narrative structure and believe that the novel upholds Claude's romanticism. But in fact, the novel interrogates Claude's viewpoint and finds it wanting almost from the very beginning: this novel represents the death of Cather's romantic voice, the voice that had been hailed by critics as the memorialist of the prairies and the "immigrant experience."

In writing *One of Ours*, Cather drew on the literary power she had established by writing about the prairies and asserted herself further by crossing the boundary between gender and genre. Just as she claimed that she wrote about the prairie before it was fashionable, so too did she claim the war as her subject before it was considered a fit subject for a woman. Claude Wheeler—whose name inverts Cather's own monogram—is a physically strong, inarticulate farm boy who longs for art and beauty but has no talent other than appreciation. He feels trapped on his family's Nebraska farm, a marked shift from the sense of liberation and grandeur that the prairie offers in *My Ántonia* and *O Pioneers!*. His experience reflects a comment that Cather made in a letter to Sergeant, in which she said whenever she visited the prairie it was only a matter of time before she began to think she would die in the cornfields (April 20, 1912, Morgan Library). In her representation of Claude's plight, Cather draws on her own sense of how oppressive bourgeois life could be, but she keeps from him the resources that allowed her to make her own escape.

Claude knows that he is a misfit in his Nebraska world, which is why enlisting seems to him a miraculous opportunity. Becoming a soldier transforms him into someone else, at least in his own opinion, and allows him to flee family, wife, and responsibility through a socially sanctioned escape hatch. While Claude's need to escape is presented sympathetically, and the people from whom he escapes are for the most part truly awful, his romantic outlook is at least partially responsible for his sense of entrapment. His romantic vision literally blinds him to the realities of his world: he cannot see, for example, that marriage to cold Enid Royce will be a terrible mistake, because he believes that all marriages were "transforming" and could change a "cool, self-satisfied girl into a loving generous one" (1078).[10] And even though the marriage is a disaster, Claude never allows himself to think about why; he merely substitutes myths about war for his marriage myths; he believes that soldiering will transform him and make his life important.

Claude's romanticism dies with him on the battlefield, but the novel has been demythologizing those romantic ideals from its very beginning. His family represents an unromantic, antipastoral vision of rural America; every member of the family is narrow-minded and parochial, each in a different way: religion, technology, money, and anti-intellectualism all become blinders. Jason Royce, Enid's father, tries point-blank to change Claude's outlook by telling him that "pretty near everything you believe about life—about marriage especially—is lies" (1059). Royce's conversation with Claude is also Cather's conversation with the ideas expressed by Josiah Royce in *The World and the Individual* (1901). Cather would have been familiar with Royce's work through her association with Annie Fields, who also knew Royce. According to Warner Berthoff, Royce believed that a "philosophy of loyalty" could solve the pressing issue of "existential trust, of whether the individual consciousness could keep its bearings and organize its own destiny against the depersonalizing expansions of modern history" (496). Loyalty, Royce argued, was the antidote for both spiritual and social alienation. Claude—the individual set adrift in the world—finds a place for himself through his loyalty to his comrades-in-arms, although ultimately he is destroyed by these beliefs. Roycean idealism dies with Claude, although Claude's mother, as I will discuss, remains loyal to Claude's memory and uses his death to keep her bearings in the postwar world. Although he tries to warn Claude against marrying Enid, Jason Royce knows that "he had no words, no way to make himself understood. He had no argument to present. . . . The dead might as well speak to the living as the old to the young." His sense of futility deepens when he sees Claude's face "with its expression of reticent pride . . . and the slight stiffness of his shoulders, set in a kind of stubborn *loyalty*" (125, emphasis added). Against Claude's loyal belief in the transformative power of marriage, Royce cannot hope to prevail. All he can do is hope that Claude will not suffer too many "heart-breaking disappointments."

In the Nebraska section of the novel, Royce's view of marriage is entirely accurate; none of the marriages appear satisfactory. And in the novel as a whole, the most satisfying emotional relationships are between same-sex couples: Mrs. Wheeler and Mahailey, Sergeant Hicks and Dell Able, Claude and David Gerhardt.[11] There is no heterosexual happiness; men and women exist in a state of perpetual misunderstanding and mismatchedness. The prewar world, in this novel, does not reveal an idyllic golden age, although Cather's comments after the war, particularly her observation that the "world broke in two in 1922 or thereabouts," suggest that she wanted to convince herself otherwise. *One of Ours* demonstrates that the world was breaking in two even before the war and that Claude and his kind are just some of many who fell between the cracks.

Even in France, where Claude feels utterly at home, Cather continues to undermine Claude's idealism and to reveal its limitations. As in other novels, in *One of Ours*, Cather juxtaposes the idyllic with the horrific, although Claude is consistently unable to see horror. Exemplifying this uneasy juxtaposition is the moment when Claude and his men find a water-filled shellhole and use the opportunity to bathe and relax in the sunshine—until Claude pulls up a German helmet from the bottom of the ditch, displacing the dead body decomposing in the mud and forcing a huge bubble of noxious gas to the surface of the water. Claude doesn't realize what he has done, even after the other men explain it to him; it is as if he is incapable of seeing evil or ugliness. Among his comrades-in-arms, Claude feels completely content; he is convinced that in France he might have the "kind of life he wanted" but could not have in Nebraska, where people were always "buying and selling, building and pulling down." His romantic exuberance finds its expression in wartime France and in his friendship with David Gerhardt, which flowers into the most passionate bond in the novel. Gerhardt, Claude realizes, is the man he has been hunting for his entire life: "some one whom he could admire without reservations; some one he could envy, emulate, wish to be. Now he believed that . . . he must have had some faint image of a man like Gerhardt in his mind" (1259). Despite his strong feelings for Gerhardt, he refuses to believe Gerhardt's comment that the war has "killed everything," including music and the arts (1265). He clings to his romantic visions of soldiers and war even when confronted with clear evidence to the contrary. When Claude leads his men through the French countryside, for example, he wears a "stoical countenance, afraid of betraying his satisfaction in the men, the weather, the country" (1217). But the narrative voice counters Claude's perspective, first by echoing Claude's naïve view of war in the comment that the men "were bound for the big show and on every hand were reassuring signs," which sounds like something that Claude would say, and then by describing a distinctly non-reassuring sight: "long lines of gaunt, dead trees, charred and torn; big holes gashed out in fields and hillsides . . . winding depressions in the earth . . . endless straggling lines of rusty barbed wire, that seemed to have been put there by chance" (1217). There is no humanity or cultivation left in the French farmland through which Claude marches so proudly, and although the narrator sees this, Claude has eyes only for the soldiers, whom he sees as "the finest sight in the world" (1217). Claude's idealism renders him unable to see the ravaged countryside; he does not see the effects of war. But although Claude is blind to this, the novel itself is not. It is, instead, a deeply ironic account of one young man's failure to shake off the illusions of youth; the entire novel is, as Merrill Skaggs has pointed out, "bathed and saturated in irony" (40).

Claude's death scene is often pointed to by critics who want to define the novel as a clichéd failure, but doing so does not take into account the myriad ways in which Cather creates a counternarrative to Claude's. One of the most famous mis-readers of Claude's death scene was Ernest Hemingway, whose biting comments contributed to the novel's poor reception. In a letter to Edmund Wilson, Hemingway wrote: "Wasn't that last scene in the lines wonderful? Do you know where it came from? The battle scene in *Birth of a Nation*. I identified episode after episode, Catherized. Poor woman she has got to get her war experience somewhere" (105).[12] Sounding like Wharton's Harold Harbard, Hemingway dismisses the possibility that in fact, Cather did know what she was doing when she created Claude's grand death scene with all its rhetorical flourishes. Claude stands on a parapet, commanding his men to hold steady against the enemy onslaught, but he is not afraid: "The men behind him had become like rock. . . . With these men he could do anything. . . . The blood dripped down his coat, but he felt no weakness. He felt only one thing; that he commanded wonderful men. . . . They were mortal, but they were unconquerable" (1292). These are Claude's last thoughts before he is shot; they are clichéd, true, but what Cather is presenting is Claude's death as he would have described it. Good soldiers, in Claude's mind, only die good and noble deaths.

As soon as Claude dies, however, the voice of the romantic vanishes and gives way to the novel's final critique of military idealism. The scene immediately following Claude's death takes place aboard a ship that is bringing his comrades back to America, but their attitudes are strikingly different from Claude's. The men aboard the ship are "not the same men who went away" (1294). The most bitter voice is that of Sergeant Hicks, whose face has taken on a "slightly cynical expression" (1295) because of "the way in which glittering honors bump down on the wrong heads in the army and palms and crosses blossom on the wrong breasts" (1295). Hicks is in mourning for his friend Dell Able, with whom he had planned to start a repair shop after the war. Now he sees that perhaps the military does not treat all men equally, that the "wrong men" get honors, and good men are left alone and disillusioned. In honor of his dead friend, he plans to "conduct a sort of memorial shop . . . with 'Hicks and Able' over the door" (1295). Like a pining sweetheart who refuses to remove the dead lover's photo from the wall, Hicks will create a sort mechanistic memento mori; he will assuage his grief by looking at the "logical and beautiful inwards [sic] of automobiles for the rest of his life" (1295). The war has swept away everything else; all that will remain for Hicks is the purity of a mechanical engine.

Hicks's plans for the future are the final words heard from a man; the conclusion of the novel belongs to Claude's mother, whose voice bids farewell to romanticism and ushers in a new world. As if to underscore the importance of female voices in this apparently male novel, the final words of the novel come from Mahailey, who believes that Claude is in heaven with God, which in Mahailey's cosmology means "directly overhead, not so very far above the kitchen stove" (1297). Claude—and God—are both domesticated, transformed into kitchen gods, Mahailey's own personal Penates, the twin Roman household gods of the storeroom.[13] Mahailey's observation brings the war story and the war hero home, makes him a subject for her own kitchen musings. Cather based Claude on her cousin, who had died on the French battlefields, but she dedicates the novel to her mother, which means that Claude's story is flanked by women's voices, by mothers. Sharon O'Brien suggests that "the dedication [implies] that the mothers . . . and the daughters . . . may both appropriate and pass on the power to tell men's stories" (200). The most important woman telling men's stories is Cather herself. She will go on to range even further afield, as if licensed by having told Claude's story, telling the stories of Bishop Latour, Professor St. Peter, and Frontenac. Claude's death, the death of the romantic hero, offers Cather a new beginning.

The novel's final section, which takes place "by the banks of Lovely Creek where it all began," also illustrates the beginnings of Cather's new style, the "novel démeublé," the unfurnished novel. The only people left in this final section are Mrs. Wheeler and Mahailey, who "think . . . together like one person." There are no men in their world except their memories of Claude—all of the other Wheeler men have vanished. When the War Department representative calls with the news of Claude's death, he asks to speak to Mr. Wheeler, but he is not there to take the call. Mr. Wheeler never reappears and neither do his sons, although there is no mention of them enlisting, being drafted, or dying— they are all just absent. Despite her grief at Claude's death, Mrs. Wheeler is glad that Claude has been spared the fate of other returning soldiers, whom she reads about in the newspapers: "Airmen whose deeds were tales of wonder, officers whose names made the blood of youth beat faster . . . one by one they quietly die by their own hand" (1296). Wartime romanticism, it seems, can kill, and although the war may produce heroes, ultimately heroes don't survive: women do.

Mrs. Wheeler and Mahailey have clearer ideas than the Wheeler men about what the war meant from its earliest mention in the newspapers. When Mrs. Wheeler and Claude discuss the possibility of the United States entering the war, Claude thinks that "party politics" will have nothing to do with military decisions, but Mrs. Wheeler observes that she's "never yet found a public question in which there wasn't party politics" (1106). It is "the women, American and foreign-born," who dig around in attics and closets, "hunting for a map" in order to follow news reports about the war. And Mahailey, the Wheeler's hired "girl" (although she is well into middle age), is the only one in the household who had "seen war with her own eyes," and her dim memories of the Civil War are very different from Claude's idea that war can be fought without rage. Mahailey knows that war results in women "huntin' for somethin' to cook with . . . [having] no stove nor no dishes nor nothin'" and boys dying "by inches" of gangrene. She has seen soldiers with "bleeding feet" and backs "raw as beef" where they have scratched their lice bites (1138, 1107). Through

her portrayal of Mrs. Wheeler and Mahailey, Cather also further dero-
manticizes life on the farm. At harvest time, while the men work in the
fields, Mahailey and Mrs. Wheeler "always lost weight . . . just as the
horses did" because they work in kitchen baking "pies and cakes and
bread loaves as fast as the oven would hold them . . . the range was stoked
like the fire-box of a locomotive" (1065). They work like animals or factory hands, a far cry from the glorious images of Ántonia and Alexandra.
Mrs. Wheeler and Mahailey have the novel's last words; it is their clear,
slightly bitter vision that guides the novel's final pages.

The final scene of the novel thus gives the postwar world to women
like Cather herself: a middle-aged woman living with a slightly subordinate female companion.[14] In constructing the conclusion to her novel,
Cather quite literally strips her narrative of almost everything; all that remains is the two women and the farm kitchen wherein they work end-
lessly, feeling Claude "always there, beyond everything else, at the farthest
edge of consciousness, like the evening sun on the horizon" (1295). The
ending of the novel reveals the beginning of Cather's new voice, the "unfurnished" style that she called for in "The Novel Démeublé," which she
published in the *New Republic* five months prior to *One of Ours*.[15] In this
essay she argues that a novel needs the "inexplicable presence of the thing
not named, of the overtone divined by the ear but not heard by it." This
intangible aura gives fiction its "high quality," but it also implies that a
novel needs a good reader, which is how Mrs. Wheeler reads Claude's letters: she "*divines* so much that he did not write . . . knows what to read
into those short flashes of enthusiasm" (1296, emphasis added). Mrs.
Wheeler reads Claude's printed words, but like the reader in "The Novel
Démeublé," she divines what is not there, as well; her ear catches the
overtones, the emotional aura of Claude's "flashes of enthusiasm." Cather
ends the "The Novel Démeublé" by citing Dumas's comment that "to
make a drama, a man needed one passion, and four walls." In the emotional drama between Mrs. Wheeler, Mahailey, and Claude's memory,
Cather demonstrates her theory; it is this "unfurnished" aesthetic that
governs the conclusion of *One of Ours*, and that creates the design for
Cather's other novels of the twenties.

"The Novel Démeublé" also demonstrates Cather's desire to forestall
criticism about *One of Ours;* the essay is her opening salvo against those
who patrol the gender–genre boundary. In addition to calling for an "unfurnished" style, Cather reminds her readers that journalism and fiction
are separate and distinct genres that should not be confused with one another. Instead of worrying about authenticity in their fiction, writers
should worry more about emotional accuracy, about creating that "inexplicable presence." A novel, she contends, "cannot be at the same time a

vivid and brilliant form of journalism" (*Not Under Forty* 48). "Mere verisimilitude" is not enough to create a convincing fiction; novels should not just "minutely and unsparingly describ[e] physical sensations." In making these distinctions, Cather attempts to teach people how to read her novel, reminding them that what matters is how well "literalness" becomes part of the "emotional penumbra of the characters themselves" (48). Reviewers and critics, however, were generally unwilling to allow her novel this imaginative leeway, and the novel was lambasted on the grounds she had attempted to eradicate: it was deemed an unrealistic presentation of the war.

III

Both *A Son at the Front* and *One of Ours* are inspired by the death of a young man whom the authors knew (Ronald Simmons and G. P. Cather, respectively), and both describe the war through the eyes of a man, although Cather combines Claude's narrative with other voices, including Mrs. Wheeler's. With its "unfurnished" ending, *One of Ours* gestures toward Cather's new style, an implicit new beginning that Wharton's novel makes explicit. Her novel ends with the word "began," as her artist-hero starts a new piece of work. And like Mrs. Wheeler, the protagonist of *A Son at the Front* is a middle-aged parent whose son dies in the war, leaving him behind to inherit the postwar world. John Campton is a successful painter, one of Wharton's only successful artist figures, who, much like Wharton herself, has found his niche both socially and artistically only after reaching middle age. Campton and his ex-wife Julia are much concerned with the fate of their son, George. Because of circumstances beyond his parents' control, George was born in Paris and thus, as a French citizen, will be mobilized when the French declare war on Germany. When George joins the army, Campton, Julia, and Julia's second husband, Anderson Brant, scheme to keep him away from the fighting. George goes along with this scheme, pretending to have an office job and sending letters home to that effect, although he has in fact joined the troops at the front (telling only his stepfather and an old family friend, Adele Anthony). George is wounded once, recovers, is wounded again and dies from complications following the second injury. The title of the novel notwithstanding, Wharton's novel actually does not spend much time at the front, although she had visited the front lines a number of times. Paris during the war is a world inverted: society women become nurses, foppish men become heroes, pacifists become warmongers, and artists become charity workers. Wharton's novel details the effect the war has—for both good and ill—on those who don't fight and dramatizes what would become one of the central issues for the writers of the high modernist period: how do art and war coexist?

Until the war in Europe begins, Campton has always isolated himself from the world around him, including his family; he believes that emotional ties interfere with his art. Because of this he has allowed Julia and Brant to raise George, although he resents Brant's money and is jealous of George's affection for his stepfather. Adele Anthony supports his rationalization by telling him that "if you'd let everything else go to keep George you'd never have become the great John Campton: the *real* John Campton you were meant to be. And it wouldn't have been half as satisfactory for you—or for George either. Only . . . somebody had to blow the child's nose, and pay his dentist and doctor . . . you ought to be grateful to Anderson for doing it. Aren't there bees or ants, or something, that are kept for such purposes?" (117). Her observation dryly reduces Brant to a drone, someone who does the dirty work, like the French peasant women who clean Campton's studio and prepare his food. Eventually, however, the novel demonstrates that Campton's isolationism is untenable, and he moves out of his artistic solipsism. Campton's position reflects America's neutrality at the beginning of the war, which Wharton despised as cowardly; she wrote to Minnie Cadwalader Jones in 1915 that President Wilson's neutrality policy made her "not very proud just now of being an American" (qtd. in Benstock 313).

Campton, like Wharton herself when the war began, is a celebrity in the world of high society; after years of struggle his work has achieved a critical success that he is beginning to parlay into financial security. Among the wealthy international residents of Paris, it has become a mark of social standing to be "done by Campton," although he makes it "as difficult and as expensive as possible . . . it was known that one had to accept the master's conditions or apply elsewhere" (5). Campton desires artistic celebrity because it brings wealth, which he wants so that he can woo George away from Brant's money. In his elitist fashion, Campton assumes that his wealth is somehow culturally and morally superior to Brant's, which comes from pedestrian things like banks and investments. Campton's fame brings with it an unexpected set of difficulties when the war begins, however: people seek him out because he is a public figure, hoping that he will lend his name—and his art—to their various war-related causes. Whenever he ventures out of his studio, he is "waylaid by flustered compatriots [saying] . . . 'Oh, Mr. Campton, you don't know me, but of course all Americans know *you!*'" (82). His carefully cultivated public image as a curmudgeon notwithstanding, he is asked to chair committees, to visit wounded soldiers in the hospital, to donate his work to charity bazaars. Campton dreads these demands, particularly the request to donate work to auctions: "No artist had a right to cheapen his art in that way," he thinks. He is afraid that if he suddenly begins to paint all the "unpaintable people" whose commissions he refused before the war, he will start "turning out work that would injure his reputation and reduce his sales after the war" (130). Both Campton and Wharton are aware that reputation and image must be carefully cultivated, protected, and preserved, but that preservation takes energy away from creating art.

Campton's struggle to maintain artistic independence in the face of pressing community need suggests Wharton's own ambivalence about being a public figure. On the one hand, she needs the financial security that comes with being a best-selling novelist, but on the other, being popular may cheapen her reputation and make her the victim of public desire. In the preface to *Ghosts* (1937), Wharton wrote that "I believe that most purveyors of fiction will agree with me that the readers who pour out on the author of a published book . . . floods of interrogatory ink pay little heed to the isolated tale in a magazine. The request to the author to reveal as many particulars as possible of his private life to his eager readers is seldom addressed to him till the scattered products of his pen have been collected in a volume" (*Uncollected* 271). Being a successful novelist brings with it an increased demand to reveal oneself to readers, which in turn creates an increased need for a public self that acts as a dam against the "interrogatory ink." Campton presents himself as a crank in order to stave off public attention; Wharton retreats to her country houses and immerses herself in relief efforts.

Campton feels that he is constantly subject to public scrutiny, but in fact he is more often the observer than the observed. The primary object of his observations is George, whose portrait was the hit of Campton's first big exhibit. George is Campton's favorite subject, but he hoards the work George inspires; he doesn't want anyone else to have the same pleasure in George's image that he does. Judith Sensibar notes that Campton's jealousy over the affection between Brant and George forms the novel's central love triangle (paralleled, on a lesser note, by the triangle between George, Mrs. Talkett, and her husband). This triangle demonstrates that Wharton, like Cather, was interested in probing what Sensibar calls the "homoerotic motifs and conventions of the Great War's masculinist literary canon" (195). Campton's jealousy of Brant consistently leads him to misread George's rather gentle stepfather. When Brant wants to buy Campton's first portrait of his son, Campton gives it to the Museum of Luxembourg, "with the object of inflicting the most cruel slight he could think of on the banker" (58). Campton finds satisfaction in thwarting Brant's desires, particularly where George is concerned; he lives in fear that "the picture might be sold [after his death], and fall into Brant's hands" (59). Although Campton had been rather uninvolved with George as a boy, now that George is a young man, Campton wants to lay the "foundation of a complete and lasting friendship with his only son, at the moment when such understandings do most to shape a youth's future" (12). Campton's desire is fueled by both love and rivalry; he adores his son, but he also wants to get George "finally and completely over to his side" (40), away from Anderson Brant. Before George leaves for the army, Campton hovers over him almost constantly, sketching him as often as he can, even when the boy is asleep. Looking in at his sleeping son, Campton sees "the sheet, clinging to his body, model[ing] his slim flank and legs. . . . For a long time Campton stood gazing . . . then . . . he began to draw, eagerly but deliberately . . . fascinated by the happy accident of the lighting and of the boy's position" (53). His adoration makes him into a voyeur, unable to resist watching his son even in his most private moments.

Looking at Campton looking at George, Wharton thus inverts Harbard's disdainful comment to Ivy Spang: Wharton, one of "we novelists," finds her "inexhaustible field" in beautiful men dressed in military uniforms—or sleeping apparently naked, covered only by a thin sheet. Harbard's remark was intended to confine Ivy to her photograph, and to chastise her for venturing into territory that only a man could really know or understand. In *A Son at the Front*, Wharton offers a rebuttal to Harbard's limited and limiting remark by bringing Campton and his son within the frame of her gaze. Women in this novel are secondary, peripheral characters, and the emotional and physical dynamics of men take center stage. Thus Campton's vaguely prurient stance over his son reveals Wharton's mastery of the field; she turns both the beautiful boy and his unhappy father into her primary objects of novelistic scrutiny.

Campton occasionally finds inspiration in women, but only rarely: once in Adele Anthony and once in Mrs. Talkett, a society woman who, unbeknownst to Campton, is having an affair with George. The sketches he does of Mrs. Talkett help him return to painting, which he had given up when the war started and George joined the army. Mrs. Talkett tells him that the charity work he has been doing is "dummy's work" and reminds him that George "would tell you to go back to your painting" (226). It is not her words that move him, however, but the shape of her body when she stands to put on her hat: "It had never before occurred to him that she was paintable; but as she stood there . . . the long line flowing from her wrist to her hip suddenly wound itself about him like a net" (227). Caught in the same net that has captured his son, although with a different desire, Campton decides that the war is "an old European disease" and begins again to paint. He loses himself in painting, seeing the world only as "lines, images, colours," experiencing a physical, sensual joy: "he felt a strange ease in every renovated muscle, and his model became like a musical instrument on which he played with careless mastery" (227). Mrs. Talkett's body helps him to regain "the lost world which was the only real one"—his art—but in that process she is reduced to an object, an "instrument" for Campton's pleasure.

Mrs. Talkett is beautiful but has a "thin personality"; his old friend Adele Anthony, on the other hand, has a strong personality but is quite plain. Mrs. Talkett volunteers as a nurse but quickly gives it up; Adele administers a relief foundation and aids newly arrived soldiers, but she is one of very few women so employed. Women, in this novel, are either beautiful or useful, and most of them are only beautiful. Like Ivy Spang, who has more success with her photo than with her writing, most of the women in Wharton's novel succeed only as beautiful objects; they fail when they try to assert themselves as anything else. Through the failed attempts of society women to transform themselves into useful workers, Wharton both satirizes those who dabble and illustrates how difficult it can be for women to find roles for themselves that are appropriate during wartime.

Perhaps not surprisingly, given Wharton's own incredibly successful efforts at relief work, it is the young women who are the least helpful and the middle-aged women who find meaningful work. Adele Anthony, whose "long pink-nosed face" was one of Campton's first critically acclaimed portraits, works at numerous war relief efforts with "humourous pertinacity." She can answer the American soldiers' "most disconcerting questions about Paris and France (Montmartre included) . . . [and] easily eclipsed the ministering angels who twanged the home-town chord and called them 'boys'" (417). Even Julia, Campton's shallow, middle-aged ex-wife, who is more interested in fashion and bridge than in war, has learned to be helpful: "Her experience as a nurse, disciplining a vague gift for the sickroom, had developed in her the faculty of self-command" (208). On the other hand, the younger women who volunteer as Red Cross nurses become "not the majestic figure of the Crimean legend, but the new version evolved in the rue de la Paix: short skirts, long ankles, pearls and curls . . . haggard with the perpetual hurry of the aimless" (143). Wharton's disdain for the Red Cross came from her own encounters with the organization in the course of her war work. She became so disenchanted with the organization that she wrote to Lewis Cass Ledyard, "It is impossible for me to collaborate any longer with the Red Cross. . . . I am quite determined not to give my name to organizations which, in the hands of the Red Cross, no longer represent my methods of dealing with the poor" (qtd. in Price 136). Wharton's "pearls and curls"

nurses, most of whom soon abandon their volunteer work, eventually affiliate themselves with a loose-knit group of speculators and profiteers,
who line their own pockets with money skimmed from charity or from
mysterious international involvements. Mrs. Talkett and her friends flirt
with being useful but ultimately cannot reinvent themselves as anything
other than decoration.

As the war drags on, Campton wrestles with his own version of the
same problem: during war does art become mere decoration? How can
he, an artist, be of use to the war effort? He is caught between his need
to spend "long solitary hours, in the empty and echoing temple of his art"
(373), and his desire to help, even indirectly, the cause for which George
is fighting. He stops painting when the war begins, telling himself that
the faces he saw "might be interesting to paint . . . if ever painting became
again thinkable" (175). But he also believes that the war is being fought
to protect France and thus, indirectly, art and artists: France had always
been "a luminous point about which striving visions and purposes could
rally . . . to thinkers, artists, to all creators, she had always been a second
country" (366).[16] This idealized vision of France makes the war into a
high-minded endeavor waged over aesthetics rather than empire; it also
rationalizes Campton's need to paint by implying that ceasing to paint
would be a betrayal of the very cause for which George is fighting.

Wharton believed that the war was worth fighting, but the novel criticizes Campton's aestheticized and abstracted image of war. The novel is
equally critical of extreme ideological positions, such as knee-jerk patriotism and do-nothing pacifism, which prove to be just as ineffective as
Campton's aesthetics. Wharton regards extremists of all stripes with particular suspicion and almost always finds their motives wanting. Mr.
Mayhew, for example, who begins the novel as a pacifist (en route to an
unnamed convention at The Hague), turns into a warmonger after he is
detained by the German government. Mayhew's anger at Germany is
aroused because his imprisonment feminizes him; he is forced into a position similar to that in which Harbard places Ivy. While in The Hague,
Mayhew was put in a German prison, along with "common thieves and
vagabonds—with—prostitutes." When he is released he is "kept . . .
under strict police surveillance, like . . . like an unfortunate woman . . . for
eight days: a week and one day over!" (140). Being reduced to an object
of scrutiny—becoming, as it were, the feminized object of Germany's "inexhaustible field"—so infuriates him that now he vows to "rouse public
opinion in America against a nation of savages who ought to be hunted
off the face of the globe like vermin." His patriotic sentiments are under-
mined, however, by the fact that he soon becomes one of those who
"speculate in war charities" (333). The desire for profit supersedes any

ideological convictions. Mayhew's ire demonstrates the connections between an imperiled masculinity and an overzealous nationalism that can lead to violence. Ultimately, none of Mayhew's responses to the war are satisfactory.

Mayhew's beliefs are obviously suspect, but the novel also scrutinizes the patriotism of those whose motives seem scrupulously pure. Mayhew's nephew, Benny Upsher, who wants so badly to fight that he lies about being Canadian in order to enlist with the English, is "mad," a madness to which even George is susceptible. When George tells his father that he is going back to the front after he has recovered from his first war wounds, Campton sees in his eyes a look "inaccessible to reason, beyond reason, belonging to other spaces, other weights and measures, over the edge, somehow, of the tangible calculable world" (359). George and Benny are lost to the rational world; being soldiers has rendered them unfit for existence anywhere other than at the front. While this may in fact be an accurate assessment of what happens to men at war, it also implies that—as with the end of Cather's novel—it is best that George dies, because he would be unable to live in a world not at war. Claude cannot live in the postwar world because he is too romantic; George cannot live in it because he is too much of a soldier.

George's death helps Campton find a balance between the demands of his art and the demands of the community. His initial response to George's death is rage and withdrawal; he hoards his grief the way he hoards his portraits of George. His only solace is wandering the streets of Paris looking at the faces of the newly arrived American soldiers: "He began to spend his days among the young American officers and soldiers, studying them . . . and then hurrying home to jot down his impressions" (412). He feeds on the soldiers' collective youth and energy like an artistic vampire, "haunting for hours every day one of the newly-opened Soldiers' and Sailors' Clubs," looking at "gaunt and serious or round and babyish young American faces," but he will never share the work he produces: "when their portraits were finished [he intended] to put them away, locked up for his own pleasure" (416). The soldiers are now his "one passion, his sustaining task"; all he wants to do is sketch "their *inexhaustibly inspiring* faces" (418, emphasis added). The soldiers have become Campton's inexhaustible field, and he uses them as instruments with which to soothe his grief.

Certain that no one grieves for George as deeply as he does, Campton initially rejects Brant and Julia's request that he create a memorial for George: "Suffering, suffering! What did any of them know about suffering?" (416). As he thinks further about Brant, however, Campton finds himself in sudden sympathy with his despised rival. He begins to see that in fact Brant will miss George more than either Campton or Julia, because Brant has nothing with which to fill the gap left by George's death. Campton has art and Julia will "fill up the void with the old occupations, with bridge and visits . . . at the dressmaker's" (423). Forced to confront his newfound sympathy for the man he had regarded as his rival for George's affections, Campton decides that "the only thing that helps is to be able to do things for people" and agrees to create George's memorial. Campton has been changed by the war, forced to see his relationships with others in a new light.

Campton's shift in attitude leads him to experiment with new media: the memorial will be not a painting but a sculpture, something the painter has never tried before. The novel's final paragraph illustrates his newfound energies: "The painter moved back to his long table. He had always had a fancy for modelling—had always had lumps of clay lying about within reach. He pulled out all the sketches of his son from the old portfolio, spread them before him on the table, and began" (426). Wharton ends her war novel—her final piece of fiction about the war—with a beginning, as if following Pound's dictum to "make it new." Campton's new project literally forces him to think in new dimensions; he moves from the two-dimensional surface of a canvas to the three-dimensional surface of a sculpture. In a letter praising Wharton's novel, Gale linked Wharton to her protagonist: "Your touch thrills me always with something beyond—delight . . . even though a book about war, tears me with our madness. And you *paint* with what quiet power all the waste and the wildness of it" (May 29, 1924, SHSW, emphasis added). After this novel, Wharton did go on to "paint" in a new way: almost all of her postwar novels, with few exceptions, address the contemporary postwar world, rather than the world of Old New York. After the war, both Wharton and Campton pull out their "old portfolios" but move in new directions, with new work, finding in their explorations a counterweight to the war's destruction.

Wharton experienced an explosion of artistic energy during the war years, despite her prodigious war relief work. During the period in which she wrote *A Son at the Front*, Wharton was writing "so much and so variously that she periodically lost track" and she had to divide letters to her publishers "into categories, a dozen or more per letter, most of them bearing the title of works in progress" (Lewis, *Wharton* 456). Like Campton for Brant, Wharton also developed new-found sympathy for that which she had once despised—in her case, American contemporary culture, which would increasingly become the subject of her postwar novels. Dale Bauer argues that after the war Wharton was increasingly "embroiled with and indebted to" an American culture that she could no longer "criticize . . . with the absolute certainty of her early fiction" (18). The conclusion of *A Son at the Front* shows Wharton's middle-aged artist firmly in control of his métier, willing to use his art to help others and to take artistic risks. This final scene offers a challenge not only to the Harold Harbards of the literary world but also to the Ivy Spangs, both of which might consider Wharton to be passé.

IV

Wharton's novel ends with an assertion of artistic power, but Wharton's own authority was severely questioned by reviewers, who greeted her novel much the way Harbard greets Ivy's story. The reviews for both Wharton's and Cather's novels fall into a pattern: when the reviews are positive, there is little or no mention of the war; but when the reviews are negative, the war becomes the central issue—and the cause for the novel's failure. As if in anticipation of this pattern, both Wharton and Cather attempted to present their novels as being about something other than the war. In a letter to a friend, Cather described how discouraging it was to have Claude thought of as a sentimental glorification of war when he was so clearly just a farm boy. She went on to say that she had tried to tell Claude's story without any literariness but that almost no one was able to read it as just a story of a boy; everyone, she complained, wanted to see it as a presentation of *the* American soldier. *One of Ours* was just a work of imagination, she argued, and not a piece of reporting (September 19, 1922, Morgan Library). Cather refuses the feminizing badge of sentimentality and—as always—claims that her work is just the artless transcription of someone's experiences. She did not write a war novel, but merely the story of a farm boy who becomes a soldier and goes to France and dies. Wharton argued with Scribner's that *A Son at the Front* was not "a war novel . . . but a study of French-American life in Paris in 1915–1916 . . . somewhat on the scale of the social studies of *The House of Mirth*" (Benstock, *Gifts* 355–56). Wharton attempts to build on the success of *The House of Mirth* as protection for *A Son at the Front,* hoping to avoid precisely the sort of commentary she had already anticipated in "Writing a War Story."

The positive reviews of both novels use language that, even as it praises, also subtly belittles the writers. One of the strongest reviews that *A Son at the Front* received was from the *New York Times,* which characterized the novel almost exclusively in terms of its emotional power: Wharton's "great talent was inspired by the keenest observation directed by the qualities of the human heart." The reviewer goes on to say that "if a man should find his eyes moist, if he should be touched to the heart by

the truth and beauty of Mrs. Wharton's last pages, it would teach him
what the effect of reality is when interpreted in the terms of life by a great
artist. . . . [The novel] pierces easily to the very depths of human joy and
sorrow" (qtd. in Tuttleton 329). On the grounds of its affective power, its
sentiment and emotion, the novel succeeds brilliantly, but the reviewer
mentions the war only in his description of the novel's plot. Dorothy
Canfield Fisher did the same thing in her review of Cather's novel, ignoring most of the war scenes and commenting instead on the novel's
"feelings" and the sympathy and honesty with which the central character was portrayed.[17] The terms on which the novels succeed are the terms
traditionally used to describe women's writing—moving, honest, touching, sentimental, sympathetic. The novels themselves, while admirable,
are "minor documents"; have a "temporary, an immediate appeal"; are
"deeply interesting but—not . . . great."[18] Writing about a supposedly
masculine subject hyperfeminizes both writers; they cannot be read as
anything other than "lady authors."

When the reviews are negative, on the other hand, the war becomes
the central issue and all three writers are found sadly lacking in their abilities to do justice to the subject. The fact that Gale criticizes all aspects of
militarism, while Wharton's and Cather's heroes happily fulfill their duties as soldiers and even espouse militarist rhetoric, becomes irrelevant.
The language used to criticize all three writers becomes remarkably similar, as do the grounds for critique. *Heart's Kindred*, for example, illustrates
the "threadbare desire" to connect fiction "to the European war," writes a
Boston reviewer in 1915, while Wharton is criticized for the same thing,
eight years later: she is a "soul belated," and the novel is "lugging in an old
nightmare." Cather, according to Sinclair Lewis, is just too old to write
about the war: if the novel had been written by "an experimenting young-
ster, [it] would stir the most stimulating hope . . . yet from Miss Cather
it is disappointing." Gale's pacifist novel is "treacle" and lacks "hard work
and vigorous creative thought"—comments that reiterate the common
association of pacifism with feminization. Cather's pro-war hero comes in
for the same criticism, however: Gilbert Seldes called him "Claude Bovary" and Heywood Broun claimed that the entire novel displayed a "sentimental attitude toward the war." Following this same line of reasoning,
the reviewer for the *Independent* claimed that Campton's character "can
hardly prove interesting—at least to men." If a woman creates the characters, then inherently the only interested readers will be women. O'Brien
notes that in the reviews of *One of Ours* "for the first time, Cather was explicitly judged as limited because of her gender" ("Combat Envy" 244).
Women's war writing caused male—and female—reviewers to fore-
ground gender, as if the gender of author became a more pressing issue

when the subject was war. Whether women write about war or peace, their timing is always off and they are capable only of sentimental—feminine—responses. Joseph Hergesheimer claims that women and feminine sensibilities are to blame for "why the stories of the late war written here, were such tinsel claptrap" (721). No matter what their approach, it seems, their mode of representation is wrong. The reviews clearly delineate the gender–genre boundary and find each writer guilty of crossing that line.

What Cather, Wharton, and Gale are most guilty of, however, is their lack of authentic knowledge about both the war and current trends in fiction. Notwithstanding Wharton's firsthand knowledge of the front line, illustrated by the articles collected in *Fighting France: From Dunkerque to Belfort* (1915), Robert Morss Lovett claimed that *A Son at the Front* "suggests the automobile excursions of American Red Cross girls in Paris to visit the graves" (qtd. in Tuttleton 333). His comment reduces the novel to an inauthentic joy ride, a cheap thrill, rather than a serious meditation about the consequences of war. The novel has an "almost antiquated air," wrote the *New Republic*, while another reviewer asks, "Where in the world has Mrs. Wharton been all this time?" According to the *Chicago Post, Heart's Kindred* will not please either "popular-book-loving people" or "the lover of real literature" because of its "loose construction, the near-psychology, [and] the poor character drawing." H. L. Mencken suggested that Cather would have done better to read Dos Passos's *Three Soldiers*, because it is "meticulously true" and portrays the war with "bold realism"—the implication being that Cather's novel is neither true nor real. Mencken's final comment, which must have been particularly galling to Cather, was that her novel's final sections ranked with "a serial in the *Ladies Home Journal* . . . it is precious near the war novel of the standard model of lady novelist" (qtd. in Schroeter 10). Writing about the war is the purview of (young) men, these reviews suggest, because only men who had been at the front possess the "real" knowledge about war. Even though much male-authored fiction about the war did not mimetically reproduce frontline experiences, having military experience gave these writers the license to interpret the war as they saw fit, and their interpretations became the models used to judge women writers—and find them wanting.

The reception of all three writers' war texts exemplifies the misogynistic response to women's writing that a number of critics have described as a hallmark of the modernist period.[19] Embedded in these reviews is a knotted cluster of issues—about gender and generational conflicts, assessments of aesthetics and prose forms—that form the outlines of high modernism. Janice Radway points out that the "authoritative status of the modernist high literary . . . was increasingly dependent . . . on the practice of marking the critical difference between that conceived as the bona fide and the authentic and that which merely masqueraded as such" (218). The reviews of Wharton's, Cather's, and Gale's war fiction enforce this distinction by implicitly, and sometimes explicitly, linking the inauthentic with the feminine. Suzanne Clark argues that during the postwar period "modernism excluded whatever was associated with the fatally popular ladies. Doing so, it represented an exaggeration of the split between popular and elite culture in American letters" (16). The intellectual experimentalism of writers like Joyce, Pound, and Eliot established an aesthetic that disavowed sentimentality, romanticism, and popularity, all terms associated with women's writing. What is troubling about this link between women and mass culture is not, as Andreas Huyssen points out, "the desire to differentiate between forms of high art and depraved forms of mass culture and its co-options. The problem is rather the persistent gendering as feminine of that which is devalued" (53). Because "popular" and "feminine" became almost synonymous terms during this postwar period, and were linked in turn to the world of magazine publishing, it became increasingly difficult for best-selling fiction by a woman writer to be taken seriously by reviewers and critics. One of the reviews of *Peace in Friendship Village*, tellingly, bemoaned Gale's "apparently complete submersion in the 'glad' school of magazine fiction," while Mencken disparaged *One of Ours* by a reference to *Ladies Home Journal.* Waldo Frank called the fiction that appeared in women's magazines "pseudo-literature," in an angry essay that used Wharton and Cather to illustrate his point: Writers like "Mrs. Wharton" and "Miss Cather," he claimed, make books that are the "straw food of fashionable letters," and in no way contribute to the "creative life of the mind and of the spirit" (47). The supposed failures of Wharton and Cather, in particular, become the same reasons that women's writing in general was excluded from the canon of high modernism. Writing about war became the acid test for modernist aesthetics, a test that women were bound to fail in the eyes of their judges, because their responses were always already feminized—and thus sentimental, emotional, romantic, "straw food."

Critical ire notwithstanding, these war novels represent a significant expansion of what "women's writing" could include in its purview. The novels challenge conventional expectations of war fiction and thus blur the gender–genre boundary that their contemporary critics worked so hard to preserve. These war novels also mark significant shifts in each author's individual career: all three writers move in significantly different directions after they write about the war, continually challenging critical expectations. Gale's work, as exemplified by *Miss Lulu Bett* and *Preface to a Life*, becomes much more cynical about small-town life. *Light Woman* (1933), the last novel published in Gale's lifetime (*Magna* was published posthumously, in 1939), depicted a couple happily living together without being married and satirizes small-town politics; the novel caused a small scandal among Gale's readers, who were used to more conventional portrayals of relationships. Among the novels that Cather wrote in the 1920s are those often thought of as her masterpieces—*A Lost Lady* (1923), *The Professor's House* (1925), *Death Comes for the Archbishop* (1927)—all of which reflect Cather's desire to escape traditional definitions of theme and genre, as do her more neglected late novels, *Lucy Gayheart* (1935) and *Sapphira and the Slave Girl* (1940). And in the novels *The Mother's Recompense* (1925) and *Twilight Sleep* (1927), Wharton tackled contemporary issues like eugenics, fascism, and divorce. Further, after she published her war fiction, each writer found a new publisher who promised her increased sales and more dynamic promotion. *One of Ours* is Cather's first novel with Knopf; Wharton firmly broke with Scribner's after *A Son at the Front,* which she gave to them in order to fulfill an old contract, and published her subsequent novels with Appleton; after *Peace in Friendship Village,* Gale left Macmillan and published *Miss Lulu Bett* with Appleton. Knopf and Appleton helped each writer to bridge the divide between "serious" and "popular" insisted upon by the cultural elite; both firms were considered to be in the forefront of "modern" publishing methods, and both helped their writers to achieve serious financial rewards. Breaking through the gender–genre boundary enabled each writer to move out of her critically sanctioned niche—happy villages, high society, prairie nobility—into new territory that she could define in her own terms.

CONCLUSION

MAKING HISTORIES

Why is Zona Gale still such an obscure figure? Her work belongs in anthologies about women's regionalism, critical discussions of women's radical and revolutionary writing in the 1930s, feminist reconsiderations of women's war writing and the pacifist movement, and explorations of black–white relationships in the early twentieth century. And yet at most there is only a quick reference to her Midwestern brand of socialism in *Better Red* (Coiner, 1995), a brief mention of her as an observer of a Washington, D.C., suffrage parade in *American Suffragist* (Weatherford, 1998), and a few glancing references to her in *The Harlem Renaissance in Black and White* (Hutchinson, 1995). How does a writer who was considered such a significant figure that her death in 1937 occasioned a eulogy on the editorial page of the *New York Times,* disappear so completely?[1]

The reasons for Gale's gradual disappearance from the literary history of the early twentieth century are linked to two important developments in U.S. literary study: the rise of New Criticism, which significantly influenced the shape of literary history for decades; and the powerful challenges to the New Critics that emerged in the early 1970s from feminist scholarship. Wharton and Cather continued to be read within the structures of both New Criticism and feminism, although with very different emphasis in each case, while Gale slid ever further into obscurity. Looking at the downward spiral of Gale's reputation from 1945 onward, in conjunction with what happens to Wharton's and Cather's reputations at the same time, illustrates the consequences of choosing sisterhood as a model for literary authority: Gale has become at best a footnote, while Wharton and Cather studies are thriving.

The emergence of U.S. literature as a discipline is a relatively recent phenomenon; there were almost no courses offered in colleges and universities

in the 1910s and 1920s, which reflects the academic consensus that U.S. literature did not warrant scholarly study. In the late 1920s and early 1930s,
however, this began to change. Sharon O'Brien argues that "after 1930
scholars, critics, and reviewers were increasingly concerned with defining
and codifying an American literary canon, the establishing of which could
both reflect and justify their own professional expertise." She goes on to
point out that in the process of creating this canon, scholars "systematically
overlooked or excluded women writers . . . defining their work either as
minor or as major but second rank: if Americans were to have a first-rate
canon to compete with that of the British, it would have to be male" ("Noncanonical" 249). During this canonization process, women writers were
derogated in language similar to that used in the reviews of Wharton's,
Cather's, and Gale's war fiction: women's writing was sentimental, popular,
inauthentic, minor. As O'Brien's comment illustrates, the male scholars
who were establishing their credentials as Americanists needed to prove
themselves by working on "hard" literature, serious literature. As a result,
they jettisoned anything that might make them—or their emerging discipline—look soft or unprofessional.

The 1963 edition of the *Literary History of the United States* (*LHUS*)
exemplifies the canonization process that O'Brien is talking about: fewer
than fifty women are included in the volume, which is over one thousand
pages long. Most of the women, including Gale, receive only a sentence
or two of discussion, while Wharton, Cather, Stowe, Edna St. Vincent
Millay, and Emily Dickinson are given slightly longer descriptions. Gale
is briefly noted as a "brilliant analyst" of U.S. daily life who wrote "far too
little." While the "far too little" seems odd for a writer who published
fourteen novels, seven plays, six collections of short stories, and numerous
essays, she is mentioned nevertheless. Wharton and Cather warrant
longer discussions, although more is not necessarily better, in this case.
Cather's work is, in the final word, "a small art," and Wharton is the
"memorialist of a dying aristocracy." Each is seen as inferior to the male
writer with whom she is compared—Sinclair Lewis and Henry James, respectively. The *LHUS* illustrates the shifts that were taking place in the
literary landscape of the United States: during the years it was compiled,
published, and then thrice revised—the years from 1940–1974,
roughly—the study of American literature had become firmly entrenched
in the academy, and U.S. women writers had been shifted to the margins
of literary history.

In *Professing Literature* (1987), Gerald Graff argues that the theorists
of American literature from the late 1930s through the 1960s "substituted
an academic tradition for a popular (and populist) one, taking the side of
'high' art over 'masscult.' They overthrew the naturalistic canon of the

twenties and thirties." Popular literature, Graff claims, was useful to these critics only for the contrast it presented against the "'complex' . . . high-brow tradition. And when [critics] did embrace writers in the popular tradition such as Cooper, Hawthorne, and Twain, they did so in ways that depopularized their work, emphasizing the elements of ambiguity, obliquity, and unresolved conflict" (222). The popular and the serious became rigidly oppositional terms, so that Twain no longer merely spun yarns, nor Hawthorne romances; they became instead artistic chroniclers of America's past who asked profound, perhaps unanswerable questions about the nature of the American psyche. It was during this same period, says Graff, that Emerson and Whitman "underwent a devaluation process . . . criticized for their 'innocence' and lack of 'tragic vision'" (223).

Like Dreiser, whose work was also devalued during this period because of his concern with "a specific form of society rather than with the 'idea' of society" (Graff 223), Gale's specificity prevents her work from being considered seriously. Critics failed to register the intensity of her political beliefs and did not hear her wry humor as a form of cultural critique. Exemplifying this critical shortsightedness are comments made by her biographer, Harold Simonson, in 1962: "One squirms at the innocence in Gale's blithe assumptions," he writes. "One wishes to confront her with the screams of Roderick Usher or the maniacal laughter of Ethan Frome. She had yet to discover the terror compacted into those nineteenth-century American symbols of the raven, the white whale, and the scarlet letter" (44). She is a "spinner of literary lace," whose ideas have a "cotton-wool fuzziness"; there is no "cosmic terror" in her writing, which also lacks the "impressive splendor [that is] in Melville, Hawthorne, parts of Twain, much of James" (113, 114). Serious literature, truly American literature, it would seem, is terrifying, impressive, precise, concerned primarily with men hovering on the brink of madness. In Gale's books almost no one ever dies, suffering is often alleviated, and there is a general feeling that society is going to change for the better, all of which become signs of her inability to grasp the inherently "tragic" quality of life in the United States.

Wharton's and Cather's work, at first glance, share a bleaker vision than Gale's; suffering, in their novels, is often left unchecked. The novels of Wharton and Cather that receive critical attention in the 1940s and 1950s are those that display the "ambiguity, obliquity, and unresolved conflict" that become the hallmarks of "serious" fiction: Wharton's *The House of Mirth*, *Ethan Frome*, and *The Age of Innocence*, and Cather's *A Lost Lady* and *The Professor's House*. Because some of their fiction was thought to display those qualities that come to be associated with "real art," Cather and Wharton remain, somewhat tenuously, within the canon of American literature. The process of inclusion, however, is highly selective; it leaves out almost all of Wharton's work written between 1911 and 1920, and that produced after *The Age of Innocence;* all of Cather's novels after *Death Comes for the Archbishop;* and the war writing done by both writers.[2] Each writer also suffers from pointed criticism that undermines the "serious" qualities of her work. Wharton is disparaged as a society lady who wrote several good novels, merely an acolyte of Henry James. Cather's two prairie novels, *O, Pioneers!* and *My Ántonia,* which seemed to lend themselves to the nationalist project of glorifying the American past, also remain the subject of critical discussion, although her work more generally gets dismissed as "antiquarian, content with much space in little room" (*LHUS* 1216).

Wharton's and Cather's late novels reflect writers who are much more engaged with their contemporary society than the *LHUS* descriptions suggest. Wharton observes the contemporary literary world in *Hudson River Bracketed* (1929) and *The Gods Arrive* (1932) and finds most of it sadly lacking in any "authentic" artistic merit; these novels also call into question the viability of the artist as "solitary genius," as if inviting readers to see Wharton herself differently. In the two-volume story of Halo Tarrant and her lover, the budding literary genius Vance Weston, Wharton issues warnings to younger novelists who think that one smash success will guarantee their literary futures. Halo's old friend Frenside, a book reviewer and dispenser of book-world wisdom, tells Vance that "nothing is as disintegrating as success. . . . And to young fellows like you, after you've made your first hit, the world is all one vast blurb" (*Hudson* 393). Weston's quest for artistic success in a money-hungry literary marketplace illustrates Wharton's own ambivalence about the book business and her dissatisfaction with the kind of work that the real-life Vance Westons around her were publishing to great acclaim. Vance is told by his publisher that they don't like his new, short novel; they would rather "have an elephant to handle, like 'Ulysses' or 'American Tragedy' . . . [because] when readers have paid their money they like to sit down to a square meal" (395), a comment that makes these novels sound like they had been written on a dollar-per-word basis to the specifications of an insatiable public. The publisher also tries to dictate Vance's subject matter by telling him that readers are fed up with "sky-scrapers and niggers and boot-leggers and actresses. Fed up equally with Harlem and with the Opera, with Greenwich Village and the plutocrats" (415). This list demonstrates Wharton's keen awareness of literary fashion and sets *Hudson River Bracketed* apart from mere literary fads. As she slyly skewers her literary contemporaries, Wharton asserts her own authorial power: *she* is subject to neither publisher dictates nor audience demands.

The sequel to *Hudson River Bracketed, The Gods Arrive,* was considered "too vigorous" for publication in *Ladies Home Journal* because of its sexual frankness: Halo and Vance live together in Europe, Vance has affairs with other women, and at the novel's end, Halo is happy, unwed, and carrying Vance's child. Halo is the novel's most insightful critic and reader; she shrewdly sees the difference between the imitative and the authentic, unlike Vance, who is often taken in by poseurs. Like Carry Fisher in *The House of Mirth,* Halo has a house and a child of her own. She does not care about social convention or male approval and asks her ex-husband why he "can't understand that a woman should want to be free, and alone with her child?" (*Gods* 360). Alone in her house on the Hudson, Halo "follow[s] her own way, neither defiantly nor apologetically, but as if it were of more concern to herself than it could possibly be to others" (424). Halo's radical independence dominates the conclusion of the novel, and her peaceful maternity suggests a creative authority that far outweighs Vance's belief that an artist "ought to be free and unencumbered" (*Hudson* 521).

After a dalliance with the crass and beautiful Floss Delaney, Vance returns to Halo, claiming that "I'm not fit for you yet, Halo; I'm only just learning to walk" (*Gods* 432), to which Halo replies that she will then have "two children to take care of"—her first admission to him that she is pregnant. Reduced to this infantile state, Vance bows at her feet. The novel concludes with the image of the narcissistic male artist kneeling in front of an independent and self-sufficient woman, which may explain both the novel's bad reviews and critics' reluctance to include it in the list of Wharton's best books. What these two novels demonstrate, however, is that far from being the "memorialist of a dying aristocracy," Wharton is an astute observer of the modern world, occupied with the same subjects as her male modernist counterparts, although her perspective sheds a less than flattering light on these writers and their world.[3]

Cather's last novel, *Sapphira and the Slave Girl* (1940), similarly challenges the image of the author that critics had established with their selective list of her serious fiction. *Sapphira and the Slave Girl* demonstrates Cather's sophisticated manipulations of genre and form, which, while perhaps more subtle than Faulkner's labyrinthine sentences and looping plotlines, nevertheless offer similar epistemological challenges to the reader. Cather's novel, again similar to Faulkner's work, wrestles with the legacy of slavery and with Cather's own conflicted attitudes about her family history and the history of the country. Ostensibly based on a true story that Cather pieced together as a child, the novel describes how Nancy, the "slave girl" of the title, escapes from her horrible mistress, Sapphira Colbert (a thinly veiled representation of Cather's maternal great-grandmother), who has schemed to have Nancy raped and then sold.[4] Cather does not mention that these events are based on true stories until the novel's autobiographical epilogue and coda, both of which call into question the structure of what has come before. If, as the epilogue and coda would have us believe, Nancy's story is true, then is *Sapphira and the Slave Girl* not a novel at all? Or should the autobiographical "I" of the epilogue be regarded as another fiction, another of Cather's always-unreliable narrators, like Jim Burden or Nellie Birdseye?

Set twenty-five years after the action itself, the epilogue documents Nancy's first return to Virginia after her successful escape and describes the fascination that she held for Cather's child-self. At the time of Nancy's return to Back Creek, Cather is about five, and she likes nothing better than to sit with Nancy, Nancy's mother Till, and Sapphira's daughter Rachel Blake as they gossip in the kitchen of Cather's childhood home (there is no indication, curiously, if Cather's own mother was present at these gatherings). The women talk about old times in a scene that appears to radiate tranquility, domestic harmony, and racial integration—Till and Nancy, ex-slaves, sit comfortably with white Rachel Blake and her granddaughter, the future author. The child-narrator says that she was "allowed to sit with them and sew patchwork. Sometimes their talk was puzzling, but I soon learned that it was best never to interrupt with questions—it seemed to break the spell. Nancy wanted to know what had happened during the war . . . and so did I" (935). Despite their wishes, however, the novel never quite explains what happened during the war; we are told only that the "war had done away with the old distinctions" (929). No questions are permitted about how these distinctions were eradicated, because that would break "spell" of storytelling. As if suggesting the enormous difficulty of finding a narrative capacious enough to contain the war, Cather elides it almost entirely, confining the "war years" to a three-page interchapter that concerns itself primarily with the returning farm boys, who tend to their neglected fields in "whatever rags were left of their uniforms" (929).[5]

Disquietingly violent stories about the Colbert family slaves lurk in the margins of Cather's postbellum romanticizing, however. Stories such as Jezebel's treatment on the slaver that brought her to Virginia from Africa, Tansy Dave's broken heart, the unanswered question about how Uncle Jeff became a "capon man," and Till's willingness to send her daughter away to keep her safe, invalidate any possibility of casting the antebellum world in a rosy glow. Even the tranquil scene of women sitting in the kitchen is less positive than it seems: Nancy and Till do not eat with the rest of the family on the night that Nancy returns but dine instead in the kitchen; Till continues to do all the housework and the cooking, despite her advanced years. Some of the "old distinctions," it seems, still remain. There are also unsettling connections between Cather and her vindictive great-grandmother, Sapphira. On the day that Nancy arrives, Cather is immobilized by an illness, as was her great-grandmother, and in order to see Nancy dismount from her carriage, Cather must be carried to the window, just as Sapphira must be wheeled from place to place. Before Cather goes to sleep, her mother brings her an eggnog to quiet her—the same remedy that Nancy brings to Sapphira to soothe the mysterious anger that Sapphira has for her, which ultimately forces Nancy to flee. Even as the epilogue attempts to smooth over the ugliness of the past and to insist that all's well that ends well, running underneath the surface is a very different version of history—both national and familial—that reflects the difficulty of making peace with the past.

Although both Wharton's and Cather's late novels are more complicated than these brief comments can convey, it should be clear that the shape of their careers looks quite different when these novels are added to the discussion. Looking at the late work suggests that neither writer was as out-of-touch or as elitist as she was made out to be by mid-century critics, but this work was only rarely discussed in the 1940s and 1950s. The public images that Wharton and Cather had constructed for themselves paradoxically worked against them, making it difficult for their later fiction to be seen as anything other than a falling away from the earlier work with which each writer had created her authorial persona. At the same time, however, because these public images anticipated aspects of post–World War II critical thought, both Wharton and Cather remained within the ongoing discussions about U.S. literature.

The public authorial selves that Wharton and Cather created anticipated the ideas of "the artist" that R. W. B. Lewis situated in an American context in his influential 1955 study, *The American Adam.* Lewis explains that "novelists were to discover . . . that the story implicit in American experience had to do with an Adamic person, springing from nowhere, outside time, at home only in the presence of nature and God, who is thrust by circumstances into an actual world and an actual age" (89). The American Adam is "the young innocent, liberated from family and social history or bereft of them" (127). Although Adam is an outsider in a "curiously staunch and artistically demanding manner," his outsider status is not caused by being one of the "dispossessed, the superfluous, the alienated, the exiled" (128). Both Cather and Wharton prefigure Lewis's formulation through their creation of public personae that were positioned as outsiders: Cather as prairie writer in the city, Wharton as the moral arbiter—and thus an aloof observer—of the urban upper-class. Because their public authorial personae meshed so easily with the ideas about "the artist" that Lewis and others helped to institutionalize, Wharton and Cather survived what the first-generation feminist critics called the "masculinizing" of American letters, while Gale became, at best, a literary footnote.[6]

It is difficult to see Gale as a version of the American Adam, because she wrote as an insider, as someone who lived among the people of small villages and rural outposts; and she participated willingly and publicly in collaborative, collective movements. Gale cannot be "liberated from social history" because of her public affiliation with the female tradition and with other women writers, as well as her lifelong commitment to pacifism; she was obviously very much a part of social history. Her work, therefore, could not be depoliticized or dehistoricized the way that Cather's and Wharton's work could be, which became particularly important as New Criticism became "the" critical approach of both reviewers and academics. The historicized settings of Wharton's and Cather's novels notwithstanding, critics found in some of their novels the ambiguity and obliquity that characterized "serious" fiction. In *Cultural Capital* (1993), John Guillory observes that for the New Critics "the language of poetry, and of literature in general, was intrinsically *difficult*. . . . If 'difficulty' names the condition of poetic language more specifically signified by the terms 'paradox,' 'ambiguity,' or 'wit,' the valorization of difficulty as the general quality of poetic language was always an integral part of the New Critical agenda of canonizing the modernist poets" (168–69). The rise of New Criticism was conjunct with the creation of a high modernist canon, which the New Criticism defined as above and against "mass culture . . . [and] popular modernism" (172). Even more than at the beginning of the twentieth century, in the years following World War II, "popular" and "serious" fiction were understood to be irreconcilable categories. Gale's popularity and social conscience work against her, as a comment from Simonson illustrates: "It may be, of course, that if [Gale] had removed herself further from current hassles, she would have strengthened her art" (64). Gale, like Wharton and Cather, bridged the perceived gap between popular and serious, however, either with novels that were both critically and popularly successful, such as *Miss Lulu Bett*, or by alternating back and forth between critical and popular successes.

The writers who fit the New Critics' vision of modernism were described as resolutely noncommercial and uninterested in popular success. This vision of modernist writers as being uninvolved with marketplace considerations still has significant critical currency, as the editors of *Marketing Modernisms* (1996) discovered when they solicited essays for their collection. Included as an epigraph to the collection is the response they received from a "senior academic," who rejected their invitation because "the phrasing [of the prospectus] betrays a concept that belittles. Joyce, Woolf, Ford, et al. were after all not junior academics with a way to make" (1). This scholar retains the idea that thinking about modernist artists as interested in money sullies their reputations and their art. By the same token, Wharton and Cather studies have only recently begun to discuss how the two authors fashioned their images—and eventually their celebrity—for public consumption, as if thinking about them in this context would lessen either writer's achievement.

The canonical vision of high modernism not only excludes women from its pantheon but also rules out fiction that is anything other than experimental or avant-garde.[7] Because of her terse novella *My Mortal Enemy* (1926) and "The Novel Démeublé," Cather was occasionally included within the modernist ranks, but Wharton and Gale were not, in part because of the traditionally narrow definitions of both modernism and experimentalism. Rita Felski challenges these traditional views, arguing that "the question of what counts as innovative or radical art cannot simply be read off from a formal analysis of the text in question, but requires a careful account of the particular contextual locations and systems of value within which meanings are produced" (203). Thus writing about the war and challenging the boundaries of genre become experimental acts, for example, as do Gale's attempts to represent in prose the transcendent experiences of spiritual awakening, and Cather's stripping the stage of the novel at the end of *One of Ours*. Without this expansion of what innovative fiction might look like, Wharton, Gale, and to a lesser degree, Cather, all suffer a similar fate: they are relegated to the margins, the scribes of minor subjects. The language of Wharton reviews is particularly instructive in this regard: her post–World War I novels are repeatedly praised as competent, well crafted, well executed, as if she is a machine that produces a well-made but unexciting product. Her very competence precludes the possibility that her work could be innovative or experimental; a craftsman does not take risks but merely executes a preexisting blueprint.[8]

As Felski's comment indicates, definitions of literary modernism have begun to broaden, and the once unbridgeable divide between popular and serious fiction has been crossed and recrossed. Indeed, my comments about modernism and my repositioning of Wharton, Cather, and Gale, accordingly, owe a great deal to the interventions of critics such as Felski. *Not in Sisterhood*, in fact, would not have been possible without the groundbreaking, critically paramount work of the feminist scholars who have come before me. The work now being done on U.S. literary modernism emerges from the so-called second generation of feminist criticism; the first generation, as Lisa Rado observes, "stayed clear [of modernism] and wrote instead about the great Victorians: Jane Austen, the Brontës, George Eliot" (4). It is this first generation that established the paradigms used by subsequent scholars but they also institutionalized the tensions between sisterhood and authority, between public and private, that Wharton and Cather adhered to throughout their careers.

Two of the earliest exercises of feminist literary criticism, Ellen Moers's *Literary Women* (1976) and Patricia Meyer Spacks's *The Female Imagination* (1975), demonstrate the difficulties inherent in creating a more inclusive vision of literary history. The language of both texts betrays an ambivalence about powerful female predecessors that echoes the ambivalence felt by Wharton and Cather themselves. Moers's description of Woolf, Stein, Cather, and Colette, a group she hails as the "peak of achievement" for women writers, is particularly telling. She writes that "there is something imposing, even alarming about the four of them. As a company, I can't help visualizing them blocked out together in stone as a sort of Henry Moore grouping—massive sculptural forms, somber, solid, and remote, with heavy shoulders, strongly modeled skulls, and perhaps a hole—in the Moore style—where the heart is" (234). These monolithic women led "comfortable, unencumbered lives on the whole, alongside companions (male or female) devoted to their creature comforts. They made a decisive choice for the literary over the lady's life, and the world rewarded them with public ceremonials, pilgrimages, prizes, collected editions, medals, degrees, and honors in an abundance never showered on literary women before" (234). Their achievements and successes make these women worthy role models, but they are also imposing, intimidating, remote, and heartless—ultimately rather terrifying examples of literary foremothers. Moers limits their power, however, by describing them as objects of an artist's scrutiny: they are Henry Moore sculptures, the raw material for a male artist to shape into art. Even as she praises their unconventional successes, Moers's words betray her anxiety about this group's power, which both inspires and overwhelms, and thus needs to be contained.

Curiously, Wharton is absent from this stony grouping and from Moers's book completely. It seems an odd omission, given that Wharton, like the four women Moers describes here, wrote frequently and with great passion about motherhood. Writing about motherhood, in fact, is what Moers points to as the significant literary achievement of these writers: "no generation ever said more, or with greater complexity—about Motherhood"(236). Wharton's absence from Moers's list may be explained by the fact that the novels in which Wharton focused most sharply on motherhood are the novels that fell out of favor in the 1940s and 1950s, in part due to their subject matter: *Glimpses of the Moon*

(1922), *The Mother's Recompense* (1925), *Twilight Sleep* (1927), *The Children* (1928), *Hudson River Bracketed* (1929), and *The Gods Arrive* (1932).[9]

Like Moers's book, Spacks's *The Female Imagination* demonstrates a similarly ambivalent attitude toward the literary women that are its subject, although Spacks gives a detailed account of Wharton and entirely omits Cather. Spacks's Wharton is not a heartless granite statue but an upper-class narrator of society novels that are not quite as good as those of George Eliot but that are equally devoted to portraying the myriad ways in which a patriarchal society crushes the female imagination. Only one of Wharton's "motherhood" novels, *The Mother's Recompense,* is included in Spacks's discussion, which deals primarily with *The House of Mirth* and *The Age of Innocence.* Wharton, more so than Eliot, "refuses to acknowledge even that the female imagination can surmount or transform society's restrictions" (239). Both Wharton and Eliot illustrate what for Spacks is the most salient feature of work produced by the female imagination: "Anger . . . shapes serious considerations of the relation between women and society . . . it sounds the most authentic woman's response: a response to bafflement, to dead ends bumped into, to society's failure to speak to women's needs" (319–20). Spacks's comment helped to establish the idea of the angry and alienated female writer/heroine that became central to first-generation feminist literary critics. At the same time, however, this comment further marginalizes Gale: anger is the mark of authenticity, and Gale's fictional voice is seldom angry.

Both *Literary Women* and *The Female Imagination* represent turning points in the study of women writers; they brought the fervor of "women's lib" into the world of academic study, initiating new subjects for literary discussion and opening the ranks of the professariat to women. Their work engendered the exploration and recovery of women's literary traditions, but the prefatory remarks of both books reflect an uneasiness about the scope of their projects. Neither writer seems to want to take full responsibility for the structure of her book. Spacks locates her literary authority within a very specific intersection between her imagination and her reader's: the choice of what writers to include in her book is "like all such choices . . . arbitrary . . . [and] reflects the operations of my own imagination; the meaning of the book as a whole must depend partly on the implications of the *special conjunctions* achieved through a *particular sensibility*" (4, emphasis added). Sounding an equally nineteenth-century note, Moers positions herself as a recorder, merely transcribing the thoughts of the writers she studies: "The literary women themselves, not any doctrine of mine, have done the organizing of the book—*their* concerns, *their* language. . . . As I understand it, my principal obligation is to record without simplification what it has meant to be at once a woman and a writer" (x). Carolyn Heilbrun strikes a similar chord in the preface of *Toward a Recognition of Androgyny* (1973): "Probably no one in the learned world of the university is less qualified than I in certain ways for the task I have undertaken. My sense of history is meager, my knowledge of languages more so" (xix). These critics disavow their own authority in precisely the fashion that Wharton, Cather, and Gale worked so hard to avoid, and thus this important feminist criticism carries within it the ghost of nineteenth-century "lady authors."

The initial burst of feminist energy that fueled Moers and Spacks also fueled the search for "role models" that often marks the beginning of any new movement, literary or otherwise.[10] It is this quest that leads Carolyn Heilbrun, in *Reinventing Womanhood* (1979), to chastise Wharton and Cather for not being feminist enough. In a chapter entitled "The Failure of the Imagination," Heilbrun takes both writers to task for having failed to "imagine autonomous women characters" (71) and professes to find it "extraordinarily puzzling that the identity crisis through which an accomplished woman author passes with evident success should so strongly resist imaginative recreation" (82). Marilyn French, almost ten years later, asks another version of the same question: "Why [have] women writers tended to grant their heroines fewer choices and greater constriction than they themselves experienced?" (219). In "Emphasis Added: Plots and Plausibilities in Women's Fiction" (1985), Nancy K. Miller offers an answer to these questions. Miller claims that "the plots of women's literature are not about 'life' and solutions in any therapeutic sense, nor should they be. They are about the plots of literature itself, about the constraints the maxim places on rendering a female life in fiction . . . the difficulty of curing plot of life and life of certain plots" (356). I agree with Miller's assessment, although as I have shown in my discussions of *The House of Mirth* and *My Ántonia*, it is possible for a woman writer to show the constraints of certain plots, and how to undo these constraints within the boundaries of one novel.

Whether or not Wharton and Cather are found wanting as feminist exemplars, the fact remains that unlike Gale, they were available for scrutiny and reconsideration because some of their work survived the institutionalizing—and masculinizing—process of the 1940s and 1950s. Gale was not found by this first generation of feminist scholars because, as Sharon O'Brien has pointed out, "we simply do not read writers whose work has not been published, evaluated, preserved, and transmitted by social, economic, and literary institutions of some sort" ("Noncanonical" 255). Feminist attentions to Wharton and Cather are thus made possible by Wharton's and Cather's "masculine" attributes, which in turn have been integrated into feminist representations of female literary authority in the United States.[11]

The vision of "sisterhood" that Moers and Spacks both invoke throughout their books implies a communal and supportive bond among women, a mid-twentieth-century version of the "community of spirit," perhaps. In *Communities of Women* (1978), Nina Auerbach not only follows the examples of Moers and Spacks, but also praises them for their sororal mission: Moers and Spacks exemplify "scholars in all areas [who] are discovering not a new sisterhood, but sisterhood as a newly perceived fact of life" (13). Despite this invocation of sisterhood as a positive force, the feminist work produced during the early 1970s and 1980s has a curiously equivocal attitude about sisterhood, particularly literary sisterhood. As Moers's description of the four heartless modernists suggests, acknowledging the power and the success of those who have come before can be a daunting project. The modernist-era women writers are particularly alarming, not only because of their historical proximity but also because of their success as independent and self-sufficient women in a male-dominated world that Moers and her cohort were only beginning to challenge. These writers chose the "literary over the lady's life, and the world rewarded them"—but would the world similarly reward scholars like Moers, who wanted to make the same choice? The relationship that this first generation of feminist critics established with their literary predecessors looks like a latter-day version of the ambivalent public stance that Wharton and Cather established with both their female peers and precursors.

Not surprisingly, the constructions of literary history that were produced by this first generation of feminist critics reflect this ambivalence. On the one hand, these feminist scholars envisioned a linear, coherent narrative of female literary authority in which each generation of women writers feels empowered by those who came before; but on the other hand, the writers who get singled out for particular attention are those who come the closest to the romantic ideal of the solitary genius. Although the conflict between authority and sisterhood is never made explicit, these critical studies suggest that literary authority cannot be found in literary sisterhood. The rhetorical insistence on a mutually supportive sisterhood within this work notwithstanding, the writers who are most subject to feminist scrutiny during this period—Wharton, Cather, Stein, Dickinson, and Woolf—are those who were publicly most ambivalent about affiliating themselves with their female peers. Gilbert and Gubar note that when Woolf writes about her female precursors, for example, her writing is "at times more than implicitly dismissive" and that she tends to "concentrate on their bodies rather than their books . . . evading a serious consideration of texts whose powers might make her tremble" (254). Although Woolf affiliated herself quite publicly with feminism and with pacifism, her relationships with literary women—peers and precursors—were not always as supportive as her politics might suggest.

Despite the efforts of feminist critics to bring women writers back into literary history during the great "recovery" process of the 1970s and 1980s, Gale's work nevertheless stayed stubbornly hidden. One explanation is suggested by Margaret Ezell's book *Writing Women's Literary History* (1993), which challenges conventional definitions of "early" women's literature in England. Ezell points out that the first wave of feminist literary history drew heavily on the characterization of the "female writer . . . as an individual at odds with her society and with herself because her creative drives require her to resist accepted 'feminine' roles" (26). Continuing this line of thought, Ezell observes that the image of the "angry and alienated female artist" adheres to "a nineteenth-century male image of authorship" (26). It is possible to see Wharton and Cather as "angry and alienated," but it is more difficult to characterize Gale in this way. Gale's political work demonstrates her lifelong awareness of social inequities and her commitment to alleviating social injustice, but her affiliations with like-minded women (and men) helped to allay whatever feelings of alienation or anger she may have had. Working with and within these various communities may have also contributed to Gale's optimism about the possibility of change, which again works against her. Her belief that people, society, and governments will improve prevents her from fitting the mold of the "madwoman in the attic."

Thus the short answer to the question I asked several pages ago—why does Gale disappear so completely—is that she does not fit into any of the critical paradigms that have been used in the last sixty-odd years to discuss U.S. literature and authorship for women or men. She is not the Adamic artist, isolated on the outskirts of society; she is not a paradoxical poet; she is not the madwoman in the attic; she is neither angry nor alienated. Cather and Wharton, by contrast, have been scrutinized within most of these paradigms, in some form or another.

As I write this, I can hear the immediate protest: "Gale must not be good enough and that's why she's disappeared." My first response to this would be to say that she is indeed "good enough" for critical discussion. Certainly she is as good—or better—than any number of women writers who have come to critical attention in recent years, many of whom Gale considered friends, peers, and precursors: Sarah Orne Jewett, Harriet Beecher Stowe, Mary Wilkins Freeman, Kate Chopin, Dorothy Canfield Fisher, Jessie Fauset, Georgia Douglas Johnson, Tess Slesinger, Meridel Le Sueur, Anzia Yezierska. Leaving questions of aesthetics aside, Gale is important in literary historical terms as well, as a writer who helped to shape the literary and political world of the early twentieth century. Revising revisionist histories is difficult work, however, because revisionists—like those who came before them—are understandably wary about having their work challenged.[12] But these challenges can make things much more interesting, as I think is the case when we bring Gale back into conversation with Wharton and Cather, which in turn facilitates a connection between these two writers, whose awareness of one another was so acute that they could not acknowledge it.

Wharton's and Cather's deliberate refusal to affiliate themselves publicly with "women's issues" or with a community of women writers strikes me as related to the late-twentieth-century phrase "I'm not a feminist but . . ." in which the statement's conclusion asserts a desire for some long-held feminist goal: equal pay, equal opportunities, affordable childcare, access to birth control and family planning, and so on. Similarly, Wharton and Cather partake of the successes created by twentiethcentury suffragists but do not acknowledge their debt. In both cases, the perception seems to be that feminism and female success are at odds, rather than conjoined. Addressing this apparent diminution in feminist power, Cathy Davidson argues that "opponents of affirmative action deploy rhetoric that encourages white women to think of themselves not as 'women' but as 'nonblacks' in order to elicit their vote against affirmative action—even though an end to affirmative action stands, potentially, to hurt them as women, as much as it will hurt any other group. . . . One could argue that if women had a more solid sense of themselves as a separate, identifiable political category this racially divisive tactic could not work. What, one should ask, has happened to feminist politics here?" (454). It seems to me a valid question.

Through the shifting tides of literary criticism in the years since their deaths, Wharton and Cather have become iconic figures of twentiethcentury white female authorship. Although critical perceptions of them have changed somewhat—Cather's public silences have become a resonant trope for discussions of early twentieth-century lesbianism, and Wharton's interests in science and in travel writing are finding a new audience in gender and cultural studies—they remain firmly ensconced in the pantheon of "serious" writers. As a result, their strategies for gaining literary authority have been uncritically accepted as examples of what women writers had to do to survive. Adding Gale to this discussion, however, demonstrates that expressions of literary sisterhood could—and did—contribute to the development of a powerful literary voice. Her disappearance points to the unfortunate fact that literary history does not yet know how to account for a career like hers: one of the lessons learned from Gale's vanishing is that literary authority is still at odds with literary sisterhood.

NOTES

INTRODUCTION

1. Due to a clause in Cather's will, none of her letters can be cited directly. This letter is from Cather to Mr. Bain, January 14, 1931. For a further discussion of Cather's will, see Chapter One.

2. This image has been scrutinized and revised in a number of important ways. For example, in *Doing Literary Business,* Susan Coultrap-McQuin has demonstrated that many of these successful nineteenth-century literary women saw themselves as ambitious professionals and demanded to be treated as such. A number of critics have argued that sentimental fiction possessed a tremendous cultural authority, an argument made most famously, perhaps, by Jane Tompkins in *Sensational Designs.* For further discussion of the sentimental or domestic novel and its authors, see Baym, Romines, Fetterley and Pryse, Jordan, and Romero.

3. Women editors suffered a fate similar to nineteenth-century women writers: their numbers declined significantly at the turn of the twentieth century. Helen Damon-Moore points out that in the early 1800s there were a "number of active women editors," but this number declined by the late nineteenth century. By the early twentieth century, there were no female editors of major mass-circulation magazines in the United States, a pattern that continued with very few exceptions until the 1960s. The few exceptions to this rule are Gertrude Battles Lane, who edited *Woman's Home Companion* from 1912 to 1941; Beatrice Gould, who with her husband Bruce, coedited *Ladies Home Journal* from the 1930s to the 1950s; and Freda Kirchwey, editor and eventual owner of the *Nation.*

4. For more discussion about the gradual professionalization of the literary world, see Wilson, West, Ohmann, and Jean Lutes's informative dissertation, "Expert Inventions."

5. I have in mind here such critics as Ellen Moers, Carolyn Heilbrun, and Patricia Meyer Spacks, whose work will be discussed in detail in the Conclusion.

6. Discussing unpublished letters is different from discussing published texts, I realize. One consideration is the difficulty of offering alternative

readings of the letters, which are not easily available. Therefore, I quote a number of letters at length, in order to provide as full a context as possible for the comments I make.

7. One of the few studies that focuses solely on Wharton and Cather is Judith Fryer's *Felicitous Spaces: The Imaginative Structures of Edith Wharton and Willa Cather.* Fryer's book does not integrate the work of the two writers in any thematic way, however. Other books that contain discussions of both Wharton and Cather are either anthologies or a series of separate critical essays linked by a thematic introduction. The result is that Wharton and Cather remain separate, steadfastly individuated from their literary sisters. See, for example, Ammons, *Conflicting Stories* and Wheeler, *'Modernist' Women Writers and Narrative Art.*

8. After 1920, Susan Ware points out, the women's movement did not decline but diversified into smaller groups, focusing around such issues as pacifism, the newly-founded League of Women Voters, and the Equal Rights Amendment. In *Beyond Suffrage,* Ware argues that in the 1930s "many of women's expectations beyond suffrage finally found fulfillment" through involvement in Roosevelt's New Deal administration (4). The women involved in the New Deal, claims Ware, "took an active interest in furthering the progress of their sex. They recruited women for prominent government positions . . . and generally fostered an awareness of women as a special interest group with a substantial role to play in the New Deal" (7).

9. Typical of this oversight is Guy Reynolds's recent book about Cather, *Willa Cather in Context* (1996), which omits any mention of suffrage or women's rights, despite the fact that the U.S.—and many other countries—was convulsed over the question of whether or not to make women into citizens.

10. For further discussion about the connections between mass culture and women, see Huyssen, Graff, Levine, Ohmann, and Radway.

CHAPTER ONE

1. All the letters cited in this book, unless otherwise noted, are from the Zona Gale Collection at the State Historical Society of Wisconsin, in Madison, Wisconsin. Future references will be noted parenthetically in the text by date, if available, and the abbreviation SHSW.

2. In *Edith Wharton's Women: Friends and Rivals,* Susan Goodman comments that "Wharton's . . . efforts to separate herself from other women writers [make her] acknowledgment of the value and power of Norton's lines seem all the more remarkable" (43).

3. The correspondence between these women goes unremarked in biographies of both Cather and Wharton, a separation maintained by Gale herself, who seems never to have spoken of Cather to Wharton or vice versa. Gale's correspondence with Wharton, and her dinner engagements with

Cather, are mentioned only in passing by Gale's two biographers, August
Derleth (1940) and Harold Simonson (1962).

4. Cather spent her college years in Lincoln, Nebraska, writing theater and
literature reviews for the local newspaper, and she wrote about fiction
while she was managing editor at *McClure's*. But after she began to publish her own work regularly, she ceased to comment about other writers
almost completely. Wharton mentions Henry James and his cohorts a
number of times in her nonfiction, and refers occasionally to other writers, although she seldom has anything positive to say about the women
writers she mentions. Neither Wharton nor Cather ever commented
publicly on Gale's work, as I will discuss. For examples of Cather's essays
and reviews, see Curtin, Slote and Faulkner, and Bohlke. For Wharton's
commentary on other writers, see Wharton, *The Writing of Fiction;* Wegener; Lewis and Lewis.

5. In *Imagined Communities,* Benedict Anderson argues that communities
are "to be distinguished, not by their falsity/genuineness but by the style
in which they are imagined" (6). Anderson discusses this idea in terms of
nations and nationalism, but his point here is also useful for my argument. Wharton and Cather imagined the community of women writers
as a limiting context, while Gale saw the same community as contribut-
ing to her literary and cultural authority. I am interested in how these differently imagined communities affected each writer's authorial strategies
and her subsequent status in literary history.

6. In *Conflicting Stories* (1991), Elizabeth Ammons states emphatically that
Wharton and Cather are part of a group of women writers at the turn of the
century who were "never a 'community.'" She goes on to assert that "ambitious turn-of-the-century women writers tended to work through problems
individually, partly because of the era's intense emphasis on individualism . . .
and partly because of the particular model of the artist to which most aspired
and which by definition implied solitary struggle" (192). Because she does
not examine feminist organizations such as Heterodoxy or friendships between writers, Ammons's book replicates the opposition between "artist" and
"community" that is one of the unspoken tenets of mid-twentieth century
feminist criticism, as I discuss in the Conclusion. In *Modernist Quartet*
(1990), Frank Lentricchia offers a different version of this same idea; he asserts that "the missing term in modernist thinking . . . is community: something larger, something more valuable than isolate selfhood" (291). But
because Lentricchia can only imagine this large and nurturing community
in the context of religious organizations—"fundamentalist Muslims . . . and
monasteries and convents"—he decides that "in the absence of religious
commitment, the choice of my modernists for radical disconnection seems
right" (291). Both Lentricchia and Ammons, despite fundamental differences in their arguments about the relationships between literature and culture, end up in the same place: splitting literary authority away from
community, privileging the individual over the group.

7. As examples of a more socially engaged model, consider the careers of Dorothy Canfield Fisher, Jessie Fauset, Zora Neale Hurston, Virginia Woolf, Elizabeth Bowen, Charlotte Perkins Gilman, Mina Loy, Mabel Dodge Luhan, or slightly later, Tillie Olsen, Meridel Le Sueur, and Dorothy Parker.

8. Several days prior to this letter to Gale, Wharton wrote Sinclair Lewis about *Babbitt* (1922), which Lewis dedicated to Wharton. She tells him that "at every page I found something to delight in, & something to talk about" and invites him to "jump on a steamer" so they could discuss his work. Her letter is laudatory and flattered, but she does not establish the sort of personal bond here that she does with Gale—there is no admission that she and Lewis are doing the same sorts of things in their novels. She thanks him for "associating my name with a book I so warmly admire and applaud" but goes no further than that (*Letters* 454–55).

9. For instance, in her review of *Glimpses of the Moon*, Rebecca West says that "an artist can be anything he likes except an echo . . . [but Mrs. Wharton] would be content to write books that are exactly like the books of Henry James. She wants to be able to achieve just exactly the beauty he did; she wants to express just exactly the wisdom he did; and she succeeds astonishingly. Thus she feels she is in touch with a rich and worthy tradition. But then, also she withholds the treasures of discovery which should have been made by such an unusual talent" (qtd. in Tuttleton 314). West's review praises Wharton for her "unusual talent" but the bulk of the review dismisses Wharton's work as being able only to ape the conventions of James. It is to this sort of commentary that Gale's admiration provides an antidote.

10. Wharton, Cather, and Gale all share long literary apprenticeships: Wharton published *The Decoration of Houses* (1897) when she was about thirty-five; her first short-story collection, *The Greater Inclination,* came out two years later. Cather published *The Troll Garden,* a collection of short stories, in 1905, when she was thirty-two, and her first novel, *Alexander's Bridge,* when she was thirty-nine. Gale's first novel, *Romance Island,* was published in 1906, when she was thirty-two. Wharton was born in 1862, Cather in 1873, and Gale in 1874; when Gale and Wharton began their correspondence, Wharton was almost sixty and Gale close to fifty. Sinclair Lewis, on the other hand, was born in 1885 and could really be considered a member of a generation younger than Wharton's.

11. Wharton's attitude about the gender of genre may have emerged from the popular press and not just from her own feelings of inadequacy. *The Bookman* ran an article in 1908 entitled "Some Recent Women Short-Story Writers" that declared "women *ought to be* among the best writers of short stories, especially those modeled upon the French style, the story of character rather than that of incident, the successful seizure of an emotional moment . . . and there are writers who, like Mrs. Wharton and Miss Cather, are particularly good in that line" (152, emphasis added). Gale is

mentioned at the end of the article as one of those "whose work is constantly to be met in the pages of the periodicals" (161).

12. Wharton expands on her own critical fortunes in a 1928 essay, "A Cycle of Reviewing," published in the *Spectator*, in which she says that critics originally "deplored" the absence of plot in her novels and then later urged her to "emancipate [herself] from the incubus of 'plot'" (*Uncollected Writings* 161).

13. Leda's affliction sounds similar to the continuing bouts of tendonitis and neuritis that Cather suffered. Given that by 1923, Gale knew and was friendly with Cather, it seems possible that Leda is partially based on Willa.

14. Wharton criticizes Lewis on similar grounds in the letter she writes to him about *Babbitt:* "In your next book, you should use slang in dialogue more sparingly. I believe the real art in this respect is to use just enough to *colour* your dialogue, not so much that in a few years it will be almost incomprehensible. It gives more relief to your characters, I'm sure, than to take down their jargon word for word" (*Letters* 455).

15. This same letter thanks Wharton for introducing her to Proust, saying that she didn't know "that Proust had used that form . . . until I had used it in two longish stories." Gale refers to an unnamed article about Proust that she enclosed with this letter to Wharton. In a letter to H. L. Mencken, Gale explains her idea about dialogue this way:

I have adopted a form which I think I shall not leave—that of integrating most talk, instead of giving a line or two, or more, to observation and replies. This permits those quotations which for any reason should stand out instead of their all being evaluated alike. . . . I have used very little paragraphing—and the paragraphs depend usually not on a change of subject or scene but on quite other considerations—as matters of tempo and emphasis, or as a fortuitous sentence which deserves a little pause. (n.d., SHSW)

Gale organizes *Preface to a Life* (1926) in this manner. The truly important ideas, like Bernard Mead's descriptions of his epiphanies, stand out in greater relief because other, less important conversations, are looped into the paragraphs without any breaks. I discuss this novel in more detail in Chapter Two.

16. In a similar example, Wharton wrote to John Hugh Smith in 1925 that "it *is* of course what an English reviewer (I forget in what paper) reviewing it jointly with Mrs. Woolf's latest, calls it: an old-fashioned novel. I was not trying to follow the new methods as May Sinclair so pantingly and anxiously does; and my heroine belongs to the day when scruples existed" (*Letters* 480). The Wharton novel is *The Mother's Recompense,* and the Woolf novel, *Mrs. Dalloway.* Wharton's disparaging remarks create a distance between herself and the two English writers: they are panting,

anxious women, while Wharton herself is serene, unruffled. Wharton professes to be untouched by literary trendsetting, although this letter clearly betrays the same anxieties about being old-fashioned that mark her letters to Gale.

17. Wharton made an exception to her usual rule against "blurbing" other writers in the case of Anita Loos's *Gentlemen Prefer Blondes* (1925). She allowed herself to be quoted calling the book "*the* great American novel," a comment that was used in advertisements along with equally laudatory comments by James Joyce and George Santayana. Wharton wasn't friends with Loos, although she did attend a luncheon in her honor at the Paris Ritz, but the novel seems to have struck a chord with her, in part because she believed that Lorelei Lee, Loos's heroine, "vindicated" Undine Spragg, the heroine of *The Custom of the Country* (1913). For further discussion of Wharton and Loos, see Benstock, *No Gifts From Chance;* R. W. B. Lewis, *Edith Wharton: A Biography;* and Wolff, *A Feast of Words.*

18. The second novel she refers to in her title is *Song of the Lark* (1915), which Cather says took "the wrong road" through no fault but her own. Curiously, whether through an editorial mistake or through deliberate misinformation given to them by Cather, when Cather's novel *A Lost Lady* was serialized in *The Century* magazine in 1923, *O Pioneers!*, not *Alexander's Bridge*, is noted as Cather's first novel in the "notes on contributors" section. *A Lost Lady* had been preceded in the pages of *The Century* by Gale's *Faint Perfume*, leading Carl Van Doren, then the magazine's fiction editor, to tell Gale that "I have, as fiction editor, had remarkable luck so far" (December 28, 1922, SHSW).

19. Given Pater's influence on Cather's ideas about art and writing, using him to describe Jewett is high praise indeed. I have discussed the connections between Cather and Pater in "Losing Nothing, Comprehending Everything: Learning to Read Both the Old World and the New in *Death Comes for the Archbishop.*"

20. Marilee Lindemann argues that the "family" Cather creates through her selection of great books "begins to build a model of American literary history as a sexually egalitarian and happy family" (*Queering* 97). To create this family, in which there are no siblings, Cather needed to look beyond her contemporaries. Tellingly, the only other essay that Cather wrote specifically about another woman writer is her piece on Katherine Mansfield, which she did not publish until after Mansfield's death from tuberculosis.

21. Because of this stipulation, I follow the model established by generations of Cather scholars, and paraphrase the letters in the text, followed in parentheses by the date. This problem is a familiar and vexing one to anyone who has worked on Cather materials, as Janis Stout has recently summarized: "Without full and definitive publication [of the letters], the uses that are made of the letters are not conveniently subject to verification. . . . Moreover, the temptation to incorporate Cather's own language—for after all, no paraphrase, however skilled, can ever convey the

meaning of the letters as well as her own words—has at times proven too great for researchers to bear, with the result that passages from the letters have been incorporated verbatim into published books and essays without quotation marks or with only nominal alteration" ("Restudying" 44). Lindemann astutely links the "peculiar situation" surrounding Cather's letters with Judith Butler's ideas about Cather's fiction and sexuality. Lindemann argues that the prohibitions around the letters "serve to prove and extend Butler's claim that lesbian sexuality is 'produced through the very historical vocabularies that seek to effect its erasure'" (18). Cather's sexuality, like her private letters, attains the status of an open secret, and through her desire to eradicate all traces of the private self, she may have in fact created greater distortions than had she done what Wharton did before she died: leave a neat stack of notebooks labeled "for my biographer."

22. Gale's mother died in 1923 and her father died in 1929, several months after Gale's marriage. Meridel Le Sueur bitingly claims that Gale "married her own father" when she chose Llelwyn Breese, a widowed banker with a teenage daughter, as her husband. Le Sueur and a number of Gale's other feminist friends were deeply (and in some cases unhappily) surprised that Gale chose to marry at all.

23. For a discussion of the "unencumbered individual" in a political rather than a literary context, see Sandel.

24. For more about the relationship between Yezierska and Gale, see Louise Henriksen's biography, *Anzia Yezierska: A Writer's Life* (1988). Henriksen reports that Yezierska's unpublished autobiography has a chapter about Gale entitled "Saint in Cellophane," not an entirely flattering comment. Le Sueur reflects some of this same ambivalence, noting that although Gale enabled her publishing career, she also had "some of the destructiveness of 'mothering'" (231).

CHAPTER TWO

1. This essay anticipates Gale's dictum in "Allotropes," published the following year, that art "reveals" rather than invents; artistic revelation occurs through and because of the artist's "imaginative interpretations." "The United States and the Artist" was part of a series that ran in the *Nation* in which the magazine asked American writers for their response to the question, "Can a literary artist function freely in the United States?" According to the tag that ran at the end of the article, Gale's was the fourth essay in the series, preceded by Mary Austin, Theodore Dreiser, and Sherwood Anderson. Cather, among a number of other writers, is mentioned as one of the forthcoming contributors.

2. Gale would have been familiar with Cather's essay not only because of her friendship with Cather but also because Cather's essay appeared with

Gale's in an essay series titled "The Novel of Tomorrow," published in the *New Republic*.

3. For broad discussions of the Progressive Era, see Diner, *A Very Different Age*, and Lasch, *The True and Only Heaven;* for a discussion of the intellectual ferment of the period, see Kloppenberg, *Uncertain Victories*. Robyn Muncy has argued that the "trustbusting" image of the Progressive Era is not an accurate generalization of the period. She notes that neither African Americans nor women had much to say about trusts or corporate reforms, which leads her to conclude that the debate over trustbusting, which is often thought to be at the center of Progressivism, "is very race- and gender-specific" (31). Examining progressivism in this way suggests that corporate reforms were thus only one aspect of the era, not its totality.

4. In 1880, approximately 288 women worked as journalists, a figure that jumped to 2,193 by 1900; by the 1920s there were nearly 12,000 women journalists, mostly in the women's or features sections (Parker 45).

5. A "Lucy Stoner" was any woman who kept her name after marriage, as did the suffragist Lucy Stone. In 1921, Ruth Hale, a Heterodite and wife of Heywood Broun, and Jane Grant, who cofounded the *New Yorker* with her husband Harold Ross, founded the Lucy Stone League as a way to encourage other women to keep their own names. In her dissertation about the Lucy Stone League, Mary Lou Parker notes that "women wanting to keep their names were accused of being mentally unstable" in the popular press and public opinion, which suggests why women who kept their names might want to start a support group (142). The "Lucy Stone-ers" counted among their membership the writer Janet Flanner and her lover, Solita Solano.

6. Judith Schwarz's book *Radical Feminists of Heterodoxy* is an invaluable resource. She notes that Grace Nail, the wife of James Weldon Johnson, was a longtime Heterodoxy member, as were the radical labor activists Rose Pastor Stokes and Helen Gurley Flynn. Among the lesbian couples, Schwarz names Elisabeth Irwin and Katherine Anthony, Dr. Sara Josephine Baker and Ida Wylie, Helen Hull and Mable Louise Robinson, Helen Arthur and Agnes Morgan. Other Heterodites included Fannie Hurst, cartoonist Lou Rogers, journalist Rheta Childe Dorr, and Robert La Follette's daughter, Fola.

In "The Heterodoxy Club and American Feminism," which examines Heterodoxy from a sociological perspective, Kate Wittenstein writes that "club members insisted on a distinction between feminism and suffragism and very self-consciously regarded themselves as pioneers in forging a new feminist theory and practice. Indeed, it was Heterodoxy's elaboration of the relationship between theory and practice that gave feminism its unique shape during the 1912–1930 period" (3).

7. In "Putting Children First: Women, Maternalism, and Welfare in the Early Twentieth Century," Linda Gordon describes "maternalism" as the

process by which activist women constructed motherhood as "women's claim to respect and power" (65). Maternalism should not, however, be confused with actually bearing children—Gale, like a great number of her activist feminist cohort, was herself childless (although late in life she adopted a young girl). On another front, sidestepping maternalism altogether, NAWSA supported the College Equal Suffrage League in order to encourage suffrage among younger women. Irwin cofounded the League with the help of her friend Maud Wood Park, who would go on to help found the League of Women Voters.

8. In "Manifest Domesticity," Amy Kaplan also talks about the links between domesticity at home and in the nation at large, but with a different emphasis. Kaplan is interested in making an argument about the structural role that domesticity plays in the "institutional and discursive processes of national expansion and empire building" (583). Kaplan's essay is part of a special issue of the journal *American Literature,* entitled "No More Separate Spheres," which—as its title indicates—debates the accuracy and efficacy of the "separate spheres" ideology. In the introduction to this issue, Cathy Davidson observes that "one could even say that a generation of women historians who felt marginalized by the neglect of women's history used the separate spheres metaphor to write about neglected women who had turned their marginality into a source of power" (446). I agree with Davidson's hypothesis, although I would add that these historians contributed immeasurably to our knowledge of the female experience in the United States. Because the challenges to separate spheres ideology are fairly recent, much of the scholarship about women's history still exists within this paradigm, a fact that I point out only to explain why, despite my own questions about this way of thinking, I draw on the work of feminist historians whose studies seem unquestioningly to accept and build on this separatist argument.

9. In "Making a Spectacle of Suffrage," Sarah Moore notes that suffrage organizers paid close attention to the "decorative effect" of their parades and pageants as a way to challenge the image of suffragists as "socially deviant" (92). The leader of the 1913 parade in Washington, D.C., Inez Milholland, for example, was chosen as much for her beauty as for her commitment to radical politics.

The effect of the mainstream suffrage campaign, observes Sara Hunter Graham, was to "replace the stereotypical image of masculinized fanatic with a nonthreatening feminine heroine imbued with domestic virtues" (48). As the suffragist movement in the United States became increasingly an organization that—at least publicly—spoke to and for predominantly white, middle-class women, it lost sight of its abolitionist and working-class roots. Much of the present-day divisiveness in feminism can be traced directly back to this turn-of-the-century shift in focus, which anticipated the homophobia and racism that undercut the liberatory activism of Friedan-era feminism. Thus the question of how to create a feminist movement that can justly address the needs of a varied constituency has been a part of the movement almost since its inception.

10. In a 1912 issue of *The Remonstrance,* for instance, the editors argued that "if [a woman] is expected to exercise independent political judgment, this will promote domestic discord and weaken family ties . . . it would be bad if it stopped here; but in order to make her vote effective, she must act with some organization, frequently supporting some other man against her husband. She must meet, confer, canvass, consult and also learn the low practices and little dirty deceits of politics. . . . What of the children who are growing up while father is working . . . [and] while mother is out until midnight . . . whooping it up for Jones" (qtd. in Burt 73). Suffrage corrupts the family, the country, and the suffragist herself, who is sullied by her contact with politics. Suffragists countered by arguing that if women were to get involved with the political process, they would eradicate its corruption.

"Antis" were difficult to fight because their opposition to suffrage took many forms: it was variously thought that suffrage would lead to Prohibition, the overturning of Jim Crow, or the destabilization of industrial interests. For an overview of these various regional arguments, see Eleanor Flexner's groundbreaking study of suffrage, *A Century of Struggle.* A speech that Marie Jenney Howe made in 1912 satirizes the protean nature of antisuffrage arguments. Made as part of a forum that she organized, "Twenty-five Answers to the Antis," Howe's speech used antisuffrage rhetoric against itself to illustrate—she hoped—the absurdity of the antis' position. She told her audience that her arguments came in pairs, "in such a way that if you don't like one you can take the other." So, for instance, she links one "anti" idea—that "women are angels"—with its opposite, saying that "if you don't like that argument try this one. Women are depraved. They would introduce into politics a vicious element which would ruin our national life." She goes on to argue that suffragists "interfere too much" and talks about a Nurses Settlement in New York, where trained nurses "go forth to care for sick babies and give them pure milk." As a result, she says, only a few babies died in one summer, whereas in the past, hundreds of babies had died: "Now what are these women doing? Interfering, interfering with the death rate! And what is their motive in so doing? They seek notoriety . . . and if sixty women who merely believe in suffrage behave this way, what may we expect when all women are enfranchised?" (qtd. in Schwarz 110–12).

11. Pryse makes a useful distinction between *local color* and *regionalist,* terms that are often used synonymously. She argues that "literary regionalism . . . features an empathic approach to regional characters that enfranchises their stories and cultural perceptions" while "local color" fiction "represents regional life and regional characters as objects to be viewed from the perspective of the nonregional, often urban Eastern reader, and frequently offered for that reader's entertainment" ("Reading," 48). Al-

though she does not say so explicitly in this essay, Pryse is arguing with Richard Brodhead's *Cultures of Letters*. Brodhead does not distinguish between *regionalism* and *local color* writing but uses these terms interchangeably to disparage the authors most associated with these genres. He argues that both genres emerged in response to the growing leisure class in the U.S., who were newly enamored of vacationing in "unspoiled" areas. Regionalism, he contends, was "*not* produced for the cultures it was written about . . . it was projected toward those groups in American society that made a considerable investment in literary reading" (122). He points out that these stories were often published in "highbrow" magazines like *The Atlantic* and *Scribner's*, which can be "searched in vain for articles that address the interests of factory workers, immigrants, farm laborers, miners, clerks, shopgirls, and secretaries." What can be found in all of this fiction is the "short piece of touristic or vacationistic prose, the piece that undertakes to locate some little-known place far away and make it visitable in print" (125). A place like Sarah Orne Jewett's fictional Dunnet's Landing, he claims, is only a "world realized in a vacationer's mental image" (145). While Brodhead's book establishes what it meant to be a reader in late-nineteenth-century America, it also remarginalizes the women's writing that he discusses. There is a large and lively body of work about women writers and regionalism. See for example, Fetterley and Pryse, Romines, Jordan, Inness and Royer, Pryse, McCullough, and the special issue of *American Literature* mentioned in note 8.

12. For more about women's clubs, see Sara Evans's essay "Women's History and Political Theory: Toward a Feminist Approach to Public Life." Evans argues that women used their clubs "to critique male stewardship of the public realm" and that the organizations provided "an essential link" between the "state and domestic life, having characteristics of both the public and the private. . . . Women themselves construed these as public not private environments, though they were often small and usually all-female" (129). Gale's novel illustrates this point: the Ladies Sodality use their organization as a way to involve themselves in the civic affairs of their town and to find their public voice.

13. In "The Domestication of Politics," Paula Baker notes that the WCTU linked so-called feminine values and traditionally defined politics. Thus while it took "traditional domestic concerns seriously, the WCTU taught women how to expand them into wider social concern and political action. With greater success than any other nineteenth-century women's group, it managed to forge the woman's sphere into a broadly based political movement" (638). The connection between suffragists and temperance advocates, however, was often used by antisuffragists, who claimed (rightly) that if women got the vote the whole country would go "dry."

14. Graham breaks antisuffrage sentiment into two different but interrelated arguments. On the one hand are what she calls the "traditionalist" arguments, which played on the nineteenth-century notion of the feminine

ideal. Enfranchising women put into jeopardy both family stability and women's health: women would become "hard, harsh, unlovable, repulsive" (14) and families would deteriorate without maternal influence. On the other hand are the "tory" arguments against suffrage, which argued that "democracy was experimental and should be limited to responsible, dutiful citizens who would exercise suffrage in the interest of society at large" (16). Gale's novel implicitly rebuts both sets of arguments.

15. For more about feminism and utopia, see Jennifer Burwell's *Notes on Nowhere: Feminism, Utopian Logic, and Social Transformation.* All utopian literature, she claims, "implicitly critiques existing conditions" (3) and also "*thematizes* a set of wishes and dreams in its construction of an imaginary alternative society" (40).

16. Bell includes in his essay the perhaps apocryphal story of Stowe's insistence that it was God who wrote *Uncle Tom's Cabin,* a comment that represents Stowe as some sort of divine secretary. In *Uncle Tom's Cabin and American Culture,* Thomas F. Gossett suggests that Stowe may have been "possessed with a prolonged spell of religious hysteria" when she made this claim. Even if she did not in fact think of herself as God's stenographer, Gossett writes, Stowe did believe that "God gives specific missions to people on earth" (94–95).

17. Gale's story anticipates the turmoil that would be created when her (white) protégée, Margery Latimer, married Jean Toomer, the African American writer. When news of their 1931 marriage was covered in *Time* magazine (on the "National Affairs" page under the heading "Races"), the couple became the subject of national scrutiny which resulted in their receiving hate mail and death threats. Despite the outcry, Gale's support never wavered, although her friendship with Latimer grew strained for other reasons, including Latimer's anger at what she thought was the other woman's literary overprotectiveness. Le Sueur believes that Gale's Victorian attitudes about sexuality felt punitive to the younger writer, who painted a scathing portrait of Gale in the story "Guardian Angel." Le Sueur claims that Gale "preached that sex was brutalizing, bestial, enslaving. And in her time it was" (231). The letters between Gale and Latimer indicate that something disrupted their friendship, but no specifics are described. Le Sueur's portrayal of Gale's sexual attitudes is quite different from the description of Gale contained in a letter that Ridgely Torrence wrote to his parents about her: "I have to laugh at your telling me to marry a girl like Zona Gale. She would be as unfaithful a creature as you could possibly get hold of" (qtd. in Clum 57).

18. Charlotte Perkins Gilman, for instance, despite her concentrated efforts on behalf of women's economic and political rights, limited her concerns to white women. In *White Women's Rights,* her study of racism and feminism, Louise Newman points out that for Gilman and other suffragists "white supremacy was entirely consistent with a belief in equality between the sexes. . . . Like other white progressives in the early twentieth century,

[Gilman] downplayed blackness as a permanent category of social inferiority: Negroes were not branded uncivilizable as a race but judged individually on the basis of their adherence to middle-class, gendered social norms" (134). Gilman's emphasis on the individual echoes Sedgwick's willingness to accept an *exceptional* member of the race—with the implicit understanding that such an exceptional individual would model middle-class white values and standards.

The suffrage movement underwent a divisive internal battle over whether or not the organization should support enfranchisement for *all* women, regardless of race, a battle ultimately won by conservative white women. There are a number of excellent discussions about the tensions between white suffragists and African American women—and NAWSA's dismaying decision to jettison African American women's interests in its pursuit of the vote. See Newman, Flexner, Graham, Giddings, Chafe, Marilley, Frankel and Dye, Harley and Terborg-Penn.

19. Although there are no records in Gale's papers about what happened to "The Reception Surprise," "Dream" seems to be a revised version of that story, in which Gale downplays the interracial marriage, but preserves the intermingling of blacks and whites. It is difficult to know precisely how Gale revised "Dream" because the original manuscript did not survive. There is only one small mention in "Dream" that Mr. Burton Fernandez is not white, a reference so slight that it could easily be overlooked. Gale may have added this detail in an effort to get the story past an editor's eye without completely abandoning her original vision.

20. This phrase comes from Langston Hughes's autobiography, *The Big Sea* (1940); it is the title of the section in which he describes the period known as the Harlem Renaissance.

21. For further discussion of African American theater, see Hutchinson.

22. Writers whose careers Fauset fostered include Hughes himself, Claude McKay, Jean Toomer, Countee Cullen, George Schuyler, and Nella Larsen, among others.

23. Georgia Douglas Johnson, the African American poet, essayist, and dramatist, dedicated her third book of poems to Gale and shared the manuscript of her play *Blue Blood* with her. In a letter to Arna Bontemps, Johnson wrote that "often I am conscious of a feeling of transcendent thanksgiving that I am living—that I have the privilege of contacting, even from afar, certain superb people. Among that number was Zona Gale, a precious woman [who] . . . makes you feel conscious of the finest and most beautiful emotions. She has passed on but there are others still among us with hearts of gold—hearts big with understanding, sympathy—love!" (qtd. in Hutchinson 491).

24. There is no record of whether Gale actually sent the story, or if she did, what Wharton thought of Hurston's work.

25. In "Modernism and Modernity," Rita Felski argues that feminist critics need to explore and expand "such oppositions between the old-fashioned

and the absolutely new in order to grasp the shifting valences of particular techniques of representation in the history of women's art" (202). Felski's essay addresses a number of issues that pertain to the current status of both Fauset and Gale.

26. This letter is written on notepaper with an interesting detail: printed onto the stationery in the upper left-hand corner are two women's heads, in silhouette, each wearing an old-fashioned sunbonnet, with her hand up near her face as if to shield what she is saying. Underneath the women's heads is the caption "Don't tell," written in copperplate script. It is an odd choice—but perhaps a telling one—for a letter in which one writer is discussing the logistics of getting another writer to write a forward for her book. This curious notepaper also suggests the traditional transmittal of women's knowledge—through whispered conversations and hidden communications, through behind-the-hand gossip.

27. A recent edition of Gilman's *The Yellow Wallpaper* that situates the novella in its cultural contexts replicates Gale's erasure from Fauset's career. Gale is mentioned nowhere in the otherwise informative introduction to Gilman's novella and the collaborative effort that produced Gilman's autobiography is reduced to a single sentence in the chronology: in 1935, Gilman "revises her autobiography and selects pictures for it" (38). Despite her strong belief in communities of women and feminist networks, Gilman is thus preserved as a singular heroine.

28. The 1924 National Origins Act placed quotas on immigration that effectively closed the door to emigration by Italians, Poles, and Russians; the law also completely excluded Asians. Gale's inclusive politics would have been outraged by such an exercise in xenophobia.

29. In *Terrible Honesty* (1995), Ann Douglas argues that the omission of spiritualism from literary history needs to be remedied: "The serious study of Spiritualism as a historical phenomenon and a literary influence has only begun; its importance will inevitably prove to be enormous" (514).

30. Gale supported the Wisconsin chapter of the Boys Conservation Bureau, contributed to the Friends of Native Landscapes, lobbied for the creation of parks, and allowed her one-act play *Neighbors* to be performed by any theater organization, without paying copyright or permissions, if the organization would plant a tree in the community where they were to perform.

31. Gale was notorious for being a very light eater. Her diet anticipated a number of late-twentieth-century trends: she believed that "one should not eat preserved fruits and jellies, white sugar, white flour, vinegar, heavy desserts, salt after forty, and meat" (Simonson 54). Given her strict dietary rules, Bernard's increasing girth becomes a sign of his moral turpitude, as does Laura's transformation from a pretty young woman into a "fat, white shape." In 1926, the ideal body for a woman was the breastless, hipless figure of the flapper, a shape to which Gale's own svelte figure conformed quite readily.

32. The townspeople have no tolerance for mysticism, despite living in a town that draws its name from the French "Pâques," meaning Easter, which marks the most mystical date on the Christian calendar. I am grateful to Shireen Patell for this observation.

33. These descriptions of Bernard's awakening also reflect the influence of Walter Pater, whose *Studies in the Renaissance* (1873) was one of Gale's favorite books in college. Bernard's apprehension of an experience as a process rather than a point reflects Pater's observation that life "fines itself down" to the "passage and dissolution of impressions, images, sensations, that analysis leaves off—that continual vanishing away, that strange perpetual weaving and unweaving of ourselves" (60).

34. Packer comments that Emerson, like others in the Transcendental Club in the 1840s, "feared that there was something 'effeminate' about American art," a fear that was particularly troubling because he had given the editorship of *The Dial* to Margaret Fuller. "It is not always clear," Packer writes, "whether Emerson thought American art lacked manliness because it was imitative or whether he feared that all art lacked manliness," but his opinions of writers like William Cullen Bryant and William Ellery Channing are clear: they have a "*feminine* or receptive" cast (447, 449). In her portrayal of Bernard Mead being penetrated by a goddess spirit that moves him to a transcendent apprehension of the world, Gale brings Emerson's fears to fruition and articulates a version of transcendentalism that echoes Fuller's plea, in "The Great Lawsuit," that boundaries not be determined for either sex.

35. In *Emerson and Asia*, Frederic Carpenter notes the relationships between Emerson, Thoreau, and Whitman and various strands of what he calls the "Orientals." He notes that Rabindrabath Tagore—one of Gale's favorite writers—declared, "No American has caught the Oriental spirit so well as Whitman." All three writers, according to Carpenter, shared "the stimulus which the ancient East gave to the progressive thought of America" (250–51). Given her long-standing interests in both Eastern philosophy and nineteenth-century American writers, it is likely that Gale both read and agreed with Carpenter's study.

CHAPTER THREE

1. Through their involvement in the Society of Midland Authors (which Butcher claims was the longest-lived group of writers in the country), Butcher was good friends with Gale; she knew Cather, who was very appreciative of Butcher's reviews. Butcher became friendly with Wharton late in Wharton's life, after Butcher interviewed her at home at Pavilion Colombe.

2. The 1913 NAWSA suffrage pageant, staged on the steps of the Treasury Building the day before Woodrow Wilson's inaugural, "marked a turning

point in suffrage activities in the United States," argues Moore, because of its "carefully choreographed and public challenge to fundamental standards of feminine behavior and propriety and recontextualization of feminine allegorical imagery" (101). She contends that this pageant and others like it "forged a connection between art production, politics, and the construction of femininity which resonates to this day" (101). In *Selling Suffrage* (1999), Margaret Finnegan observes that having well-known actresses perform in suffrage dramas and march in suffrage parades helped to sell the cause to the country: "An enormous flurry of attention . . . accompanied suffrage events hosted by professional performers" (88) Fola La Follette's popularity—and later, her notoriety—was increased by the fact that Robert La Follette, the Wisconsin progressive senator, was her father. When Bob La Follette voted against declaring war on Germany, he was reviled, as was his entire family. One of the only places where Fola could find refuge was Heterodoxy meetings.

3. Maureen Honey argues that New Woman fiction was a mainstay in a number of the popular magazines, including *Ladies Home Journal, McCall's,* and *Woman's Home Companion.* These stories "deal seriously and progressively with many contemporary feminist issues: lack of professional advancement, sexual harassment, prostitution as alienated labor, enfeebling marital dependency, and the importance of female solidarity. Above all, they endorse a woman's right to meaningful paid work outside the home" (26). These "New Woman romances," as Honey calls them, were often in conflict with the more conservative editorial position espoused by women's magazines, as Nancy Burkhalter points out in "Women's Magazines and the Suffrage Movement" (1996). Burkhalter examined two women's magazines, *Ladies Home Journal* and *Good Housekeeping,* and two general interest magazines, *Literary Digest* and *The New Republic,* and found that the women's magazines dealt with suffrage "in a safe way, focusing . . . on how it could make the woman's life at home easier, or how it could help her do her job more efficiently. No radical reforms were called for, no weighty arguments debated" (19). As NAWSA modified its public image, however, suffrage and suffragists become, in editorial eyes, "easily fused with traditional values." Burkhalter contends that the general interest magazines were much more openly supportive of the suffrage movement. Despite the fact that women's magazines were reluctant to promote suffrage on their editorial pages, suffragists publicized their causes in many other ways. Finnegan describes a wide range of suffrage commodities, including "hats, blouses, badges, pins, valentines, Kewpie dolls, playing cards, drinking cups, luggage tags, fans, hat pins, and much more" (112).

4. In *Sentimental Modernism,* Suzanne Clark points out that for many women writers in the early twentieth century, "the women's tradition was all too coherent . . . it was risky for a writer to appeal to a community of readers which identified her with the feminine. . . . But popular appeal

was precisely what was risky. . . . The feminine community, however populous, was nonliterary and nonauthoritative by definition" (34). It is in the teens and twenties that this distinction solidified into the distinctions between high-brow and low-brow and, as Janice Radway has so cogently illustrated in her book about the Book-of-the-Month Club, yet a third category, the middle-brow. It is in part because the club disrupted what had seemed to be clear distinctions between high and low that initial response to the BOMC was so violent.

5. For discussions of the novel in these terms see, among others, Elaine Showalter's *Sister's Choice;* Elizabeth Ammons's *Edith Wharton's Argument with America;* and Alice Kinman's unpublished dissertation, "Becoming a Citizen in the 'Land of Letters': Edith Wharton's Early Work, 1891–1905."

6. A number of critics discuss the connections between Wharton's interest in architecture and her writing, among them Judith Fryer, in *Felicitous Spaces: The Imaginative Spaces of Edith Wharton and Willa Cather,* and Sarah Luria, in "The Architecture of Manners: Henry James, Edith Wharton, and The Mount." Luria notes that Wharton praised "cozy rooms where one could sit by the fire and write a letter or have an intimate chat" (299), a description that fits both the drawing room in Carry's house, where Lily sees Rosedale playing with Carry's daughter, and the guest bedroom where Lily sleeps, which has a fireplace with a pillowed lounge next to it, where Carry sits to give Lily advice about her situation.

7. This is probably the same photograph that Gale found in a magazine and responded to so passionately.

8. The distinction between serious and popular was represented as a gendered distinction, more often than not, in the popular press: men write serious fiction and women write popular novels. Thus Wharton could not see herself as a popular, best-selling novelist without imagining a concomitant loss of literary authority. Wharton's later novels, which were quite popular and were serialized in women's magazines, are generally considered inferior to her earlier (and less commercially successful) work. Similarly, Cather's best-selling novel, *One of Ours,* was also one of her most disparaged novels.

9. In "Corporate Thinking: Edith Wharton's *The Fruit of the Tree,*" Jennie Kassanoff makes a similar point, arguing that the concluding scene "suggests that authorial intent, the very agency behind textual production, has been dangerously dislocated: the author can no longer control her own production" (53). It is this loss of control that Wharton most fears, but while Kassanoff sees Wharton becoming "incapacitated" by her loss of control, I think that these anxieties led Wharton to create a public authorial self that she deploys to satisfy her readers. Wharton's public persona, like Cather's, becomes a kind of scrim, behind which she can do as she pleases. If the public self is a fiction, then it matters less if it is misread by her audiences.

10. Cather finds in the prairie what Edith Wharton finds in New York: fitting
    subject for her pen. Each writer's mentor—Sarah Orne Jewett and Henry
    James, respectively—told her to find her own subject: to "explore the
    parish," in Jewett's words (qtd. in O'Brien 345), or in James's advice to
    Wharton, to utilize "the American subject . . . *Do New York!*" (Lewis 71n).

11. Lena Lindgard, unlike Tiny, has been the subject of a number of critical
    discussions, most of which tend to focus on Lena's sexuality, whether het-
    erosexual or homosexual, and how that sexuality functions in the novel.
    See for instance, Blanche Gelfant's *Women Writing in America;* Judith
    Fetterley's *"My Ántonia,* Jim Burden, and the Dilemma of the Lesbian
    Writer"; Judith Butler's *Bodies That Matter,* which has a brief discussion
    of *My Ántonia* and a longer discussion of the early short story, "Tommy
    the Unsentimental"; and Marilee Lindemann's essay, "'It Ain't My
    Prairie': Gender, Power, and Narrative in *My Ántonia,*" among others.

12. Tiny's adventures in the gold fields echo the actual experiences of a num-
    ber of female adventurers, whose autobiographies and memoirs were
    quite popular in the early years of the century. See, for example, Mary
    Hitchcock's *Two Women in the Klondike* (1899) and E. L. Kelly's tales of
    her exploits in the Klondike, which ran in *Lippincott's Monthly.* For more
    information about women and the gold rush, see Melanie J. Mayer's
    Klondike Women: True Tales of the 1897–98 Gold Rush and Frances Back-
    house's *Women of the Klondike.*

13. When Elizabeth Sergeant told Cather that she was reading McClure's
    story as it appeared in *McClure's,* Cather "admitted to having a hand in it"
    and boasted with a chuckle that "she could . . . write a better and truer
    McClure than McClure himself" (Sergeant 125). For a discussion of Mc-
    Clure's and Cather's ghostwriting collaboration, see Williams, "Hiding in
    Plain Sight," Woodress, Thacker, Lee, or O'Brien. See the memoirs of
    Edith Lewis and Sergeant for more firsthand accounts of Cather's reac-
    tions to McClure's stories.

14. Not surprisingly, recent attempts to revise Cather's image by investigating
    her psychosexual makeup and by stressing the innovative complexity of her
    fiction have met with considerable resistance. For example, in a 1995 *New
    Yorker* essay, Joan Acocella rails against all types of Cather criticism, but
    particularly against critics who are "tendentiously political"—by which she
    means, it seems, "wild-eyed" feminist critics generally and those who read
    Cather as a lesbian in particular. Acocella concludes her essay with the plea
    that Cather "become a non-topic again" and leave her books to "those who
    really care about them." If we "really cared" about Cather, Acocella's logic
    goes, we would pay no attention to things like sexuality, politics, or con-
    text. Acocella recently published an expanded version of this essay, *Willa
    Cather and the Politics of Criticism,* in which she argues that "political" crit-
    icism ignores "the profundity of [Cather's] vision, her originality, her *ear.*"
    Continuing her equation of "political" with "feminist," Acocella goes on to
    ask, "What do they have left of her . . . once all that has been ignored in

order to turn her into a feminist?" (74). As I have argued elsewhere, it is Acocella's logic—not feminist criticism—that makes aesthetics and discussions of literary style irreconcilable with considerations of gender and sexuality. See my "Hiding in Plain Sight: Willa Cather and Ghostwriting."

15. Cather leaves Houghton Mifflin for Knopf in a move that Marilee Lindemann describes as "clearly shrewd and necessary." She claims that "Cather, who needed to earn a living and whose years with *McClure's* had given her a healthy respect for the value of publicity, had long been dissatisfied with what she described to [Ferris] Greenslet as the cautious spirit with which the firm handled her work." Lindemann also notes that Cather's letters to Greenslet contain a "modern vocabulary of economic self-interest and the commodification of the book and the author" (*Queering* 87).

16. Cather told Fanny Butcher that she chose Knopf as her publisher because when she used to go to concerts in midday she noticed "in the predominantly feminine audience, . . . a handsome Spanish-looking young man who was plainly listening . . . with his whole being." Cather told Butcher that when "I found out that he was a book publisher . . . I decided then and there that any young man who would neglect his business to listen to music in the afternoon was the publisher I wanted" (366). Typically, Cather downplays her interest in making money at writing and asserts that her interest in Knopf was purely aesthetic. In her description of Knopf as "Spanish-looking," there is both a not-so-veiled reference to Knopf's Jewishness and to Julio, the guide over whom Cather rhapsodized during her trip to the Southwest in 1912. Julio, she wrote to Elizabeth Sergeant, looked like an Aztec sculpture, with skin the color of very old gold (June 15, 1912, Morgan Library Collection).

17. Porter's remark is quoted in Stout, "Katherine Anne Porter's 'Reflections on Willa Cather'" 724.

18. In "Cather, Woolf, and the Two Mrs. Ramsays" (1998), I point out that contrary to Cather's public disdain for "experimental" writers, she in fact has a deeply complex relationship with Virginia Woolf, a relationship that provides the subtext for *Lucy Gayheart* (1935).

19. Cather was quite aware of the reputation that the Village had, as a joke that she made in a 1919 letter to Greenslet indicates: she wrote him that it was impossible to get a new phone in an apartment except in cases of emergency, such as having a child. Such a situation, she observes wryly, could easily create the occasion for a village farce. (I am grateful to Bob Thacker for passing along this anecdote.)

20. Sexuality in *The House of Mirth* and *My Ántonia* is more complicated and less clearly rewarded. Ántonia, at the end of the novel, is more like a grizzled she-bear, and her sexuality seems to have been subverted into motherhood. Lena and Tiny's flirtatious behavior makes them subject to scandal in Nebraska; they can only establish their West Coast version of a Boston marriage in San Francisco, away from wagging tongues. Lily

Bart is punished both for being too publicly sexy (as in her *tableau vivant* portrait) and for not being promiscuous enough to channel her sexuality into shelter or profit. Carry is spicy and twice-divorced but can flourish only on the margins of society, not at its center.

21. This strange choice for a premiere occurred because David Belasco, the theater impresario, had just donated a theater space to the prison. Gale's play was chosen to inaugurate the new stage.

22. A poster advertising the movie highlights Lulu's abject position by showing her crouched on the ground scrubbing the floor, while Dwight towers over her yelling, "Get to work! Is this what I support you for?" Released by Paramount and directed by William DeMille (Cecil B.'s brother), the movie starred Lois Wilson, Milton Sills, Theodore Roberts, and Helen Ferguson.

23. Heywood Broun, writing in *The Bookman*, argues that the revised ending can be explained by the fact that Gale "loved her valiant young spinster to the top of her bent, that she was more anxious that Lulu should be similarly understood and loved by a lot of people than lost through misunderstanding, that she would have redrawn the portrait a hundred times, if necessary, to make it clear, and that she would, by these tokens, have upset heaven and earth sooner than bear it false witness." Broun accurately claims that Gale wanted Lulu's story to be *heard* at all costs.

24. Gale wrote to Robert La Follette that she was "too much of a socialist" to be of use to any traditionally partisan politics (September 20, 1920). In the rest of this letter she explains that she did not want the Wisconsin suffragists to affiliate themselves with partisan politics, because she wanted them to be part of a "third party movement." She also explains that she would never be "identified outright with the Republican party!"

25. One possible exception to this tendency to marginalize the community of spirit is the relationship between Tom Outland and Rodney Blake in *The Professor's House* (1925). Although this relationship ends with what Tom thinks is Rodney's betrayal—he sells the Native American relics they had discovered without consulting Tom first—the months they spend together, first in a cattle camp and then on the mesa, are "beautiful . . . soft, sunny, like a dream" (235). Even in this instance, however, as Cather offers a portrait of idyllic domesticity and emotional rapport, there is no *sisterhood*, only brotherhood.

26. Du Breuil was a sociologist and military officer who strongly supported feminism and women's issues (*Uncollected Writings* 204). This eulogy appeared in *Revue Hebdomadaire*, May 15, 1915.

Chapter Four

1. His name is reminiscent of *H. Rider Haggard*, whose novel *She* (1887) was a turn-of-the-century best-seller. One of the protagonists in that

novel is *Horace Holly*. Sandra Gilbert and Susan Gubar contend that Haggard's novel epitomizes "the complex of late Victorian anxieties that were exacerbated not just by the battle of the sexes . . . but also by a series of other key cultural changes" (*Sexchanges*, 7). By making Harbard/Haggard the voice of authority in her story, Wharton concedes the still-current pressures exerted on the literary world by men made anxious about female power, but the ending of her story, as I will discuss, demonstrates Wharton's sense of mastery over these men.

2. For further description of these and other images, see Banta; Gilbert and Gubar, *Sexchanges;* Minter; and Reynolds.

3. As we saw in her letters to Gale, Wharton was sure that she was thought of as a dead Victorian, an idea that was echoed in the reviews that *A Son at the Front* received. Similarly disparaging comments were made about Cather's novel, which will be discussed later in this chapter. This dismissive attitude about women writers continued in critical writing that emerged *about* World War I literature, which privileged the soldier-writer at the expense of all other voices. Lynne Hanley points out that in Paul Fussell's influential book *The Great War and Modern Memory,* for example, that "women are nowhere to be seen. They are not at the front, they are not in the rear, they are not tending the home fires, they are not writing their memoirs. . . . The only memorable woman is . . . the enthusiast recalled in Robert Graves's *Goodbye to All That*" (31).

   Only relatively recently have critics begun to pay attention to women's literary responses to war in ways that move the writing beyond the idea of the "war between the sexes," which, while an important idea, limits the extent to which women can be seen to engage not only with questions of literary authority but also with questions about militarism itself. In talking about the battle over the rights to literary representations of the war, I do not mean to reduce the violence of war into merely a trope for the war between the sexes. It is nevertheless important to realize that even as the "great war" was being waged in Europe, the war over women's rights continued in both Europe and the United States, where gender roles/identities were very much contested categories in the years surrounding the war. For further discussion about women and war, see Hanley, Cooper, Raitt and Tate, and Gilbert and Gubar, *No Man's Land.* For a discussion of the pacifist movement in particular, see Alonso, Steinson, and Kuhlman.

4. In the same way that Gale used her celebrity to help raise money, so too did Wharton, although with a different goal. Her fund-raising project, *The Book of the Homeless* (1915), raised over fifteen thousand dollars for her charitable organizations in France, and was created by Wharton's abilities to bring together important artists and military figures. Using one of her favorite metaphors, Wharton describes the book in terms of a house, with herself as the housekeeper or hostess: "I appealed to my friends who write and paint and compose, and they to other friends of

theirs . . . and so the Book gradually built itself up, page by page, and picture by picture. You will see from the names of the builders what a gallant
piece of architecture it is, what delightful pictures hang on its walls, and
what noble music echoes through them. But what I should have liked to
show is the readiness, the kindliness, the eagerness, with which all the
collaborators, from first to last, have lent a hand to the building. Perhaps
you will guess it for yourselves when you read their names and see the
beauty and variety of what they have given. So I efface myself from the
threshold and ask you to walk in" (xxiv-xxv). Wharton worked tirelessly
on behalf of refugees, raising thousands of dollars, starting schools and
hostels for women and children, and encouraging Americans to donate
supplies to hospitals and orphanages. For her labors, she was awarded the
French Legion of Honor.

5. Prior to the convention, Inger has read in the paper that a group of
   women are meeting in Congress under the headline "Sob Session Likely."
   Coverage of the WPP was similarly dismissive—when it was mentioned at
   all. One article, in the Washington *Post*, claimed that "women loved
   fighting men" because they wanted a "warrior's virile reproductive powers" (qtd. in Steinson 45n, 55). A woman's desire to bear virile children
   would ultimately outweigh her desire to rid the world of war, according
   to this logic.

6. Germany invaded Belgium in early August, 1914, en route to France.
   Belgium was all but destroyed by the invasion, and tales of German atrocities against civilians circulated widely. The atrocities were verified by the
   Bryce Report, which was later discredited as a tissue of inventions based
   on documentation and testimony that conveniently disappeared at the
   end of the war. Nevertheless, these stories were widely believed in the
   early days of the war, by both pacifists and militarists, and were at the base
   of much Allied propaganda. Many historians believe that because these
   tales of wartime horrors were revealed as groundless, people were much
   more resistant to the early stories of Hitler's genocidal plans.

7. In Britain, for example, more than one hundred women who intended to
   travel to The Hague conference were denied passports and thus could not
   attend the meeting (Alonso 67).

8. For a further discussion of the ambivalence with which women greeted
   the outbreak of war, see Gilbert and Gubar, *Sexchanges,* particularly
   Chapter Seven.

9. Gale's mention here of the Red Cross functions as a sort of product place-
   ment: this story first appeared in *Red Cross* magazine.

10. Maureen Ryan notes that Enid's is "the untold story" of Cather's novel.
    Ryan argues that Enid "quietly violates the norms of her time and place"
    through her decision to flee her unhappy marriage by going to China as
    a missionary (70). Ryan overlooks the fact that Enid's fervent espousal of
    "causes" makes her the object of satire. Enid is deeply committed to veg-
    etarianism, Prohibition, and Christianity but devoid of romance, passion,

and sensuality. She refuses to allow Claude to spend the night with her on their wedding night, claiming that she does not feel well. In the morning, when they are leaving the train, Claude asks her if she's forgotten anything, and Enid replies, "I never lose things on the train, do you?"—a comment that is both a bad pun and an indication that to all intents and purposes, Claude will die in France a virgin. The meals Enid prepares further indicate Cather's disdain for her attitudes: on her club nights, Enid leaves for Claude "a dish of canned salmon with a white sauce; hardboiled eggs, peeled . . . a bowl of ripe tomatoes, a bit of cold rice pudding; cream and butter" (165). The cold, gelid, qualities of this meal would have revolted Cather's epicurean sensibilities; Enid illustrates much of what Cather disdained about the "modern world."

11. A number of critics have discussed the novel's homoeroticism, a theme that it shares with many other World War I novels. Paul Fussell notes that in World War I poetry, "no one . . . can fail to notice . . . the unique physical tenderness, the readiness to admire openly the bodily beauty of young men, the unapologetic recognition that men may be in love with each other" (280). Marilee Lindemann astutely notes that "one need not diagnose Claude as homosexual (though such language would be appropriate given the novel's social context) in order to appreciate the way his queer body intervenes in American discourses of sexuality and citizenship." Lindemann goes on to argue that even as "efforts [were being made] to exclude homosexuals from military service in World War I . . . Cather turns the queer Claude into a soldier hero and an exemplary American" (*Queering* 71). John Anders traces the novel's homoeroticism through its references to Whitman and to the Greek ideal embodied in the Theban corps of soldiers known as the Sacred Band, referred to by Plato and Plutarch. In *One of Ours,* Anders claims, Cather strengthens her literary affinities with "homosexual myth and gay literary traditions" through the fact that Claude finds spiritual redemption in his friendship with David Gerhardt. Michael North discusses Claude's relationship with Gerhardt as the fruition of Claude's search for an "aesthetic proxy," the term that Cather uses to describe Claude's friendship with Gladys Farmer. As an aesthetic proxy, Gladys fulfills those behaviors that Claude himself—because of rigidly structured gender roles—cannot: enjoying beauty, caring for her clothes, being careful about her manners. Claude seeks the same thing in his marriage with Enid and fails utterly, but he finds the perfect aesthetic proxy in Gerhardt, who, argues North, "is all the more useful for being a man, representing as he does the possibility that masculinity and the aesthetic might not be utterly at odds" (188). Cather's representation of the intimate friendship between Claude and Gerhardt, as well as the other intimate bonds that flourish between soldiers, helps to establish the novel as working firmly within the literary tradition of the "Great War," despite the attempts of contemporary reviewers to invalidate her portrayals of life in the ranks.

12. The beginning of Hemingway's comment offers further context for his fury. "Look at *One of Ours*," he writes, "Prize, big sale, people taking it seriously"(105). This suggests that his vituperativeness has more to do with Cather's success than with the source of her war scenes. Her success must be dismissed at all costs, or it will, to misquote him slightly, catheterize him. Claude's death scene may also be a reenactment of something that happened to G. P. Cather, the cousin on whom Cather based the character of Claude. According to Woodress, the *New York Times* reported that G. P. Cather was cited for bravery when, "with splendid courage and coolness he mounted the parapet of a trench and directed a destructive flanking fire from two automatic rifle teams exposed to seven German machine guns" (303–304).

13. Mahailey's comment resonates with the novel's other classical references: the troop ship *Anchises;* the veiled references to Plato and Euripedes; a newspaper called the *Argus;* and so on. For a thorough discussion of these classical references, see Anders and Rosowski.

14. Edith Lewis is far more educated and sophisticated than Mahailey. But the relationship between Mrs. Wheeler, the "boss," and Mahailey, who provides both emotional companionship and labor, seems to echo the way that some biographers have constructed the Cather-Lewis relationship: Lewis is both Cather's personal secretary/assistant and dear friend. I think that the Cather-Lewis relationship was more emotional and physical than just "good friends," but the parallels between the two couples are worth noting.

15. The essay appeared in the April 12 issue as part of a series of essays entitled "The Novel of Tomorrow" commissioned by the magazine. Gale's essay, which has the same title as the general series, appeared in the same issue.

16. Dorothy Canfield Fisher, who also lived and worked in France during the war, and who published a book similar to Wharton's *Fighting France* called *Home Fires in France* (1919), disdained Wharton's French chauvinism. In a comment that echoes Wharton's own conception of herself, Fisher wrote Paul Reynolds that a character in her new novel would be "the sort of last-generation American woman, like Mrs. Wharton, who (so it seems to me) takes Europeans with a funny, prayerful certainty of their innate superiority" (90). In addition to her own book about France, Fisher helped Cather with the French parts of *One of Ours*, which has led Janis Stout to point out the number of strong parallels between Fisher's *Home Fires of France* and Cather's novel.

17. Interesting partisanship can be traced through the reviews: Elizabeth Shepley Sergeant, a longtime friend of Cather's, wrote a negative review of *A Son at the Front* for *The Atlantic;* Burton Rascoe, who admired Cather a great deal and became friends with her after *One of Ours* was published, wrote a scathing review of Wharton's novel and praised *One of Ours*. Cather arranged to have Fisher review her novel, certain that her

friend would give the novel favorable coverage—and she did, in the pages of the *New York Times Book Review*. Fola La Follette, a close friend of Gale's and daughter of the pacifist senator, wrote one of the few positive reviews of *Heart's Kindred*.

18. Unless otherwise noted, all the reviews of *A Son at the Front* are in Tuttleton.

19. There are a number of excellent discussions about the link between modernism and misogyny. See for example Gilbert and Gubar, *No Man's Land*; Scott, *The Gender of Modernism*; Rado; North; Clark; Wheeler; or Minter.

CONCLUSION

1. The *New York Times*, December 29, 1938. Another indication of Gale's status at the time of her death is the fact that in 1943, Knopf brought out "memorial" editions of the three books Gale published with them: *Portage, Wisconsin, and Other Essays; Borgia;* and *Bridal Pond*.

2. For illuminating discussions of Cather's and Wharton's late work, see Carlin and Bauer, respectively.

3. In these two novels, particularly in *The Gods Arrive*, it is possible to see indications of Gale's friendship with Wharton, particularly the fact that Weston recuperates from his grandmother's death and his breakup with Floss Delaney at the home of an old teacher of his, who lives in Belair, Wisconsin. The "solitude of the northern woods" (403), which sounds similar to the landscape around Portage, renews Weston's literary energies. When Weston remembers his grandmother's invocation of God on a particularly beautiful spring day in Euphoria, his memories spark a Gale-like reverie: "Perhaps what [his grandmother] had called 'God' was the same as what he called 'The Mothers'—that mysterious Sea of Being of which the dark reaches swayed and rumoured in his soul . . . perhaps one symbol was as good as another to figure the imperceptible point where the fleeting human consciousness touches Infinity" (*Hudson* 449). Although he sometimes thinks of his grandmother as a huckstering evangelist, after his stay in Belair, Weston realizes that she possessed a "deep central peace," and he feels "the warmth of her soul in his" (410). Gale's mysticism and belief in spiritual connection, often expressed in her letters to Wharton, demonstrated to Wharton that such beliefs were not always hoaxes perpetuated on a credulous audience.

4. The reasons for Sapphira's plotting against her young slave are deliberately ambiguous. She claims to believe that her husband is in love with Nancy, although her only evidence of this is the malicious gossip of Lizzie, the cook and a notorious liar. An alternative possibility, suggested by Sapphira's name, with its embedded link to Sappho, is that Sapphira wants Nancy for herself; she is not jealous of her husband's possible affection for Nancy, but of Nancy's affections for him.

5. Cather's handling of the Civil War in *Sapphira and the Slave Girl* is structurally very similar to Woolf's treatment of World War I in *To the Lighthouse* (1927). For more about Woolf and Cather, see Williams, "Cather, Woolf, and the Two Mrs. Ramsays."

6. In *The Resisting Reader*, Judith Fetterley states bluntly that "American literature is male." Wharton is one of the few exceptions, in her argument, to a literature that "neither leaves women alone nor allows them to participate" (xii). And in "Melodramas of Beset Manhood," Nina Baym has famously argued that white, Anglo-Saxon literary critics shaped American literature in their own image, creating a literary history that excluded women, indeed "entered her [into] literary history as the enemy" (9). Baym and Fetterley here articulate a common theme in first-wave U.S. feminist criticism. These views have since been refined and revised by a number of other scholars, including Baym and Fetterley themselves. For general discussions of canon formation, see Graff, Lauter, and Guillory. For discussions of feminist literary criticism and the academy, see Todd, Baym, Ezell, Greene and Kahn, Anderson and Fine, Fetterley, and Boxer, among others.

7. For examples of the recent trend to broaden modernist studies, see Felski, Scott, Rado, Gilbert and Gubar, and Hutchinson, among others. In her discussion about the decline of Cather's reputation in the 1930s and 1940s, O'Brien observes that "during the informal, uncodified beginnings of a profession women may play powerful roles, but the process of professionalization is also one of masculinization. Hence—just as midwives were exiled as the American Medical Association became established— women writers were required to leave the highest reaches of the canon, as if their presence there would somehow make it questionable that the American literary canon and the work of those who sought to establish it were serious enterprises" (250).

8. Radway notes that fears about standardization and mass production were also linked to fears about increased female cultural authority: "In a culture suddenly grappling not only with machines but with the prospect of non-subordinate women, women endowed with the official rights of choice and voice—the vote—and at the same time liberated sexually as dancing flappers and vamps . . . it seems clear that masculine agency was as threatened by the effects of an increasingly visible, potentially uncontrollable and uncontainable population of women as by the tireless operations of self-propelled machines" (212).

9. Bauer notes that Wharton was deeply aware of the "class connotations of eugenics debates about good and bad mothering" and that, by the end of the twenties, Wharton was particularly interested in "the ethical and social meanings of motherhood" (27).

10. "Readers want positive images and experiences with which they can identify," writes Reina Lewis about the need for "heroes" in the early stages of any cultural politics that emerges out of an oppressed, underrepresented,

or marginalized group. Lewis, who is writing about the rise of queer literary studies, points out that this search for role models can lead to inaccurate perceptions, a "quagmire of positive images" (Lewis in Munt 27). At the conclusion of their essay "Forward into the Past: The Complex Female Affiliation Complex," Gilbert and Gubar ask whether or not "we feminist critics . . . have rewritten and reappraised history in order to give it the positive inflection we desire and require?" (262). Although the importance of this question seems central to the current state of feminist literary study, reappraising these overly positive histories has been slow to happen.

11. Ezell wonders whether we should "ask ourselves whether the canon of women's literature, whenever it is constructed, should simply be a replica of the male tradition as defined by literary history" (59). Annette Kolodny articulates an earlier version of this idea in a review essay published in *Signs* in 1976, when she notes with pleasure R. W. B. Lewis's new Wharton biography, which she calls a significant departure from previous "biographical straitlacings." She cautions, however, that even in these days of "liberation," scholars and critics need to be aware that they are so "habituated . . . to the notion of artistic expression as a masculine prerogative that there remains a lingering tendency to portray women's success in this area as somehow also 'masculine' or at the very least, foreign to their nature" (419). Her review concludes with an assessment that sounds eerily familiar to those of us who remember the various celebrations of the "Year of the Woman" that occurred in the late 1990s in Hollywood. Generally speaking, these late-twentieth-century celebrations, like the one Kolodny remarks on in 1975, were "somewhat less than satisfying. . . . So much for 'The Year of the Woman'; it wasn't really" (421).

12. At the 1997 American Literature Association conference, I gave a paper that included a suggestion about ways in which feminist literary history had perhaps replicated some of the same ideological structures it wanted to replace. The chair of the panel and a woman in the audience admonished me for being disloyal—and ungrateful—to the earlier generation of feminist critics, as if by pointing out the need for continued revisions and reexaminations I was undermining the entire feminist project. Their criticism implied that all the necessary revisions had been completed, that I should be content to work within the parameters that had already been established.

WORKS CITED

Acocella, Joan. "Cather and the Academy." *New Yorker,* November 27, 1995, 56–67.

———. *Willa Cather and the Politics of Criticism.* Lincoln: U of Nebraska P, 2000.

Adickes, Sandra. *To Be Young Was Very Heaven: Women in New York Before the First World War.* New York: St. Martin's Press, 1997.

Alonso, Harriet Hyman. *Peace as a Women's Issue: A History of the U.S. Movement of World Peace and Women's Rights.* Syracuse, NY: Syracuse UP, 1993.

Ammons, Elizabeth. *Edith Wharton's Argument with America.* Athens, GA: U Georgia P, 1980.

———. *Conflicting Stories.* New York: Oxford UP, 1991.

Anders, John. *Willa Cather's Sexual Aesthetic and the Male Homosexual Literary Tradition.* Lincoln: U of Nebraska P, 1999.

Anderson, Benedict. *Imagined Communities: Reflections on the Origin and Spread of Nationalism.* 1983. Rev. ed. London: Verso, 1991.

Anderson, Mary, and Lisa Fine. *Doing Feminism: Teaching and Research in the Academy.* East Lansing: Michigan State UP, 1997.

Anon. "American Novelists Who Have Set Art Above Popularity." *Vanity Fair* [New York], January 1921, 55.

———. "The Apotheosis of Greenwich Village." *Vanity Fair* [New York] February 1921, 37.

———. "The Literary Spotlight: Zona Gale." *The Bookman* April 1923, 168–72.

Ardis, Ann. *New Women, New Novels: Feminism and Early Modernism.* New Brunswick, NJ: Rutgers UP, 1990.

Auerbach, Nina. *Communities of Women: An Idea in Fiction.* Cambridge, MA: Harvard UP, 1978.

Backhouse, Frances. *Women of the Klondike.* Vancouver: Whitecap, 1995.

Baker, Paula. "The Domestication of Politics: Women and American Political Society, 1780-1920." *American Historical Review* 89.3 (1984): 620–47.

Banta, Martha. *Imaging American Women: Idea and Ideals in Cultural History.* New York: Columbia UP, 1987.

Barlow, Judith. *Plays by American Women.* New York: Applause, 1990.

Bauer, Dale M. *Edith Wharton's Brave New Politics.* Madison: University of Wisconsin P, 1994.

Baym, Nina. *Feminism and Literary History.* New Brunswick, NJ: Rutgers UP, 1992.

Bell, Michael Davitt. "Conditions of Literary Vocation." In *Prose Writing 1820–1865*.Vol. Two of *The Cambridge History of American Literature*. Ed. Sacvan Bercovitch. Cambridge, MA: Cambridge UP, 1995. 11–123.

Benstock, Shari. "Beyond the Reaches of Feminist Criticism: A Letter from Paris." *Tulsa Studies in Women's Literature* 3.1/2 (1984).

———. *No Gifts from Chance: A Biography of Edith Wharton*. New York: Scribner's, 1994.

Berthoff, Warner. "Culture and Consciousness." *Columbia Literary History of the United States*. Ed. Emory Elliott. New York: Columbia UP, 1988. 482–98.

Bohlke, Brent, ed. *Willa Cather in Person: Interviews, Speeches, and Letters*. Lincoln: U of Nebraska P, 1986.

Boxer, Marilyn Jacoby. *When Women Ask the Questions: Creating Women's Studies in America*. Baltimore: The Johns Hopkins UP, 1998.

Brodhead, Richard. *Cultures of Letters: Scenes of Reading and Writing in Nineteenth-Century America*. Chicago, IL: U of Chicago P, 1993.

Broun, Heyward. "Miss Lulu Bett." *New York Tribune*, February 6, 1921, n.p.

Burkhalter, Nancy. "Women's Magazines and the Suffrage Movement: Did They Help or Hinder the Cause." *Journal of American Culture* 19 (Summer 1996): 13–24.

Burt, Elizabeth V. "The Ideology, Rhetoric, and Organizational Structure of a Countermovement Publication: The Remonstrance, 1890–1920." *Journalism and Mass Communication Quarterly* 75.1 (Spring 1998): 69–83.

Burwell, Jennifer. *Notes on Nowhere: Feminism, Utopian Logic, and Social Transformation*. Minneapolis: U of Minnesota P, 1997.

Butcher, Fanny. *Many Lives—One Love*. New York: Harper & Row, 1972.

Butler, Judith. *Bodies That Matter: On the Discursive Limits of "Sex."* New York: Routledge, 1993.

Campbell, Bruce F. *Ancient Wisdom Revived: A History of the Theosophical Movement*. Berkeley and Los Angeles: U of California P, 1980.

Canby, Henry Seidel. "Why Popular Novels Are Popular." *The Century Magazine* [New York], June 1922, 253–60.

Carlin, Deborah. *Cather, Canon, and the Politics of Reading*. Amherst: U Massachusetts P, 1992.

Carpenter, Frederic Ives. *Emerson and Asia*. Cambridge, MA: Harvard UP, 1930.

Castle, Terry. *The Apparitional Lesbian: Female Homosexuality and Modern Culture*. New York: Columbia UP, 1993.

Cather, Willa. *Alexander's Bridge*. Boston: Houghton-Mifflin, 1912.

———. *Death Comes for the Archbishop*. New York: Knopf, 1927.

———. *A Lost Lady*. New York: Knopf, 1923.

———. *Lucy Gayheart*. New York: Knopf, 1940.

———. *My Ántonia*. In *Early Novels and Short Stories*. Ed. Sharon O'Brien. New York: Library of America, 1987. 707–938.

———. *Not Under Forty*. 1936. Lincoln: Bison, 1988.

———. *One of Ours*. In *Early Novels and Short Stories*. Ed. Sharon O'Brien. New York: Library of America, 1987. 939–1298.

————. *O Pioneers!* In *Early Novels and Short Stories.* Ed. Sharon O'Brien. New York: Library of America, 1987. 133–291.

————. *The Professor's House.* New York: Knopf, 1925.

————. *Sapphira and the Slave Girl.* In *Later Novels.* Ed. Sharon O'Brien. New York: Library of America, 1990. 775–940.

————. *The Song of the Lark.* In *Early Novels and Short Stories.* Ed. Sharon O'Brien. New York: Library of America, 1987. 291–707.

————. *Shadows on the Rock.* New York: Knopf, 1931.

————. *Willa Cather on Writing.* 1936. Rpt. Lincoln: Bison, 1988.

Chafe, William H. "Women's History and Political History: Some Thoughts on Progressivism and the New Deal." In *Visible Women: New Essays on American Activism.* Ed. Nancy A. Hewitt and Suzanne Lebsock. Chicago: U of Illinois P, 1993. 100–118.

Charvat, William. *The Profession of Authorship in America, 1800–1870.* New York: Columbia UP, 1992.

Chauncey, George. *Gay New York: Gender, Culture, and the Making of the Gay Male World, 1890–1940.* New York: Basic, 1994.

Clark, Suzanne. *Sentimental Modernism: Women Writers and the Revolution of the Word.* Bloomington: Indiana UP, 1991.

Clum, John M. *Ridgely Torrence.* New York: Twayne, 1972.

Coiner, Constance. *Better Red: The Writing and Resistance of Tillie Olsen and Meridel Le Sueur.* New York: Oxford UP, 1995.

Cooper, Helen M., and Adrienne Auslander Munich. *Arms and the Woman: War, Gender, and Literary Representation.* Chapel Hill: U of North Carolina P, 1989.

Coultrap-McQuin, Susan. *Doing Literary Business: American Women Writers in the Nineteenth Century.* Chapel Hill: U of North Carolina P, 1990.

Curtin, William, ed. *The World and the Parish: Willa Cather's Articles and Reviews, 1893–1902.* Lincoln: U of Nebraska P, 1970.

Damon-Moore, Helen. *Magazines for the Millions: Gender and Commerce in the Ladies Home Journal and The Saturday Evening Post, 1880–1910.* Albany: State U of New York P, 1994.

Davis, Thadious M. Foreword. *There is Confusion.* By Jessie Redmon Fauset. 1924. Rpt. Boston, MA: Northeastern UP, 1989.

Davidson, Cathy N. Preface. *American Literature* 70.3 (1998): 443–65.

Derleth, August. *Still, Small Voice: The Biography of Zona Gale.* New York: Appleton-Century, 1940.

Dettmar, Kevin J. H., and Stephen Watt. *Marketing Modernisms: Self-Promotion, Canonization, Rereading.* Ann Arbor: U of Michigan P, 1996.

Diner, Steven J. *A Very Different Age: Americans of the Progressive Era.* New York: Hill and Wang, 1998.

Douglas, Ann. *Terrible Honesty: Mongrel Manhattan in the 1920s.* New York: Farrar, Straus & Giroux, 1995.

duCille, Ann. *The Coupling Convention: Sex, Text, and Tradition in Black Women's Fiction.* New York: Oxford UP, 1993.

Emerson, Ralph Waldo. *Essays and Lectures.* Ed. Joel Porte. New York: Library of America, 1983.

Evans, Sara M. "Women's History and Political Theory: Toward a Feminist Approach to Public Life." In *Visible Women: New Essays on American Activism.* Ed. Nancy A. Hewitt and Suzanne Lebsock. Chicago: U of Illinois P, 1993. 119–39.

Ezell, Margaret J. M. *Writing Women's Literary History.* Baltimore: The Johns Hopkins UP, 1993.

Felski, Rita. "Modernism and Modernity: Engendering Literary History." *Rereading Modernism: New Directions for Feminist Criticism.* Ed. Lisa Rado. New York: Garland, 1994. 191-208.

Fetterley, Judith. "*My Ántonia,* Jim Burden, and the Dilemma of the Lesbian Writer." In *Lesbian Texts and Contexts: Radical Revisions.* Ed. Karla Jay and Joanne Glasgow. New York: New York UP, 1990. 145–63.

———. "'My Sister! My Sister!': The Rhetoric of Catherine Sedgwick's *Hope Leslie.*" *American Literature* 70.3 (1998): 443–65.

———. *The Resisting Reader: A Feminist Approach to American Fiction.* Bloomington: Indiana UP, 1978.

Fetterley, Judith, and Marjorie Pryse. *American Women Regionalists.* New York: Norton, 1992.

Finnegan, Margaret. *Selling Suffrage: Consumer Culture and Votes for Women.* New York: Columbia UP, 1999.

Fisher, Dorothy Canfield. *Home Fires in France.* New York: Henry Holt, 1916.

———. "Latest Works of Fiction: *One of Ours.*" *New York Times Book Review,* September 10, 1922, 24.

Flexner, Eleanor, and Ellen Fitzpatrick. *Century of Struggle: The Woman's Rights Movement in the United States.* 1975. Cambridge, MA: Harvard UP, 1996.

Ford, Mary K. "Some Recent Women Short-Story Writers." *The Bookman* [New York], April 1908, 152–61.

Frank, Waldo. "Pseudo-Literature." *New Republic,* December 2, 1925, 46–47.

Frankel, Noralee, and Nancy S. Dye. *Gender, Class, Race, and Reform in the Progressive Era.* Lexington: UP of Kentucky, 1991.

French, Marilyn. "Muzzled Women." *College English* 20.3 (1987): 219–29.

Fryer, Judith. *Felicitous Spaces: The Imaginative Structures of Edith Wharton and Willa Cather.* Chapel Hill: U of North Carolina P, 1986.

Fuss, Diana. *Essentially Speaking: Feminism, Nature, and Difference.* New York: Routledge, 1989.

Fussell, Paul. *The Great War and Modern Memory.* New York: Oxford UP, 1975.

Gale, Zona. "Allotropes." *The Yale Review,* March 26, 1926: 282–96.

———. *Borgia.* New York: Knopf, 1929.

———. "Children's Children." Ms., 1929. In Westgate Press papers. Butler Library, Columbia University.

———. "The Colored Players and Their Plays." *Theater Arts Magazine* [New York] 1923, 158–64.

———. *A Daughter of the Morning.* Indianapolis, IN: Bobbs-Merrill, 1917.

———. *Faint Perfume.* New York: Appleton, 1923.

————. *Heart's Kindred.* New York: Macmillan, 1915.

————. *The Loves of Pelleas and Etarre.* New York: Macmillan, 1908.

————. *Miss Lulu Bett.* New York: Appleton, 1920.

————. *Mothers to Men.* New York: Macmillan, 1911.

————. "My Favorite Character in Fiction." *The Bookman* [New York], May 1926, 323.

————. *Peace in Friendship Village.* New York: Macmillan, 1919.

————. *Portage, Wisconsin, and Other Essays.* New York: Knopf, 1929.

————. *Preface to a Life.* New York: Appleton, 1926.

————. *Romance Island.* Indianapolis: Bobbs-Merrill, 1906.

————. "The United States and the Artist." *The Nation,* July 1, 1925, 22–24.

————. "What Women Won in Wisconsin." *The Nation,* August 23, 1922, 184–85.

Gallop, Jane. "Annie Leclerc Writing a Letter, with Vermeer." In *The Poetics of Gender.* Ed. Nancy K. Miller. New York: Columbia UP, 1986. 137–57.

Gelfant, Blanche. *Women Writing in America: Voices in Collage.* Hanover, NH: UP of New England, 1984.

Giddings, Paula. *When and Where I Enter: The Impact of Black Women on Race and Sex in America.* New York: Morrow, 1984.

Gilbert, Sandra, and Susan Gubar. "Forward into the Past: The Complex Female Affiliation Complex." In *Historical Studies and Literary Criticism.* Ed. Jerome McGann. Madison: U of Wisconsin P, 1985. 240–65.

————. *Letters from the Front.* Volume Three of *No Man's Land: The Place of the Woman Writer in the Twentieth-Century.* New Haven: Yale UP, 1994.

————. *Sexchanges.* Volume Two of *No Man's Land: The Place of the Woman Writer in the Twentieth-Century.* New Haven: Yale UP, 1989.

————. *The War of the Words.* Volume One of *No Man's Land: The Place of the Woman Writer in the Twentieth-Century.* New Haven: Yale UP, 1988.

Gilchrist, Cherry. *Theosophy: The Wisdom of the Ages.* New York: HarperCollins, 1996.

Gilman, Charlotte Perkins. "Domestic Economy." In *A Nonfiction Reader.* Ed. Larry Ceplair. New York: Columbia UP, 1991. 157–168.

————. *Herland.* Ed. Ann J. Lane. New York: Pantheon, 1979.

————. *The Living of Charlotte Perkins Gilman.* 1935. Rpt. Salem, NH: Ayer Company Publishers, 1987.

————. *The Yellow Wallpaper.* Ed. Dale M. Bauer. New York: Bedford, 1998.

Glimpses of the Moon. Advertisement. *New York Times Book Review,* September 10, 1922: 15.

Goodman, Susan. *Edith Wharton's Women: Friends and Rivals.* Hanover, NH: UP of New England, 1990.

Gordon, Linda. "Putting Children First: Women, Maternalism, and Welfare in the Early Twentieth Century." In *U.S. History as Women's History: New Feminist Essays.* Ed. Linda K. Kerber and Alice Kessler-Harris. Chapel Hill: U of North Carolina P, 1995. 63-86.

Gossett, Thomas F. *Uncle Tom's Cabin and American Culture.* Dallas: Southern Methodist UP, 1985.

Graff, Gerald. *Professing Literature: An Institutional History.* Chicago: U of Chicago P, 1987.

Graham, Sara Hunter. *Woman Suffrage and the New Democracy.* New Haven: Yale UP, 1996.

Greene, Gayle, and Coppélia Kahn. *Changing Subjects: The Making of Feminist Literary Criticism.* New York: Routledge, 1993.

Guillory, John. *Cultural Capital: The Problem of Literary Canon Formation.* Chicago: U of Chicago P, 1993.

Haggard, H. Rider. *She.* Ed. Norman Etherington. Bloomington: Indiana UP, 1991.

Hanley, Lynne. *Writing War: Fiction, Gender, and Memory.* Amherst: U Massachusetts P, 1991.

Hapgood, Hutchins. *A Victorian in the Modern World.* New York: Harcourt, Brace, 1939.

Harley, Sharon, and Rosalyn Terborg-Penn. *The Afro-American Woman: Struggles and Images.* Port Washington, NY: Kennikat, 1978.

Heilbrun, Carolyn. *Reinventing Womanhood.* New York: Norton, 1979.

———. *Toward a Recognition of Androgyny.* New York: Norton, 1973.

Hemingway, Ernest. *Ernest Hemingway: Selected Letters, 1917–1961.* Ed. Carlos Baker. New York: Scribner's, 1981.

Henriksen, Louise Levitas. *Anzia Yezierska: A Writer's Life.* New Brunswick, NJ: Rutgers UP, 1988.

Hergesheimer, Joseph. "The Feminine Nuisance in American Literature." *The Yale Review* [New Haven], July 1921: 716–25.

Herrick, Robert. "A Feline World." *The Bookman* [New York] March 1929, 1–6.

Hoare, Philip. *Serious Pleasures: The Life of Stephen Tennant.* New York: Penguin, 1990.

Hollinger, David A. *Postethnic America.* New York: Basic, 1995.

Holt, Henry. "The Commercialization of Literature." *The Atlantic Monthly,* November 1905, 577–600.

Honey, Maureen, ed. *Breaking the Ties That Bind: Popular Stories of the New Woman, 1915-1920.* Norman: U of Oklahoma P, 1992.

Hughes, Langston. *The Big Sea.* New York: Hill and Wang, 1963.

Hutchinson, George. *The Harlem Renaissance in Black and White.* Cambridge, MA: Harvard UP, 1995.

Huyssen, Andreas. *After the Great Divide: Modernism, Mass Culture, Postmodernism.* Bloomington: Indiana UP, 1986.

Irwin, Inez Haynes. Inez Haynes Irwin Papers. Schlesinger Library, Radcliffe College.

———. *Angel Island.* New York: Henry Holt, 1914.

Inness, Sherrie, and Diana Royer, *Breaking Boundaries: New Perspectives on Women's Regional Writing.* Iowa City: U of Iowa P, 1997.

Johnson, Abby Arthur, and Ronald Maberry Johnson. *Propaganda and Aesthetics: The Literary Politics of Afro-American Magazines in the Twentieth Century.* Amherst: U of Massachusetts P, 1979.

Jordan, David. *Regionalism Reconsidered: New Approaches to the Field.* New York: Garland, 1994.

Kaplan, Amy. "Manifest Domesticity." *American Literature* 70.3 (1998): 581–606.

———. *The Social Construction of American Realism.* Chicago: U of Chicago P, 1988.

Kassanoff, Jennie A. "Corporate Thinking: Edith Wharton's *The Fruit of the Tree.*" *Arizona Quarterly* 53.1 (1997): 25–59.

Kerber, Linda K. "Women and Individualism in American History." *Massachusetts Review* Winter 1989: 589–609.

Kerman, Cynthia Earl, and Richard Eldridge. *The Search for Wholeness: The Lives of Jean Toomer.* Baton Rouge, LA: Louisiana State UP, 1987.

Kinman, Alice Herritage. "Becoming a Citizen in the 'Land of Letters': Edith Wharton's Early Work, 1891–1905." Diss., U of Georgia, Athens, 1996.

Kloppenberg, James T. *Uncertain Victories: Social Democracy and Progressivism in European and American Thought: 1870–1920.* New York: Oxford UP, 1986.

Knopf, Marcy Jo. Foreword. *The Chinaberry Tree.* By Jessie Redmon Fauset. New York: Stokes, 1931.

Kolodny, Annette. "Review Essay: Literary Criticism." *Signs: A Journal of Women in Culture and Society* 2.2 (1976): 404–21.

Latimer, Margery. *Guardian Angel and Other Stories.* 1932. Ed. Nancy Loughridge. Old Westbury, CT: Feminist Press, 1984.

Lasch, Christopher. *The True and Only Heaven: Progress and Its Critics.* New York: Norton, 1991.

Lauter, Paul. *Canons and Contexts.* New York: Oxford UP, 1989.

Le Sueur, Meridel. "Afterword: A Memoir." In *Guardian Angel and Other Stories.* 1932. Ed. Nancy Loughridge. Old Westbury, NY: The Feminist Press, 1984. 230–35.

Lee, Hermione. *Willa Cather: Double Lives.* New York: Pantheon, 1989.

Lentricchia, Frank. *Modernist Quartet.* Cambridge, MA: Cambridge UP, 1994.

Levine, Lawrence A. *Highbrow/Lowbrow: The Emergence of Cultural Hierarchy in America.* Cambridge, MA: Harvard UP, 1988.

Lewis, David Levering. *When Harlem Was in Vogue.* New York: Knopf, 1981.

Lewis, Edith. *Willa Cather Living: A Personal Record.* New York: Knopf, 1953.

Lewis, Reina. "The Death of the Author and the Resurrection of the Dyke." In *New Lesbian Criticism: Literary and Cultural Readings.* Ed. Sally Munt. New York: Columbia UP, 1992. 17–33.

Lewis, R. W. B. *The American Adam: Innocence, Tragedy, and Tradition in the Nineteenth Century.* Chicago: U of Chicago P, 1955.

———. *Edith Wharton: A Biography.* New York: Harper & Row, 1975.

———. and Nancy Lewis, eds. *The Letters of Edith Wharton.* New York: Collier, 1988.

Lindemann, Marilee. "'It Ain't My Prairie': Gender, Power, and Narrative in *My Ántonia.*" In *New Essays on My Ántonia.* Ed. Sharon O'Brien. New York: Cambridge UP, 1999. 111–35.

———. *Willa Cather: Queering America.* New York: Columbia UP, 1999.

Luhan, Mabel Dodge. *Intimate Memories: Volume Three: Movers and Shakers.* New York: Harcourt, Brace, 1936.

Luria, Sarah. "The Architecture of Manners: Henry James, Edith Wharton, and The Mount." *American Quarterly* 49.2 (June 1997): 298–327.

Lutes, Jean Marie. "Expert Inventions." Diss., U of Wisconsin, Madison, 1997.

Madigan, Mark. *Keeping Fires, Night and Day: Selected Letters of Dorothy Canfield Fisher.* Columbia: U of Missouri P, 1993.

Marcus, Laura. "Virginia Woolf and the Hogarth Press." In *Modernist Writers and the Marketplace.* Ed. Ian Willison, Warwick Gould, and Warren Chernaik. London: Macmillan, 1996. 124–51.

Marilley, Suzanne M. *Woman Suffrage and the Origins of Liberal Feminism in the United States, 1820–1920.* Cambridge, MA: Harvard UP, 1996.

Mayer, Melanie J. *Klondike Women: True Tales of the 1897–98 Gold Rush.* Athens, OH: Swallow, 1989.

McCullough, Kate. *Regions of Identity: The Construction of America in Women's Fiction, 1885-1914.* Stanford: Stanford UP, 1999.

McDowell, Deborah E. Introduction. *Plum Bun: A Novel Without A Moral.* By Jessie Redmon Fauset. 1928. Rpt. Boston: Beacon, 1990.

Michie, Helena. *Sororophobia: Differences among Women in Literature and Culture.* New York: Oxford UP, 1985.

Middleton, George. *These Things Are Mine.* New York: Macmillan, 1947.

Miller, Nancy K. "Emphasis Added: Plots and Plausibilities in Women's Fiction." In *The New Feminist Criticism: Essays on Women, Literature, and Theory.* Ed. Elaine Showalter. New York: Pantheon, 1985. 339–61.

Minter, David. *A Cultural History of the American Novel.* New York: Cambridge UP, 1994.

Moers, Ellen. *Literary Women.* New York: Doubleday, 1976.

Moore, Sarah J. "Making a Spectacle of Suffrage: The National Woman Suffrage Pageant, 1913." *Journal of American Culture* 20 (Spring 1997): 89–103.

Muncy, Robyn. "Trustbusting and White Manhood in America, 1898–1914." *American Studies* 38.3 (Fall 1997): 21–42.

Munt, Sally. *New Lesbian Criticism: Literary and Cultural Readings.* New York: Columbia UP, 1992.

Nettels, Elsa. *Language and Gender in American Fiction: Howells, James, Wharton and Cather.* Charlottesville, VA: UP of Virginia, 1997.

Newman, Louise Michele. *White Woman's Rights: The Racial Origins of Feminism in the United States.* New York: Oxford UP, 1999.

North, Michael. *Reading 1922: A Return to the Scene of the Modern.* New York: Oxford UP, 1999.

O'Brien, Sharon. "Becoming Noncanonical: The Case Against Willa Cather." In *Reading in America: Literature and Social History.* Ed. Cathy N. Davidson. Baltimore: The Johns Hopkins UP, 1989. 240–58.

———. "Combat Envy and Survivor Guilt: Willa Cather's 'Manly Battle Yarn.'" In *Arms and the Woman: War, Gender, and Literary Representation.* Ed. Helen M. Cooper and Adrienne Auslander Munich. Chapel Hill: U of North Carolina P, 1989. 184–204.

————. *Willa Cather: The Emerging Voice.* Cambridge: Harvard UP, 1987; rpt. 1997.

Ohmann, Richard. *Selling Culture: Magazines, Markets, and Class at the Turn of the Century.* New York: Verso, 1996.

Packer, Barbara L. "The Transcendentalists." *Prose Writing 1820–1865.* Vol. Two of *The Cambridge History of American Literature.* Ed. Sacvan Bercovitch. Cambridge, MA: Cambridge UP, 1995. 331–604.

Park, Sowon S. "Suffrage Fiction: A Political Discourse in the Marketplace." *English Literature in Transition* 39.4 (1996): 450–61.

Parker, Mary Lou. "Fashioning Feminism." Diss., U of Oregon, Eugene, 1994.

Pater, Walter. *Selected Writings.* Harold Bloom, ed. New York: Columbia UP, 1974.

Price, Alan. *The End of the Age of Innocence: Edith Wharton and the First World War.* New York: St. Martin's Press, 1996.

Pryse, Marjorie. "Reading Regionalism: The 'Difference' It Makes." In *Regionalism Reconsidered: New Approaches to the Field.* Ed. David Jordan. New York: Garland Press, 1994. 47–63.

————. "Sex, Class, and 'Category Crisis': Reading Jewett's Transitivity." *American Literature* 70.3 (1998): 517–50.

Rado, Lisa. "Lost and Found: Remembering Modernism, Rethinking Feminism." In *Rethinking Modernism: New Directions for Feminist Criticism.* Ed. Lisa Rado. New York: Garland, 1994. 3–19.

Radway, Janice A. *A Feeling for Books: The Book-of-the-Month-Club, Literary Taste, and Middle-Class Desire.* Chapel Hill: U of North Carolina P, 1997.

Raitt, Suzanne, and Trudi Tate. *Women's Fiction and the Great War.* New York: Oxford UP, 1997.

Reynolds, Guy. *Willa Cather in Context: Progress, Race, Empire.* New York: St. Martin's Press, 1996.

Romero, Lora. *Home Fronts: Domesticity and Its Critics in the Antebellum United States.* Durham, NC: Duke UP, 1997.

Romines, Ann. *The Home Plot: Women, Writing, and Domestic Ritual.* Amherst: U of Massachusetts P, 1992.

Rosowski, Susan. *The Voyage Perilous: Willa Cather's Romanticism.* Lincoln: U of Nebraska P, 1986.

Rourke, Constance Mayfield. "Transitions." *The New Republic,* August 11, 1920, 315–16.

Royce, Josiah. *The World and the Individual.* New York: Macmillan, 1901.

Ryan, Maureen. "No Woman's Land: Gender in Willa Cather's *One of Ours.*" *Studies in American Fiction* 18.1 (Spring 1990): 65–75.

Sandel, Michael J. "The Procedural Republic and the Unencumbered Self." *Political Theory* 12 (February 1984): 619–735.

Schroeter, James. *Willa Cather and Her Critics.* Ithaca, NY: Cornell UP, 1967.

Schwarz, Judith. *Radical Feminists of Heterodoxy: Greenwich Village, 1912–1940.* Norwich, VT: New Victoria, 1986.

Scott, Anne Firor. *Making the Invisible Woman Visible.* Chicago: U of Illinois P, 1984.

————. *Natural Allies: Women's Associations in American History.* Chicago: U of Illinois P, 1991.

Scott, Bonnie Kime, ed. *The Gender of Modernism.* Bloomington: Indiana UP, 1990.

————. *Refiguring Modernism: The Women of 1928.* Two volumes. Bloomington: Indiana UP, 1995.

Seldes, Gilbert. "Claude Bovary." *The Dial* 73 (September 1922): 343–45.

Sensibar, Judith. "Behind the Lines in Edith Wharton's *A Son at the Front*: Rewriting a Masculinist Tradition." *Journal of American Studies* 24 (1990): 187–99.

Sergeant, Elizabeth. *Willa Cather: A Memoir.* Philadelphia: Lippincott, 1953.

Showalter, Elaine. *Sister's Choice: Tradition and Change in American Women's Writing.* Oxford: Clarendon, 1991.

Simonson, Harold P. *Zona Gale.* New York: Twayne, 1962.

Skaggs, Merrill Maguire. *After the World Broke in Two: The Later Novels of Willa Cather.* Charlottesville, VA: UP Virginia, 1990.

Slote, Bernice. *The Kingdom of Art: Willa Cather's First Principles and Critical Statements, 1893–1896.* Lincoln: U of Nebraska P, 1966.

———— and Virginia Faulkner. *The Art of Willa Cather.* Lincoln: U of Nebraska P, 1974.

Spacks, Patricia Meyer. *The Female Imagination.* New York: Knopf, 1975.

Spiller, Robert, and Willard Thorp, Thomas H. Johnson, Henry Seidel Canby, and Richard M. Ludwig, eds. *Literary History of the United States.* 3rd ed. New York: Macmillan, 1963.

Spivak. Gayatri Chakravorty. "Subaltern Studies: Deconstructing Historiography." In *In Other Worlds: Essays in Cultural Politics.* New York: Methuen, 1987. 197–221.

Steinson, Barbara J. *American Women's Activism in World War I.* New York: Garland, 1982.

Stout, Janis. "Willa Cather's *One of Ours*: Another Word on the Role of Dorothy Canfield Fisher." Unpublished manuscript.

————. "Katherine Anne Porter's 'Reflections on Willa Cather': A Duplicitous Homage." *American Literature* 66 (1994): 619–735.

————. "Re-Studying Cather: Historicist and Historical Scholarship." *Willa Cather Pioneer Memorial Newsletter and Review* 43.2 (Fall 1999): 42–44.

Stowe, Harriet Beecher. *The Minister's Wooing.* In *Three Novels.* Ed. Kathryn Kish Sklar. New York: Library of America, 1982. 521–876.

————. *Uncle Tom's Cabin.* In *Three Novels.* Ed. Kathryn Kish Sklar. New York: Library of America, 1982. 1–520.

Sumner, Keene. "The Everlasting Persistence of This American Girl." *American Magazine,* 1921, 34, 137–41.

Thacker, Robert. "Willa Cather, S.S. McClure, and the Act of My Autobiography." Unpublished manuscript, 1997.

Todd, Janet. *Feminist Literary History.* New York: Routledge, 1988.

Tompkins, Jane. *Sensational Designs: The Cultural Work of American Fiction, 1790–1860.* New York: Oxford UP, 1985.

Tuttleton, James W., ed. *Edith Wharton: The Contemporary Reviews.* New York: Cambridge UP, 1992.

Wall, Cheryl A. *Women of the Harlem Renaissance.* Bloomington: U of Indiana P, 1995.

Ware, Susan. *Beyond Suffrage: Women in the New Deal.* Cambridge, MA: Harvard UP, 1981.

Weatherford, Doris. *A History of the American Suffragist Movement.* Santa Barbara, CA: ABC-Clio, 1998.

West, James L. W., III. *American Authors and the Literary Marketplace Since 1900.* Philadelphia: U of Pennsylvania P, 1988.

Wharton, Edith. *The Art of Fiction.* New York: Scribner's, 1925.

———. *A Backward Glance.* In *Novellas and Other Writings.* Ed. Cynthia Griffin Wolff. New York: Library of America, 1990. 767–1068.

———. *Collected Short Stories of Edith Wharton.* Ed. R. W. B. Lewis. New York: Scribner's, 1968.

———. *Fighting France: From Dunkerque to Belfort.* New York: Scribner's, 1915.

———. *The Fruit of the Tree.* New York: Scribner's, 1907.

———. "George Eliot." *The Bookman,* May 1902, 247–51.

———. *Glimpses of the Moon.* 1922. Rpt. New York: Macmillan, 1994.

———. *The Gods Arrive.* New York: Appleton, 1932.

———. "The Great American Novel." *The Yale Review* July 1927: 646–56.

———. *The House of Mirth.* In *Novels.* Ed. R. W. B. Lewis. New York: Library of America, 1985. 1–348.

———. *Hudson River Bracketed.* New York: Appleton, 1929.

———. *The Mother's Recompense.* New York: Appleton, 1925.

———. *A Son at the Front.* New York: Scribner's, 1923.

———. *Twilight Sleep.* New York: Appleton, 1927.

———. *Uncollected Critical Writings.* Ed. Frederick Wegener. Princeton: Princeton UP, 1996.

———. *The Art of Fiction.* New York: Scribner's, 1925.

———, ed. *The Book of the Homeless.* New York: Scribner's, 1916.

Wheeler, Kathleen. *'Modernist' Women Writers and Narrative Art.* New York: New York UP, 1994.

White, William Allen. *Selected Letters of William Allen White.* New York: Holt, 1947.

Williams, Deborah Lindsay. "Cather, Woolf, and the Two Mrs. Ramsays." *College English* 61.1 (September 1998): 29–41.

———. "Hiding in Plain Sight: Willa Cather and Ghostwriting." *Willa Cather Pioneer Newsletter and Review* 43.3 (Fall 1999): 25–31.

———. "Losing Nothing, Comprehending Everything: Learning to Read Both the Old World and the New in *Death Comes for the Archbishop.*" In *Cather Studies, Volume 4: Willa Cather's Canadian and Old World Connections.* Ed. Robert Thacker and Michael A. Peterman. Lincoln: U of Nebraska P, 1999. 80–97.

Willison, Ian, Warwick Gould, and Warren Chernaik. *Modernist Writers and the Marketplace.* London: Macmillan, 1996.

Wilson, Christopher. *The Labor of Words: Literary Professionalism in the Progressive Era.* Athens, GA: U of Georgia P, 1985.

Wittenstein, Kate E. "The Heterodoxy Club and American Feminism, 1912–1920." Diss., Boston University, 1989.

Wolff, Cynthia Griffin. *A Feast of Words: The Triumph of Edith Wharton.* New York: Oxford UP, 1977.

Woodress, James. *Willa Cather: A Literary Life.* Lincoln: U of Nebraska Press, 1978.

Woolf, Virginia. *Three Guineas.* New York: Harcourt, Brace, 1938.

Zilversmit, Annette. "Reading the Letters of Edith Wharton." *Women's Studies* 20 (1991): 93–95.

INDEX